Interior Design of the Electronic Office

The Comfort and Productivity Payoff

Interior Design of the Electronic Office

The Comfort and Productivity Payoff

Walter B. Kleeman, Jr.

with Francis Duffy
Kirk P. Williams
Michele K. Williams

VNR VAN NOSTRAND REINHOLD
New York

The Steelcase questionnaire and printout are copyrighted by E. S. S. and are reproduced by permission of Steelcase Inc.

Library of Congress Catalog Card Number 90-43538
ISBN 0-442-00613-6

Printed in the United States of America.

Van Nostrand Reinhold
15 Fifth Avenue
New York, New York 10003

Chapman and Hall
2-6 Boundary Row
London, SE1 8HN, England

Thomas Nelson Australia
102 Dodds Street
South Melbourne 3205
Victoria, Australia

Nelson Canada
1120 Birchmount Road
Scarborough, Ontario MIK 5G4, Canada

16 15 14 13 12 11 10 9 8 7 6 5 4 3 2 1

Library of Congress Cataloging in Publication Data

Interior design of the electronic office: the comfort and
productivity payoff/by Walter B. Kleeman, Jr.; with Francis Duffy,
Kirk P. Williams, Michele K. Williams
p. cm.
Includes bibliographical references and index.
ISBN 0-442-00613-6
1. Office layout. 2. Interior design. 3. Environmental
engineering. 4. Office furniture. I. Kleeman, Walter.
HF5547.2.I58 1991
658.2'3—dc20 90-43538
CIP

To the health, safety, comfort and productivity of office workers everywhere

Most organizations and most jobs in the office will tend to become more technical and more professionalized. Each individual will matter more and be capable of wielding more power. Organizations will be less unitary and will tend to split up into autonomous or quasi-autonomous baronies with minds and wills of their own. The implications for the conduct of design are formidable: we will have to accept the user as co-designer whether we like it or not. We will have to present and share our ideas with the users, in effect be their teachers.

Never have offices been so central to society; we would do well to take their design seriously.

—Francis Duffy

Contents

PART *III*

Interior Design Needs in Office Environments 75

PART *IV*

Office Interior Furnishings 141

PART *V*

The Productivity Payoff 207

Preface

Experts estimate that two-thirds of American workers devote their time to handling information and that most of them work in offices. ''Handling information'' once meant just that—doing it by hand. Now, information is being processed in offices with the aid of an increasing number and variety of electronic machines, principally the computer and its associated electronic devices.

Moreover, there is a continuing procession of advances and changes in these devices and the methods of using them. As this process continues, it will continue to change office workers' jobs as well as their expectations. The increase in the importance of this segment of the work force is creating a strong worldwide drive for greater office comfort and productivity.

This book is intended as a practical guide through the maze of problems we face in designing the electronic office. We will talk about the ways that office workers are reacting to technological innovation and how this relates to the interior design of the office; and we will explore some practical ways these problems can be solved by design.

Because the computer revolution is happening everywhere, we have made a conscious attempt to give this book an international flavor by searching the world for design problems, research studies, and solutions. We have made use of valid research results wherever we've found them. Contributions are included from France, The Netherlands, West Germany, Sweden, Italy, Japan, Austria, Canada, Australia, Singapore, Switzerland, and many other countries, while the bulk of the material in the book comes from the United States and Great Britain.

This book has been written from a multi-disciplinary point of view. The principal sources of information are the disciplines of interior design, architecture, human factors/ergonomics, management theory, computer technology, information technology, facilities management, anthropometry, and architectural psychology.

I feel most fortunate to have had the help of my co-authors, Dr. Francis Duffy; Michele K. Williams, IBD; and Kirk P. Williams. Among the four of us we have designed millions of square feet of offices in several countries.

We would add a word of caution: what follows represents our best efforts to summarize the state of office design as it exists at this writing;

however, the pace of progress is swift and change will continue to happen.

In writing this volume, we have had important help from our colleagues, especially John Worthington of Duffy Eley Giffone Worthington (DEGW), London, UK; Dr. Peter Ellis; Gere Picasso, formerly of AT&T Communications; Bill Robinson of Steelcase; Harry Urban, Publisher of *Wood & Wood Products;* Chuck Broffman, president of *The Designer;* Muriel R. Chess, formerly editor of *The Designer* and *Professional Office Design;* Laura Haney, former editor of *The Designer;* Carl Ruff of Carl Ruff Associates; Rani K. Lueder of Humanics; Niels Diffrient, FIDSA; Peter J. Hackett, CPA; Betsy Coughron of the Quality Circle Institute; Grahame Watson of Watson Furniture Systems; Don Stuckle of TRW; Dr. Peter Mitchell of Ergo Design; Dr. Etienne Grandjean of the Swiss Federal Ergonomic Laboratories; Dr. Marvin Dainoff of Miami University and consultant to the National Institute of Occupational Safety and Health; Dr. Manfred Welsch; Dr. Tim Springer, president of Springer Associates, Inc.; Robert and John Reis of DataSafe; Peter B. Silvestri of United Technologies Building Systems; and Debra Urban, Peter Mullineaux, and Lewis Farrer of Martin Marietta Denver Aerospace.

The following are reprinted by permission from the copyright holders: Chapter 1 and a small portion of Chapter 2 were published in *Design* (no. 412); passages from ORBIT I in Chapter 3; passages from *Environment and Behavior* (14, no. 5, 593–610, Sept., 1982), Sage Publications, Inc. (other passages from this source also appear in Chapter 3); Chapter 4 is from *Facilities* (5, no. 3); Chapter 5 was published in different form in *The Designer* (25, no. 318); Chapter 6 was published in different form in *Environment and Behavior* (20, no. 5, 537–549, Sept., 1988), Sage Publications, Inc; abridged versions of parts of Chapter 8 appeared in *Wood & Wood Products* (89, no. 1 and 89, no. 2); another part of Chapter 8 appeared in different form in the Human Factors Society Bulletin, Inc. (30, no. 2, 1988); an abridged version of Chapter 15 was in *The Designer* (25, no. 330); an abridged version of Chapter 17 was in *The Designer* (31, no. 394); an abridged version of Chapter 18 was in *The Designer* (31, no. 392); passages from Chapter 18 were in the Human Factors Society, Inc. Bulletin (25, no. 12, 1982); part of Chapter 18 was included in *Anthropometry and Biomechanics–Theory and Application,* NATO Series III: Human Factors, Easterby, Ronald, Kroemer, K. H. E., and Chaffin, Don B., eds., Plenum Publishing Corp. (1982, 235–239); another version of Chapter 19 appeared in *Wood & Wood Products* (89, no. 10); Chapter 21 appeared in *Wood & Wood Products* (90, no. 9); passages in Chapter 22 were in *Wood & Wood Products* (90, no. 6); passages in Chapter 23 were published in *Facilities* (2, no. 3).

Illustrations are printed with the permission of The Alma Companies; Allsteel, Inc.; The ARC Group, Inc.; Armstrong World Industries; Baker Furniture; CenterCore; Comforto, a Haworth Co.; Councill Business Furniture; Cross Market Management Co.; DataSafe; DEGW; *Design;* Dest Corp.; Niels Diffrient, FIDSA; Hag, Inc.; Haworth, Inc.; The Harter Group; Herman Miller, Inc.; Human Factors Technologies; Interface Flooring Systems; JG Furniture Systems; Johnson Controls; Karastan Bigelow; Kardex Systems, Inc.; Knoll International; Lees Commercial Carpet; National Mount Airy; Panel Concepts, Dr. Thomas Pickett; Rangine Corp.; Sligh Furniture; Sam Sloan, AIA; Steelcase Inc.; Stow & Davis, a division of Steelcase Inc.; Tecno (UK); United Technologies, Watson Furniture Systems; Westinghouse Furniture Systems.

Contributors

Walter B. Kleeman, Jr., Ph.D., FASID, ASFD, CSI, IDEC, IFDA, High Point, NC, consultant.
Francis Duffy, Ph.D., M. Arch., AA Dipl. (Hons), ARIBA, DEGW Ltd., London, UK.
Kirk P. Williams, Martin Marietta Astronautics Group, Denver, CO.
Michele K. Williams, IBD, W. B. Wood Co., New Providence, NJ.

Interior Design of the Electronic Office

The Comfort and Productivity Payoff

PART I

History and Meaning in Office Design

Chapter 1

A History of Office Futures

Office buildings have changed our cities, and office work has revolutionized our society. Manhattan or Frankfurt or the City of London are evidence of the enormous impact the office has had upon our lives. Yet the history of the office building as a reflection of changing office organizations has hardly been attempted. Neither has a history of the development of the office as a social system.

The difficulties are formidable. We have no full theoretical understanding of the way in which buildings relate to office organizations. Why, for instance, do highly paid stockbrokers work three or four to a shared office while partners in an accounting firm work in a single room? Is it technology, social structure, or simply tradition which explains such habits?

While the study of the office as a focus for social and economic history has not yet proved attractive to historians, it could well make an important contribution to our understanding of aspects of our modern society. An investigation of office space focuses attention in a particularly acute way on a vast section of the economy and working population that is otherwise hazily and inadequately defined.

Obviously office buildings have changed in many ways during the past 100 years; each generation of new enterprise seems to have had its own organizational and technological problems to solve. What factors have prompted and accelerated change? The following questions are crucial to an understanding of these changes.

First, what were the prevailing social ideas about relationships in office organizations and, indeed, in society at large?

Second, to what extent does the form of office buildings and office interiors reveal changes in office technology and office organization? (Office technology is taken here to cover the tasks performed in the office, the machines needed to carry out the flow of work, and the pattern of communications; office organization refers to the office as a complex of relationships between people, some powerful and others weak.)

This chapter was contributed by Francis Duffy.

Third, to what degree are the form of office buildings and their interior arrangements dependent upon available construction materials and methods as well as existing real estate practice—the conditions under which office properties are bought, leased, and valued?

And, finally, what is the most powerful agent of change in office design: internal factors such as office technology and organization, which relate directly to building users, or external factors such as building technology and real estate prices, which relate to users through the medium of agents who are not directly under their control and who intervene only intermittently in their organizational lives?

Office technology, office organization, building construction, and real estate factors may be seen to be the most important influences on the development of office design. The first two are *internal factors;* the last two are *external factors.*

The relationship between internal and external influences is crucial. To examine the play of these factors on offices, four contrasted pairs of buildings have been selected. Each pair is roughly contemporary; each example reveals something of the way in which technology, organization, building construction, or real estate practice has influenced the office form.

1849–1864: Fine Houses and Space to Let

In 1849 the Sun Life Assurance Company, founded in the early eighteenth century and the world's largest insurance office, moved into new premises purpose-designed by architect C. R. Cockerell. It was relatively unusual and therefore a sign of some prosperity for a company to build its own offices. What kind of layout did it consider to be appropriate to convey a sense of corporate solidarity?

The Sun building fitted its ''small household'' organization of groups of six to ten clerks into a plan not far removed from that of a fine house with its sequence of great rooms and robust classical detailing, though it was necessary to slip in two unclassical extra floors. Because of their skills, which were scarce and hard to replace, clerks enjoyed a high status in the early nineteenth century. Their workplaces revealed little functional differentiation between home and office. Only the seating hinted at office use.

The Oriel Chambers (Peter Ellis, Liverpool 1864), differs from the Sun building in that it was designed to be let out as several small suites of accommodation suitable for very small two- or three-person firms. Architect Peter Ellis provided the ideal setting for a Dickensian world of small entrepreneurs and professionals, supported by one or two indispensable clerks. His design offered a modular plan of neat, tiny units that created a stylistic precedent for countless office buildings.

1894–1904: Paper Factories in the Sky

The Larkin Building (Frank Lloyd Wright, Buffalo, New York, 1904) was built for a mail order company. The organization was typical of the new

Sun Life Insurance Company building designed by C. R. Cockerell. (From DEGW sources.)

kinds of enterprise that sprang up at the end of the nineteenth century, and depended for successful operation upon three vital preconditions: the economies of scale that vast coordinated purchasing could achieve; excellent communications for ordering and distribution; and a large, malleable, well-organized and, above all, cheap workforce capable of handling thousands of minute transactions quickly and efficiently.

The Larkin office, built by a corporation to accommodate hundreds of clerks, was entirely different in scale to what had been usual in the nineteenth century. The technology was far more routine and factorylike; the employees were low in status (clerks sat on fixed seats that pivoted from their desks, so rigid was the space planning); the corporate owner was more dominant.

The building is the natural product of a movement which advocated that highly regimented, scientific management principles developed in industry could be applied to the growing clerical workforce. With its strict segregation of the sexes and corporate slogans on the wall, Larkin is original not just because of its design, but because it is evidence of the rapid commercial growth that transformed American society. Internally, the Larkin building is one large space proclaiming the unity of organization with everyone under the eagle eye of the office supervisor. It is a far cry from the sequential rooms of the Sun office or the simple, repetitive spaces of the Oriel Chambers.

Another type of office building developed at this time was as spectacular as Larkin, at least in its external form. This was the skyscraper, a colossal version of the tiny, speculative honeycomb of office cells that characterizes Oriel Chambers. It was a product both of real estate practice (developers began to maximize on their investment by building upwards on key, expensive sites in the central business districts of New York and Chicago) and of building technique (steel frame construction and the invention of the elevator made such offices possible).

The skyscraper was not the result of a change in the size of organizations, but it did perhaps reflect the growth in number of different enterprises. The Guaranty Building (Buffalo, New York, 1895) sums up this great development in the use of office space: its 12 U-shaped storeys provided an enormous number of small offices on a very restricted site. The contrast with the Larkin building, built nine years later in the same city, could not be greater.

The Oriel Chambers designed by architect Peter Ellis contained a number of small units. (From DEGW sources.)

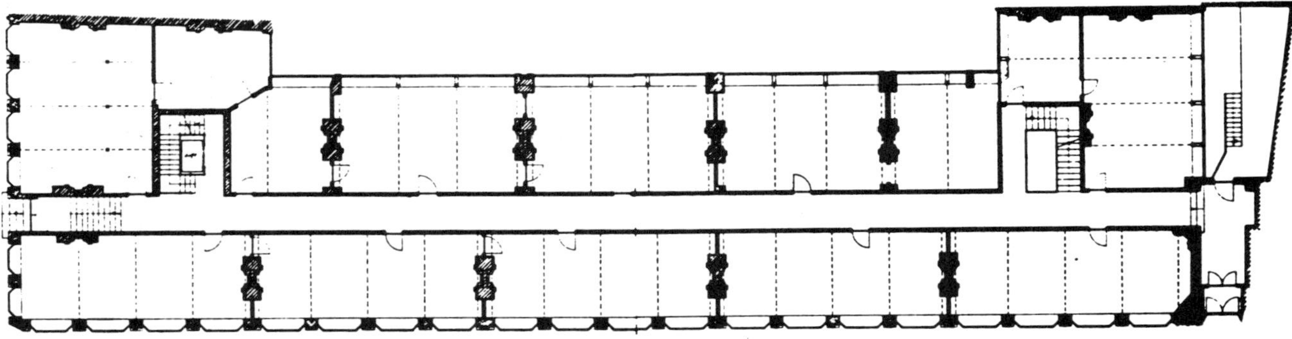

Upper ground floor plan of Oriel Chambers. (From DEGW sources.)

1954–1963: In the Vice of Corporate Control

Nearly 60 years later, the Seagram Building (New York, 1954) shows few advances from the Guaranty in terms of meeting real organizational requirements. Though it is much more refined and has the benefit of full air-conditioning, it shares the same vision of the office as one building, with one entrance, which is capable of being subdivided and leased in small units. Moving from floor to floor in the Seagram Building is a surreal experience: there are as many as 20 different firms, each tenant acting within the normal conventions of New York real estate practice by decorating in its own way. One is therefore confronted with several wildly differing corporate worlds coexisting within one structure.

But even as the Seagram Building was being constructed, a far more spectacular development in office design was taking place in West Germany. This was the invention of *Bürolandschaft,* or ''office landscaping,'' an

Pickett Coal Company Office, Beverly, Massachusetts, January, 1893. (Courtesy of Dr. Thomas Pickett.)

attempt to achieve an organic freedom both in organizational and building form.

The office landscape concept sprang from three diverse sources. The first was scientific management principles, which had had an immense impact on the Larkin building. The second factor was "human relations" thinking, which promoted a relaxed and status-free form of layout and emphasized noninstrumental aspects of work such as addressing staff by first names. The third influence, was cybernetics, specifically the concept of the office as a kind of communications device or control system.

The office landscape was developed as part of the management consultancy movement of the 1950s. It was applied particularly by the Schnelles, who invented the unforgettable imagery of random desk arrangement, plants, relaxation areas and light, portable furniture. This form of layout

Frank Lloyd Wright's Larkin building in Buffalo, New York. (From DEGW sources.)

was made possible only by an advance in building technology: the use of air-conditioning to make deep space habitable.

The Ninoflax office (Nordhorn, West Germany, 1963), the administration building for a textile company, is a typical early example of *Bürolandschaft.* Most activities are clerical, and the offices are entirely open plan. The building form breaks the modular discipline that marks the Seagram Building. Unlike Seagram, with its variety of tenants, the building is the product of a large clerical organization run with a certain corporate management style. No deviation is tolerated from this style. It is the product of a real estate tradition in which custom-built offices prevailed over speculative developments and building forms were moulded to express the intentions of the client.

Another factor that shaped the development of office landscaping was the industrial climate during a period when staff discipline and obedience could be relied upon and senior management were able to adopt ''advanced'' policies without question. These conditions no longer prevail in northern Europe. With increasing skepticism about office landscaping and

Office in the interior of the Larkin building. (From DEGW sources.)

Special space-saving furniture designed for the Larkin building and manufactured by Steelcase Inc. (From DEGW sources.)

tougher attitudes regarding real estate practice and the negotiation of working conditions by employees, Ninoflax and hundreds of similar offices became obsolete within ten years.

1973–1983: The Fruits of Industrial Democracy

Against a background in which powerful centralized management thinking could no longer be reconciled with growing white collar industrial democracy, Centraal Beheer, an insurance office designed in Holland by Herman

The *bürolandschaft* (office landscape) concept in the Ninoflax building. (From DEGW sources.)

Hertzberger in 1973, has become famous for the involvement of staff in its design. They have been encouraged to paint their own walls, put up posters, invite their families in for lunch and even bring in their pets.

The office layout of Centraal Beheer is a radical departure from most conventional forms—both open plan and traditional. Floors are not stacked up on top of each other in time-honored fashion. Instead a series of modules (3 by 3 meters [10 by 10 feet]) link together to form a friendly, ambiguous network of workspaces in which staff enjoy both privacy and a sense of belonging to the communal life of the office. The building has several approaches and entrances, not just one, and the spatial variety inside allows personal expression and well-being to flourish.

The search for humane working environments that balance corporate efficiency against personal choice and dignity is taken even further with the new four-story Union Carbide headquarters in Danbury, Connecticut, designed by Kevin Roche, John Dinkeloo & Associates. The building provides no less than 2,358 private offices, all a standard modular size (4 by 4 meters [13 by 13 feet]), all with windows and a view out to a wooded parkland (the parking lot is skillfully concealed inside the center of the building).

Fifteen different office interiors were designed, ranging from traditional to modern, and employees were invited to choose exactly what they wanted (including even light fittings and accessories) from 15 full-size mock-up models. Hierarchical power is no longer tied to physical space in an egalitarian scheme that particularly improves the lot of lower-level employees.

Anti-"landscaping," highly modular projects like the new Union Carbide building are the result of many factors, not least internal ones such as labor legislation. The most interesting crux in the evolution of the office futures is the conflict between internal organizational factors and external real estate forces.

Unlike North American projects, European office buildings have generally tended to reflect architectural or stylistic trends and, in more recent times, managerial fashions, quickly and accurately. This is because of the relative weakness of the external forces. Ninoflax in particular shows the impact of managerial style on building forms.

In the United States, despite the fertility of organizational ideas, external real estate factors have tended to dominate. Offices have been seen as negotiable commodities first, and objects for use second—the skyscraper proliferation in Chicago and New York is a good example of this.

Why external constraints were weak in one context and strong in another can be explained only in terms of fundamental economic forces. In retrospect, the offices discussed here tell us far more about the societies that build them than about their designers.

Chapter 2

Symbolism in Office Design

There are many elements of office design that are symbolic and not necessarily functional; in fact, sometimes the less functional an item may be, the more status it may indicate. Among these elements are the presence, absence, size, quantity, and/or quality of workspace, furniture, draperies, photographs, paintings, desk ornaments, sofas, bars, oriental rugs, coffee tables, bathrooms, executive dining rooms, antiques, identification signs, diplomas, plaques, certificates, and especially chairs.

Chairs

Chairs have always been rather expressive and symbolic objects. For at least 4,500 years, from the pharaohs of Egypt to the kings and queens of Europe, they were strictly seats of the mighty—literally seats of power. Not until the last ten years of the fifteenth century did chairs come into use by ordinary people, who had been using benches and stools.

Before 1490, chairs were symbols of rulers, both temporal and religious. Popes have used an ancient chair of oak, thought to be Saint Peter's throne. Cathedrals are so called because they are the places where the archbishop or bishop has his seat, throne, or cathedra: thus the phrase *ex cathedra,* meaning from the throne, chair, or seat of power. Early religious paintings and mosaics showed God sitting on a throne. There is great significance in the fact that in these works, Christ, the child, is sometimes shown in an approximate sitting position while in the womb, the first position that each of us assumes.

The symbolic meaning of chairs is still evident in expressions we use today. We talk about county seats, seats on stock exchanges, and chairpersons. We address the "chair" in meetings and legislatures and refer to judges as the "bench" on which they sit; "the bench" is usually a high-backed "judge's chair."

Chairs are used symbolically in the office as well, especially in strongly hierarchical organizations. For this kind of firm, office furniture dealers must offer a series of chairs that is carefully graded in terms of comfort, size, and back height. The chair with the largest, highest back and the most comfortable seat (sometimes called a "judge's chair") belongs to the strong person who runs the enterprise. Progressively lower, smaller backs and less comfortable seats characterize the chairs for the people in the lower ranks of the business. The height of a chair back is very important for indicating the chairperson's place in a conference setting.

When workers in a large office belong to a union, management must be careful to choose one or two types of chairs and then stick to those types. The introduction of a new type of chair has been the subject of more than one labor-management bargaining session.

Hopefully, this hierarchical approach is beginning to change for organizational reasons (see Chapter 22, A Case for Participatory Design) and for

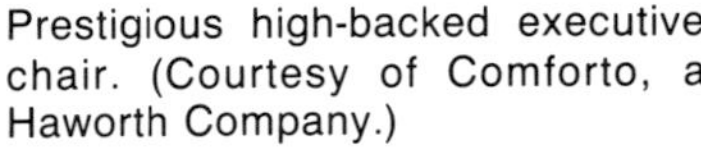

Prestigious high-backed executive chair. (Courtesy of Comforto, a Haworth Company.)

reasons of comfort and productivity. The highest styled chair, either traditional or modern, is not necessarily comfortable and comfort is becoming more important to productivity (see Chapter 23, Increased Productivity from Design). The chair and worksurface in the executive suite are often in traditional styles that are not very adjustable for comfort and productivity. The seat heights of traditionally styled chairs, for instance, usually do not adjust to a low enough point to be comfortable for women executives and smaller men.

The more these pieces are true to the styling of their periods, the less comfortable they usually are. In those times, seating was designed for appearance; comfort was secondary. Because this kind of styling seems to be so important to some executives, chair designers hesitate to innovate enough in the design of these traditional pieces to improve their comfort.

Desks

Sizes of desks are frequently awarded according to rank in the office (as are completely enclosed offices, windows, and the best views). The standard beginning size for office desks is 60 inches wide by 30 inches deep; this size probably evolved from the fact that it meets the limits of human capabilities to reach something on the desk without standing up. Where space or money is exceptionally tight, some desks 45 inches wide are found, as in automobile or real estate sales offices. From there, most manufacturers' standard desk lines increase in size in 6-inch increments until 84 inches wide by 42 inches deep is reached; that seems to be about the limit for standard executive desks. Anything larger than that is usually custom-made.

At some point in the hierarchy, desk materials and finishes begin to change. A plain melamine plastic laminate top may change to a wood-patterned laminate and that may change to real wood as rank moves upward. More exotic materials may appear in the upper echelons, such as leather, rare burls, or even marquetry inlays.

Reception desks, however, are the artifacts that really show how status is reflected in design; the more prestige an organization wants, the more elaborate and striking the reception desk will be and the more likely it will be custom-designed.

In fact, the whole reception area is often symbolic of the impression the firm inside wishes to make. One manufacturer signals a businesslike attitude with framed product photos in color on the reception room walls. A research organization uses its extensive library as a reception area to impress visitors with its store of knowledge. Another manufacturer puts just three very large custom-made chairs and an elaborate specially designed desk in a room big enough to hold four times as much furniture—to give an impression of dignity and solidity. This organization also shows original art throughout its offices for the same purpose. An insurance agency uses fire marks (plaques formerly attached to the fronts of buildings to show which company had insured the building) and old prints of fire-fighting scenes in its reception area to show that they are genuinely involved in their profession, not just interested in selling insurance. Many organizations hang portraits of their founders in the reception area to show their longevity and stability.

Panels, Phones, and Computers

The use of panels in open-plan offices may also symbolize status. Higher panels and a greater degree of enclosure for the workstation tend to mean higher rank. Cloth-upholstered and wood-veneered panels are seen to be more prestigious than plastic laminate or painted metal ones.

Even telephones, computers, and printers may show rank, which is indicated by how much equipment an individual has and the number of features on each device. A videophone on the desk may serve to demonstrate the importance of an individual.

Rare inlaid woods form the top of this prestigious desk designed by Charles Pfister for Baker Executive Office. (Courtesy of Baker Furniture.)

Haworth's prototype desk of the future features a modular top and an integrated computer system built into a box beneath the desk's work surface. An 11-inch wide, one-inch thick electroluminescent flat panel display provides the visuals, thus symbolizing a forward-looking image for Haworth. (Courtesy of Haworth, Inc.)

Space

Then there is the symbolism of space. The sizes and positions of office spaces themselves tell quite a story. Here's Dr. Edward T. Hall on the subject:

> Anyone watching the anxious faces and movements when space allocations are made prior to an organization's move can't help recognizing the tremendous importance space plays in our life. Space allocations are inevitably, and quite correctly, read as a type of communication. Both relationship and priorities can be seen in the arrangement, size and allocation of spaces. (1970)

While the amount of space allotted to an office worker is perhaps most symbolic of rank and status, the position of the workplace in relation to others is also important; in some organizations, closer to the boss is better. Spaces closest to the areas of highest activity are desirable. Windows are prized by many for access to natural light, as are corner offices. In offices occupying more than one floor usually the higher the floor, the more status it indicates.

Another symbol of prestige is access control for privacy, or the number of barriers between the worker and interruption or distraction. How many secretaries guard the entrance to the boss's office? Even the presence or absence of a door may be an indicator.

Signs

Signs have many functions in the office. As Fritz Steele (1986) points out, they can

- Identify the ownership of workspaces
- Indicate rank by showing position, title, function, and name
- Control access
- By their design carry a message about the type of organization, set a mood and influence the feelings of those who see them
- Tell who can use what
- Say what activities are permitted and forbidden
- Identify individual and group territories
- Give directions to other locations
- Warn of danger
- Help with security

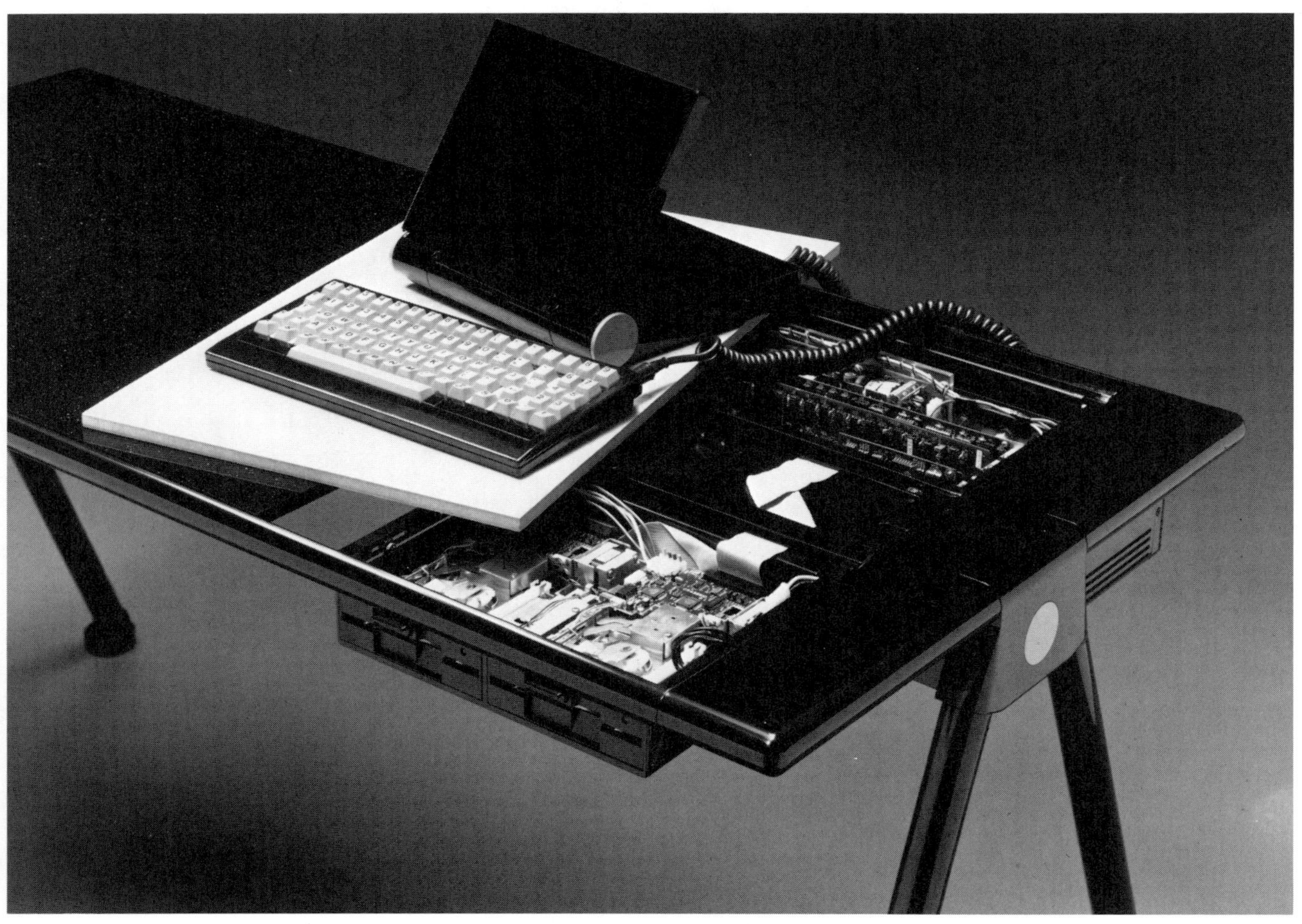

The central processing unit (CPU) for an IBM PC XT clone in Haworth's Desk of the Future is shown open for servicing with a panel of the modular top removed. The CPU also pops in and out for the same purpose. (Courtesy of Haworth, Inc.)

An Example of Hierarchical Design

One instance of an hierarchical approach to the assignment of office furniture and spaces was the interior design of the CBS building in New York, built in the mid-1960s.

The interior designer for the building refused to accept the assignment unless she could write a complete book of rules (and have them obeyed) controlling the uses of interior space, the furniture which would be allocated by rank, the exact accessories to be used by each employee, and exactly what types of personal items could be used or posted. One measure of control was the fact that tape could not be used on the steel walls.

At that time managers were given plain steel and plastic laminate desks and 100 square feet of office space. At the director levels the space increased to 150 square feet and the desk had wood-patterned plastic. Directors also reveled in two visitors' chairs with arms added.

At the vice-presidential level the square footage increased to 225. Although a real-wood desk was offered, most chose a worktable with no file drawers to show that vice-presidents don't have to tend files.

Egalitarian Design

In opposition to this hierarchical way of looking at office design, more companies today are looking at comfort and convenience for all their employees as a way of emphasizing employee participation and are more egalitarian in their approach.

An example of this way of looking at office design is General Motors Corporation's new Saturn headquarters in Troy, Michigan. Saturn managers instructed an office design firm that all of the furniture and carpeting must be the same grade and quality for *all* headquarters employees regardless of rank. The design firm didn't follow instructions and ordered much higher grade furniture and carpeting for the eight top executives.

When the executives found out what was happening, they cancelled the expensive executive furniture and carpet; in the process they saved more than $1 million. Evidently the Saturn part of General motors really believes in equal design treatment for all employees.

An important aspect of egalitarian design is employees' participation in the design of their own workplaces. As will be demonstrated in examples in the last chapter, this participation becomes a most important ingredient in the mix of measures to increase office productivity.

PART II

Changes Drive Office Design

Chapter 3

The Rush of Technology

Computer technology has advanced swiftly and industry experts say it will continue to do so. Stanford University economist Edward Steinmuller states, "If airline technology had changed as rapidly as computer technology, the Concorde would be carrying half a million passengers at 20 million miles per hour for less than a penny per passenger."

A research report from the Centre for Advanced Land Use Studies (CALUS), of the British College of Real Estate Management, says:

> If the automobile industry had developed at the same rate as the microelectronics industry over the last thirty years, it has been estimated that a Rolls Royce would cost a mere 1.39 pounds, would do 3,000,000 miles to a gallon and would develop enough power to drive the Queen Elizabeth 2. (CALUS 1983)

The first postwar Volkswagen Beetles and the first viable valve computers are contemporaneous. And yet, if the car had developed at the rate of the computer, today's Beetle would travel at 600 miles per hour, do 30,000 miles to the gallon, travel for 10,000 years between services and cost less than a dollar.

According to the Office Environment Index 1989, a survey conducted by Louis Harris and Associates and sponsored by Steelcase, 78 percent of office workers use a computer, the same percentage as in 1988. However, computer use has intensified. Workers' median use of computers increased in 1989 to four hours in the average workday as compared to three hours in 1988, and 23 percent use both a personal computer and a terminal connected to a mainframe.

At Imperial Oil in Canada, the number of personal computers in use rose from 25 to 1,100 in a five-year span. During the same period, the number of mainframe visual display terminals increased from 700 to 2,500. The company's computer storage was expanded 300 percent and instructions per second went up 252 percent.

According to Harris, the number of top executives with computer terminals or PCs in their offices increased to 57 percent in 1989 from 50 percent in 1988. Ten percent of top executives have both. For employees with more than one terminal, larger worksurfaces are needed, whether they be workers or executives.

A recent survey by Arthur Young & Company reported that 83 percent of the most senior U.S. financial executives now use their own computers. One reason executive use of terminals is increasing is that faster access is needed to raw information. In a large company an executive using his own terminal can get information that has not been screened or delayed by an entrenched data-processing hierarchy.

According to Peter Drucker (1985), an internationally known management consultant, the fact that an executive can immediately get information directly from a mainframe computer database has significantly reduced the number of middle managers. They have been phased out because their primary purpose was to process and transmit information. Now the computer does it faster, better, more accurately, and more comprehensively. Information is power and the ability to access that information through computer terminals can redistribute power. Executives don't want to get left in the lurch.

Cost and Size

According to Dr. Lewis Branscomb of IBM (1982), the price of small general computers of comparable power in dollars per instruction executed per second has been dropping at an annual compound rate of about 25 percent per year since the early 1950s. The average improvement in this rate for the largest general purpose computers has been about 15 percent per year. The

The computer enters the executive office. (Courtesy of Steelcase Inc.)

drop is less steep than for small machines because large computers offer added function as well as more computing power.

Dr. Humberto Gerola and Dr. Ralph E. Comery (1984), also of IBM, say that while computer technology has advanced rapidly over the past 20 years, continued growth at a similar pace can be expected through and probably beyond the 1990s.

It is likely that the trend will continue toward smaller, faster, and cheaper circuits made possible by improved production techniques. The speed of single-chip microprocessors is expected to increase by a factor of 10 by the end of the decade. Similar progress is anticipated in the areas of memory, magnetic storage, printers, and displays. Overall, approximately 20 percent growth annually in the capability of computing systems can be projected.

One of the necessary factors in this expected growth is the ability to put more and more circuits on a single chip. While at present it is only a dream, scientists at EMV Associates and others have been working for some time to develop organic-electronic microcircuits, so-called biotechnology chips that may be faster than present inorganic chips and 1/500 the size.

Another dream is the optical computer, which processes information encoded in light beams. If signals are processed optically, scientists studying the possibility say that this kind of a computer may offer the potential of computing at speeds measured in trillionths of seconds, up to ten times faster than today's fastest electronic computers. The optical computer also would offer vast improvements in cost, size, weight, power consumption, and reliability.

An example of what is happening in the race for smallness, is a computer NCR introduced some time ago. It is about the size of a bread box, weighs 50 pounds, and replaces a computer seven times that size; yet, the new computer is 50 percent more powerful and consumes 90 percent less electricity. It can sit on a desk or table or it can be hung on a wall.

Combined Devices

Several years ago Francis Duffy and Roger Pye pointed out that the real significance of computers, semiconductors, chips, microprocessors, and the communication they make possible comes from the fact that "what were once separate devices—typewriter, telephone, filing cabinets, copier and computer—have now become linked, not only linked, but inseparable" (1979).

One example of a combined device is the Displayphone from Northern Telecom. This is a combination of a telephone with a computer screen and keyboard, advertised as an "advanced business telephone and computer." It can call onto the screen information you need while you are talking, store much-used telephone numbers in its memory (the Displayphone will also dial them for you), use it for electronic mail, and obtain information from in-house or outside computers while you're talking on the hands-free telephone. Canon has a similar device called the Navigator.

Incidentally, electronic mail is now international and can either be electronically stored words and data or voice; it is said to end telephone tag. When Schering-Plough put in electronic mail, they drove the use of it from the top down with the idea that people have an incentive to use the system if the boss may have left them a message.

Mitel Corporation, a Canadian electronics manufacturer, has announced a similar product called Kontact™, an executive workstation that, in addition to offering the functions of the Displayphone, can be used as a word processor when a printer is attached. Competing designs have been marketed by AT&T, Compaq, and about two dozen other companies.

A further advance from combined telephones and computers is a device from Datapoint called Minx™, which combines a telephone, a personal computer with full color, and full-motion video so that face-to-face communication can also take place. Minx incorporates voice and video into an information-processing terminal that also provides word and data processing, database, spreadsheet, and shared resource capabilities.

A revolution for simple videophones may be brewing in Japan. Eight Japanese companies have introduced them and Fujitsu markets one that retails for less than $500. Sales of 2 million units per year in Japan are forecast by 1992.

Digital Equipment recently introduced a new linking product called DECtalk™, which is a speech synthesizer. The computer can be called from anywhere and asked verbally for information, which is given in any one of several synthesized voices, including a middle-aged man or woman, a young child, or a senior citizen.

Other New Devices and Their Effects

Two new devices may make the computer terminal more user-friendly and also attract more executive users.

The first is Hewlett-Packard's HP-150 personal computer, which uses infrared technology to make the human finger an instrument to reckon with. Infrared sensors tell the computer what to do when you touch pictures (icons) that appear on the screen. For example, your Personal Card File may be accessed by touching a picture of a card file. It is also noteworthy that the HP-150 screen fits onto the top of the central processing unit and that the printer fits onto the top of the screen. Without the keyboard, the rest of the system takes up just one square foot of desk top, a great advantage in the ongoing battle for desk top acreage. The touch screen can also be used for creating graphics.

The second device is a voice-activated computer that will accept English commands. A voice-activated computer has been in operation at the Massachusetts Institute of Technology for years, but until recently this type of equipment has been much too expensive for general use. Prices are coming down, however. An English firm has announced a voice-activated computer with a 4,000-word vocabulary for less than £2,000, or a little more than $3,900. The use of voice-activated computers will make tight acoustical control in the office an absolute necessity.

IBM uses infrared technology to provide cordless communication from keyboard to computer, allowing the keyboard to be moved around the office and still operate with the computer. Microwave radio is being used for the same purpose. These technologies allow great flexibility in workplace design.

Devices have been developed, primarily for the handicapped, to control computers with very slight movements, including one that moves the cursor with a shake of the head.

A Robot in the Office

An office robot developed by Bell & Howell is now in use. The Mailmobile®, equipped with a beeper and a flashing yellow light, is self-propelled with battery power and automatically guided along an invisible chemical path painted on the floor. The route can be changed by erasing the path and repainting it. In some cases it can outperform two or more messengers while increasing frequency of service and the number of dropoff points. Bell & Howell claims that with the addition of microprocessors and intelligent capabilities, the Mailmobile can "interface with elevators to serve multiple floors and perform varying stopping sequences."

Flat Panels and the Battle of the Windows

IBM and others have flat panel screens that reduce the total depth needed for the terminal significantly. Some are filled with neon and argon gases that glow when electric charges are passed through them to form the message on the screen. These devices, when coupled with appropriate printers, produce high-resolution graphics and printing. Some flat panels can also be divided into four quadrants or "windows." Each quadrant can be connected to a separate database or mainframe computer, allowing the user to work on four jobs at once. For instance, a travel agent could simultaneously check fares, seat and flight availabilities, and reservation status.

Windows have become a focus of competition. More than a dozen companies now offer software to split up computer displays into as many as six or seven windows, each representing a separate program, database, or file, meaning that the user can work on that many jobs at once. These "windows" often contain "icons" (described above) that reduce the number of keystrokes needed to activate a specific computer function.

New technologies for flat panel displays are also being developed, such as plasma panels, vacuum fluorescence, electro-luminescence, light-emitting diodes, and liquid crystals. Because of their matte surfaces, these new designs also hold the promise of not generating glare as typical screens do. Some of the more recent models also use less power.

Fax

Perhaps the most ubiquitous addition to the desktop is the facsimile machine, which may be a combination telephone and facsimile device. About 50 manufacturers competed for sales of about 910,000 machines in the United States in 1988—four times the number sold in 1986. By the end of 1989 it is estimated that there were about 3.4 million in use here.

Driving fax use are its convenience, speed of transmission, and the fact that when used late at night, it can be cheaper than USPS first-class mail. At any time of day or night it is usually cheaper than courier service for short documents.

The use of the fax in some countries is much heavier per capita than in the United States. Switzerland has 15 times as many machines; Norway, 12; and the United Kingdom, 8. Japan has 2.5 million faxes. Half of the telephone traffic between Japan and the United States is facsimile transmission.

The fax may disappear from some desktops, however. Several companies are now making easily installable boards for PCs that allow document transmission through a modem directly from one computer's disk to another computer's disk anywhere in the world. The document can be viewed on screen and/or printed out.

Competition for Space

Even with miniaturization, the use of flat screen panels, and the replacement of older devices by new ones, new devices tend to mean more machines taking up more space at every workstation. For example, substituting a word processor for a typewriter can require as much as 75 percent more worksurface.

Major changes, such as supplying workers with first-time computers in an existing office, can cause severe overcrowding. This is illustrated by what happened at one former "big eight" certified public accounting firm. The firm had a mainframe computer; it then bought a personal computer for each partner, thus crowding the partners' offices.

On one design job, the client had a variety of mainframes and then decided to purchase 500 personal computers but made no provision to plan for the extra space needed.

Among competitors for desktop real estate are the fax; the optical scanner, which reads printed pages and stores the words on standard magnetic computer disks; and the IBM Communications Module, used with the IBM typewriter to interface with "compatible typewriters, text processors, computers, and data networks."

Where did the worksurface go? (Courtesy of Sam Sloan, AIA.)

The proliferation of machines underscores the need for flexible and easily changeable workstation components. The rush of technology is so swift that some companies are changing the configuration of workstations as often as 10 times per year (see Chapter 17).

Studies of Present and Future Offices

Rapidly advancing technology continues to pose many problems for office and office building design. Two major British studies that explored these challenges have yielded some important design guidelines.

The first of the studies, ORBIT 1 *(Office Research into Buildings and Information Technology),* was conducted by Duffy, Eley, Giffone, Worthington (DEGW), architects and space planners; Building Use Studies, design researchers; and Eosys, electronic office systems specialists.

ORBIT 1 was a multi-client research project sponsored by organizations with an interest in the impact that information technology (IT) will have on the shape and function of office buildings in coming decades. The study defines IT as ''The use of computers, microelectronics and telecommunications to help obtain, store and send information in the form of pictures, words or numbers more reliably, quickly and economically'' (Duffy 1983).

Sponsors of ORBIT 1 included Steelcase (United States); Steelcase Strafor (United Kingdom); Bovis Construction; British Telecom (the British post office and telephone system); the British Department of Industry; Fletcher King (surveyors, valuers, and real estate agents); Glenrothes Development Corporation and two other Scottish New Towns (Livingston and Cumbernauld); Greycoat City Offices PLC (with Norwich Insurance Group); Jones, Lang, Wootton (chartered surveyors); Matthew Hall Mechanical and Electrical Engineers; the governments of Sweden, New South Wales, and Queensland; the town of Milton Keynes; and Prudential Insurance. Francis Duffy of DEGW is the principal author of ORBIT 1.

The second study is *Property and Information Technology: The Future for the Offices Market,* a Centre for Advanced Land Use Studies (CALUS) research report from the British College of Real Estate Management. CALUS describes a new form of office organization based on information technology as the ''information age office,'' the ''postindustrial office,'' the ''combi-office,'' and the ''post-microchip office.'' Individualism and job satisfaction are emphasized, and technology is viewed as ''the servant rather than as the master'' (1983).

Selected recommendations from ORBIT 1 and CALUS are offered below.

Though most offices are not now completely automated, the pace is swift. From ORBIT 1 we learn that when technology does arrive, it can have very fast and radical effects. Organizations or sections whose day-to-day work methods were previously unaffected can in one year reach a stage where 80 percent of workplaces have a computer terminal.

Workstation Size

A major consideration is the individual workplace, which will often have to be considerably larger, since the new machines—often bulky desk-top

Too many terminals for the amount of worksurface provided.

equipment—do not necessarily replace existing machines. Although some integration of functions occurs, new application ideas often lead to the purchase of new machines.

ORBIT 1 states that "the average size of individual workplaces is increasing by as much as 50 to 100 percent," adding that the

> ratio of ancillary or support space (i.e. shared areas for equipment, meetings, etc. rather than workplaces) is also increasing. In some organizations this increase has been at a rate of 25 percent over two years with the result that only 50 percent of net usable space in the building is occupied by workplaces. (Duffy 1983)

On this point CALUS (1983) notes that there was an increase of 45 percent in the amount of office space in England and Wales from 1966 to 1976, while the number of office employees only increased 13 percent. This difference occurred because more space was being used by each office employee. CALUS also says that in the United Kingdom and in the United States, with the increase in numbers of electronic office machines, this trend toward more space being assigned to each office worker will continue.

Building Specifications

ORBIT 1 states:

> *The specification for new buildings is more stringent than is generally assumed.* The popular conception that most information technology equipment can operate in general office areas is optimistic. While this may apply to terminals and microprocessors, powerful processors and paper handling equipment still require separation in specially controlled machine rooms. This is because the equipment will continue to require freedom from static and dust, as well as controlled humidity and even temperature.

Information technology is not easy to assimilate into office buildings. A major problem is that it generates many miles of cable. Another problem is that banks of equipment in general office areas (where staff work) generate heat.

Many existing buildings are in danger of premature obsolescence. This is because they will not be easy to modify in order to cope with the direct and indirect effects of information technology. Deep plan buildings (more than 56 feet deep) are the most clearly identifiable group in this category. . . .

Extensive and premature renovation of existing buildings will be expensive but inevitable. The cost of renovating certain types of office buildings to take on information technology may be equal to the cost of constructing new buildings. (Duffy 1983)

These worksurfaces are not sized adequately for the task. (Courtesy of Sam Sloan, AIA.)

Demand for Cellular Offices

ORBIT 1 identifies another needed building characteristic:

> The increased demand for cellular office space (private offices) with external views implies building forms with a high ratio of perimeter to floor area—i.e., building depths no wider than about 56 feet from perimeter to perimeter. Very narrow (less than 40 feet wide) or wide buildings (more than 56 feet wide) will be less flexible to use. (Duffy 1983)

CALUS essentially agrees with these dimensions and also points out that since these dimensions are about at the limit that buildings can be designed without obstructing columns, they are more flexible in terms of the way that the space can be used. These dimensions also allow almost all staff to work in natural light. CALUS forecasts that atrium buildings will become popular in Britain because they offer more natural light for office workers.

Security

ORBIT 1 has this to say about the increasing need for redundant security:

> Security will be an increasing cause of concern. Office buildings should allow visitors ready access and yet be capable of several layers of security zoning so that access is tightly controlled. It will be an advantage for office complexes to have a number of potential openings to be used as distinct ''front doors'' so that if there is more than one tenant each can have his own entrance. (Duffy 1983)

Floor-to-Ceiling Heights

ORBIT 1 states, ''Demands on services call for generous floor to ceiling heights of 9 feet and minimum floor to floor heights of 12 feet.'' The space between the floor and the ceiling is, of course, used for wiring and air conditioning and should be generous because the wiring tangles in spaces between open floors may resemble ''a nightmare in a pasta factory. . . . One workstation may require as many as five sockets.'' (Duffy 1983) As we shall see later, some workstations may require as many as ten.

Heating, Ventilating, and Air Conditioning (HVAC)

According to ORBIT 1,

> HVAC systems will need to be zoned in small areas, plus or minus 200 square feet, to cope with the problem of scattered ''hot spots'' caused by concentrations of equipment. (And the heat they produce.) Each VDT or other office device adds about the same amount of heat as a person does. (Duffy 1983)

CALUS comments that a word processor may produce as much as 10 times the amount of heat as the electric typewriter it replaced and that a large photocopier may generate 40 times as much heat as one worker does.

ORBIT 1 advises that ''the requirements of equipment have to be set against staff preferences for natural ventilation. In certain locations intermediate HVAC systems which allow a controlled mixture of natural and artificial environments will be appropriate.'' (Duffy 1983)

Ducting Capacity

ORBIT 1 notes that ''buildings which allow add-on capacity in the form of generous space for vertical and horizontal ductwork, or terraces to accommodate additional heat pumps, will be attractive.'' The study goes on to recommend that, in order to accommodate information technology, a building have a ''generous ratio of vertical ducting to floor area (over 2 percent),'' as well as ''generous and flexible horizontal ducting (raised floors, undercarpet flat wiring or good quality floor ducting), with dense outlets (at 5 foot centers). At the building scale, ample vertical ducting is required to allow for concentrations of cabling where horizontal ducts meet vertical ducts. Ducting should be dispersed rather than concentrated at one point.

Continued development is needed of a whole range of products which help to distribute cabling, such as rigid ducts, suspended service 'pods,' well-designed electrical outlet boards, and partitioning. These products will be of particular value in buildings that are hard to convert to heavy electronic use.''

The Office of the Future Is Here

Both ORBIT 1 and CALUS essentially agree that the office of the future is already in operation. ORBIT 1 says,

> *Most of the technology which will have greatest impact on office design over the next ten years already exists and is in use by leading edge organisations.* The more futuristic developments in office technology are likely to affect only a minority of organisations. Therefore present experience of information technology by advanced users is a good basis for judging future building requirements. (Duffy 1983)

CALUS makes the point differently:

> *When Information Technology is placed in a wider perspective it can be seen that the ''office of the future'' (at least during the 1990's) will certainly not be very futuristic and, it will be argued, may very well not be an office at all.* (Calus 1983)

Both studies agree that improvements in communication technology now make it possible for offices to be located almost anywhere.

As ORBIT 1 comments, ''*Information technology is changing the rules of office choice.* Locational options are increasing as communications improve. Therefore there may be more decentralisation and fewer large single tenancies in prime areas'' (Duffy 1983).

Interchangeable Buildings

CALUS discusses the new phenomenon of interchangeable buildings, with a shell so constructed that the space can easily be changed to permit use for offices, research, assembly of parts into products, light manufacturing, or other activities. Moreover, as the desired ratio of these uses changes, the spaces can easily be changed to permit whatever use is needed at any given time. Office space, for example, can become factory space and vice versa.

There has also been a blurring of some of the traditional differences among these activities. An example of an interchangeable building can be found at Plexus Computers in San Jose, California, where office workers and production employees work in the same facility.

Facilities Management

ORBIT 1 emphasizes that

> Facilities management should be given more status. More integrated management structures which bring together data processing management and space management at a high level of seniority are essential if building resources are not to be wasted. (Duffy 1983)

Challenges and Opportunities

ORBIT 1 draws a number of conclusions about the challenges and opportunities of the electronic office:

> *For developers and surveyors* the challenge is firstly to set standards for new office buildings, and secondly to work out which existing office buildings are worth renovating. Knowledge of what information technology means and willingness to help all potential tenants understand its implications should mean not only new kinds of buildings but new kinds of service.
>
> *For architects and engineers* the challenge is to devise building and servicing systems which allow change, which are sensitive to the needs of individuals and organisations, and which have the internal character, interest and quality to mature and survive short term expediency.
>
> *For builders* the challenge is to devise methods of construction which are not only quick and efficient but which allow easy access for change after the initial construction is complete. Better ways of adapting and reviving existing buildings are badly needed to save time and money. Building and adaptation are closer than ever before.
>
> *For furniture manufacturers* the challenge is to abandon old-fashioned concepts of the secondary role of office furniture and to invent not only practical solutions to office servicing but also to extend the range of furniture to include all scenery elements, such as screens.
>
> *For equipment manufacturers* the challenge is to realise the impact of their products upon buildings, organisations and individuals and incorporate this understanding in the design of their products.
>
> *For users* the challenge is to achieve the internal coordination between data processing and building management that is essential to achieve effective space management, assess what they expect their building to provide and communicate these requirements to the designers and suppliers.
>
> *For everyone* the challenge is to realise that buildings live: both long and short term design must be reconciled; design and construction must be sensitive to the dimension of time; and office design must enhance not only hardware but the software of space management. (Duffy 1983)

ORBIT 2

An advanced study, ORBIT 2 (Harbinger et al. 1985), has been completed in the United States. The thrust of ORBIT 2 was to develop a system for rating buildings by their ability to accept office information technology. The prime consultant was the Harbinger Group, a Xerox company. Associated consultants were DEGW, Dubin-Bloome Associates, and Facility Research

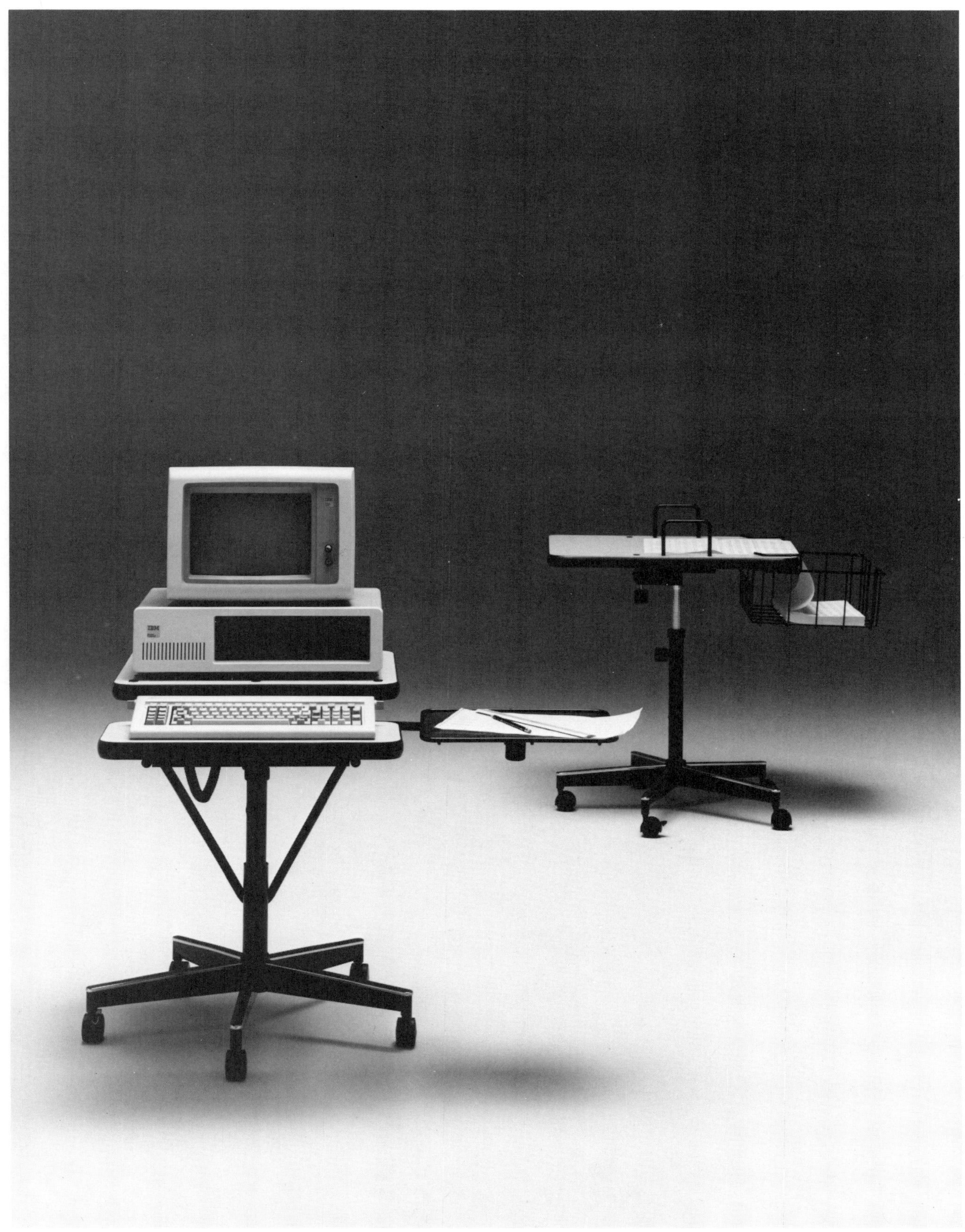

A movable, adjustable terminal table and a movable printer table. (Courtesy of JG Furniture Systems.)

Associates. American ORBIT 2 was sponsored by the World Bank, Honeywell, Mead, Interface Flooring Systems, TRW, Steelcase, Mobil Corporation, Tate Architectural Products, Xerox, Exxon Corporation, Donn Architectural Products, the Building Owners and Managers Institute, Birtcher Pacific, Public Works Canada, the Houston Design Center, the Alberta Department of Public Works Supply and Services, Mead, Arthur Young, and SunarHauserman, among others.

Each sponsor put forward one or two office buildings for experimental assessment in a wide variety of shapes, sizes, and types. The sponsors' diverse buildings and organizations also provided a test bed for the questionnaires and survey methods.

The needs defined by ORBIT 1, CALUS, and ORBIT 2 have resulted in a new phenomenon: the intelligent building. This development is the subject of the next chapter.

Chapter 4

Intelligent Office Buildings on Three Continents

Lack of depth is the usual price paid for breadth of ambition. In order to make sense of the current enthusiasm for intelligent office buildings, however, it is necessary not only to investigate what is happening in countries as widely dispersed as Japan, Sweden, and the United States but also to indulge in a rather liberal interpretation of what office buildings actually are. The first benefit of this point of view is that a great deal can be learned from contrasts between offices built in different countries (and for different organizations), particularly about values held by individuals and about the social structures that make up the modern office organization. The second benefit is that a better understanding of how offices are built and serviced—*through time*—is of great practical advantage to those who must manage rapidly changing organizations.

The phrase *intelligent building* means different things to different people. In a futuristic view one might imagine buildings that could orient toward the sun, or away from its burning rays, depending on the latitude for which they were built; buildings that could anticipate not only the extremes of climate but also the likely pattern of diurnal use so that scarce energy could be expended with the utmost parsimony; buildings that know where everything and everyone is at any time of day or night; buildings that recognize you and are sufficiently clever to hand you your raincoat and umbrella when you leave the door because they have learned from your diary that you are off on a trip to Manchester where rain, it so happens, is falling today.

Dimensions of Building Intelligence

A document produced by the newly deregulated and privatized Nippon Telegraph and Telephone Company (NTT), distinguishes three major aspects of building intelligence.

This chapter was contributed by Francis Duffy.

Office Automation

A high level of office automation is provided by the building owners, either for their own organization's use or for tenants. Such features include built-in local networks (local area networks [LANS] or "data highways") together with a wide selection of high-tech office equipment to provide word processing, large volume printing, electronic filing, electronic diaries, credit card access for timekeeping or for access to cafeteria and common office services, software support, and even "war rooms" where data is assembled and manipulated in electronic form for big decision makers.

Advanced Telecommunications

Tenants or user organizations are offered ready access to a far more up-to-date and wider range of telecommunication services than they would customarily expect. This wider range, which is achieved through digital switching and fiber optic cabling, leads not only to considerable advantages in volume and cost but also to particular services such as facsimile transmission; voice mail; and computer graphics; as well as voice, video, and computer conferencing.

Building Automation

The oldest and most reliable form of building intelligence is automation based upon the integration, through electronics, of various subsystems useful for running buildings, such as power management, security of people, and data, as well as energy.

Implications of the Quantitative Approach

NTT is quick to point out, not only in its documentation but also in its prototypical intelligent building projects, such as the new Shinagawa complex, that these three aspects of building intelligence have important implications for the way in which buildings are planned and managed. Also affected are the development of new kinds of building components (better ducting systems for cables and air conditioning, more responsive lighting and furniture, and building skins which react to light) and building techniques (life-cycle costing, fast tracking of construction, and greater responsiveness to changing demands).

There is an irony here. Despite this wonderful shopping list, the reality is that the kinds of office buildings currently occupied by organizations such as Honda, Mitsubishi, Mitsui, Daiwa, Toshiba, and Shimuzu are not only crushingly similar but, by advanced Western standards, elementary not just in quality but also in the application of information technology to office tasks. For a variety of complicated reasons (not the least of which is the refractory nature of the Japanese language, especially its characters) the bulk of office technology used in Japan tends to be centralized and allocated from the top down rather than equably distributed and dynamic. Hence the environmental stress generated in many Western organizations by PCs and LANs seems still to be rare in Japan. Perhaps this is why NTT fails to mention what to us is a colossally important aspect of building intelligence: the ability of buildings over time to accommodate changes in individual requirements and organizational demands.

Responsiveness to Change

Responsiveness is a more subtle, more qualitative aspect of building intelligence. In the 1960s the design of offices was influenced primarily by organizational efficiency (remember the endless arrays of elementary steel furniture and the appearance of the office before carpet came into general use). In the 1970s a new factor emerged that overtook but did not displace operational efficiency in office design—the need engendered by the energy crisis to cope with costs in use. Costs in use in their turn were overtaken in the 1980s, but not removed, by a new wave of concern for office quality. The timing of this development is explained by the substantial changes in the office population brought about by information technology. Obedient, poorly paid clerks have been more or less replaced by better educated, less easily satisfied professionals and managers who expect a better quality environment.

Twijnstra, a Dutch management consultants firm, has made projections that reflect the changing mission of the office building. Twijnstra argues that the office environment of the 1990s will be influenced by yet another factor, the need to stimulate creativity, to galvanize inert office organizations into greater teamwork and more demanding intellectual effort. Architectural devices such as the atrium, which are often thought of simply as spatial gimmickry, can be alternatively interpreted as a powerful means of making people in large organizations more aware of the totality of the organization and the relationships between its parts—a means, if used correctly, of stimulating organizational change.

There is little evidence of such environmental ambitions in Japan. In fact the reality is that most Japanese offices are stuck firmly in the era of operational efficiency, the only interesting feature of which is the use of the office environment to emphasize collectivity and teamwork. It is also clear, however, that the Japanese are less than happy with their existing offices. As one Japanese said to Professor Franklin Becker of Cornell, the pioneer of scientific facilities management, "Ten years ago your [American] factories were better than ours. Now ours are better equipped than yours. In ten years our offices will be better than yours." The Japanese may be prepared to tackle what NTT omitted from its otherwise extremely comprehensive list of the features of the intelligent building—the fourth dimension of intelligence, the capacity to respond to new kinds of demand.

In a time of rapid organizational and technological change, buildings cannot continue to be regarded as large, heavy, permanent entities—slow to build and expensive to run. Office buildings, in particular, are contrived by weaving together four major factors:

1. Information technology: the storage, processing and transmittal of information, primarily by electronic media
2. Organization: the social structure that holds people together to carry out office tasks
3. Building technology: the means available for constructing and servicing the building fabric
4. Facilities management: the software by which the use of buildings is programmed and managed through time.

No one building is ideal for all organizations. Depending on each user's particular mix of information technology and organizational structure, entirely different kinds of building technology and facilities management will be required. For example, contemporary Japanese and Swedish office buildings are totally different in appearance precisely because the office cultures of Japan and Sweden are so far apart. Such mixes change through time, never more so than at present, and to facilitate such change, it is enormously helpful to look at office buildings not as complete entities but as a series of imposed life cycles:

- The shell, skin, and structure, designed customarily (although this is increasingly in question) to last for at least 50 years
- The services—the primary mechanical and electrical systems, which are increasingly important and which have a life span usually no more than 15 years
- The scenery—the ceiling, partitions, furniture and finishes that constitute the fitting out necessary to accommodate a particular division or tenant. Such elements are usually cleared away within five to seven years of being installed, the customary length of a lease.

The more independent of each other these major time cycles are the easier it is for a building to accommodate change. For example, it should be possible to alter scenery without reconstructing the basic servicing structure or rebuilding the long-term shell. An interest in accommodating different kinds of tenants and different patterns in the use of building resources is of the utmost pragmatic importance in determining which building has the capacity (or the intelligence) to cope with different rates of organizational and technological change.

Building Intelligence in North America

The most intensive discussion of building intelligence in North America has not centered on building automation, although great advances have been made in energy management and in the development of automated building systems by firms such as Honeywell and Johnson Controls. What has caught the headlines is the contribution of office automation and advanced telecommunications to the aggressive marketing of real estate. The most common name for this is *shared tenant services* (STS)—value added by information technology services to multi-tenanted property. There are three reasons for this characteristically North American emphasis on tenancy and service:

1. The large scale and volatility of the North American real estate market and particularly the very important role of the speculative office developer. While such developers exist in most European countries, nowhere, except perhaps in the United Kingdom, is their importance so great.
2. The excellent North American tradition of building management, the result of a buyers' market and a much more responsive approach by landlords to tenants than exists, for example, in Britain. The importance of building management is also obviously more important in a situation where office buildings tend to be much bigger than in Europe and multitenancy is far more common. It is also true that in the United States tenants are more mobile, more sophisticated, and more demanding.
3. The deregulation of the great U.S. telephone monopoly, the Bell System, which has introduced competition and a bewildering variety of choices for users of telecommunication services. The legal reality is that not only is there competition between prime services but that each large building can, in effect, become a private utility company as far as telecommuni-

cations are concerned, run for the benefit of the tenants and the profit of the landlord.

In the United States in mid-1985, the height of the shared tenant services craze, there were approximately 100 office projects in which shared tenant services were offered and several hundred more under construction. Most were large (over 500,000 square feet) high-rise office buildings in major urban centers such as Houston, Dallas, and Atlanta, cities that were overbuilt after the 1982 recession and that continue to exhibit high vacancy rates. No one has yet become wealthy through providing shared tenant services and there is considerable doubt about the profitability of some already installed. There have been some notable failures and a gradual realization not only that some tenants resist the concept of sharing (they have their own preferred systems) but also that the management of shared tenant services is a considerable and labor-intensive necessity. The movement tends to be vendor driven by a combination of anxious developers and eager telecommunications salesmen, and there is little evidence of a ground swell of demand on the part of critical end users. Recently, however, the most active

An intelligent building, the $330 million Tabor Center in Denver. (Courtesy of United Technologies.)

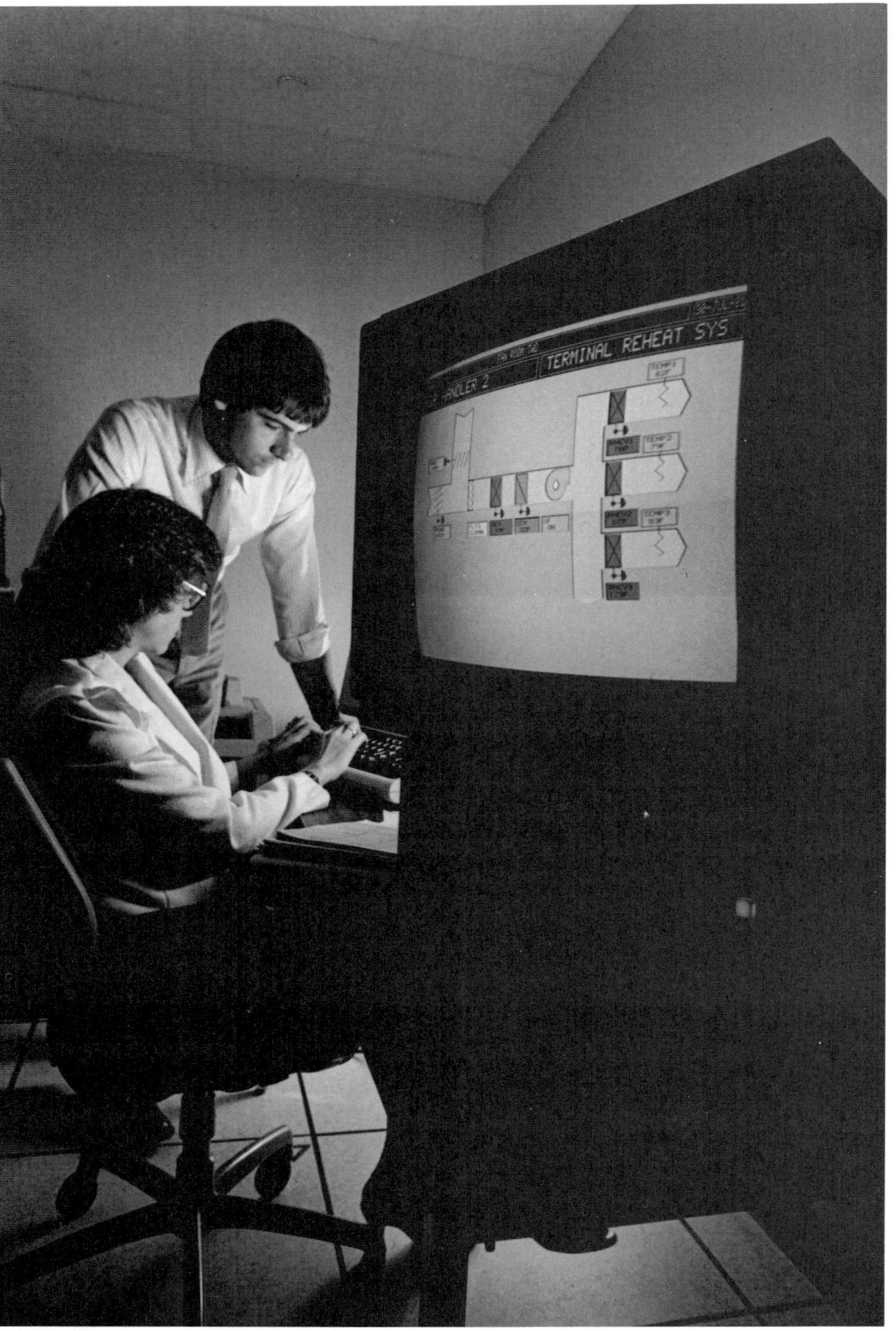

Facilities managers monitoring the computer in an intelligent building. (Courtesy of United Technologies.)

of the associations in this field, the International Intelligent Building Association, seems to be moving in a consumerist direction. To Europeans, used to monopolistic and slow-moving postal, telephone, and telegraph systems (PTT) and very often custom-built office buildings, the amount of hype has been astonishing. Nevertheless it is quite clear that shared tenant services are likely to survive as a long-term concept. In cities such as Dallas, STS has become a feature that no prime value office development can be without. The chief achievement is a product of the integrating culture of the communications age—the linking of two entities that had been conceptually quite distant, real estate and telecommunications.

Building Intelligence in Japan

There is considerable interest in Japan in what intelligence means for building design. At least one of the three factors that explain the rise of the intelligent building in the United States exists in Japan: the deregulation of the telephone monopoly, NTT, in late 1986. The paradoxical context is a society that is dependent on trading in high-tech products and not yet using them as extensively as many firms in North America and Western Europe. Office space in Tokyo includes some advanced buildings but many others of poor quality, which are at least as vulnerable to obsolescence caused by information technology as those in Britain. There are many firms with conservative and labor-intensive forms of office organization that are nonetheless extremely effective.

The outsider is struck by a number of differences in the Japanese approach to building intelligence:

- The vision, expressed frequently in brochures and publicity, of organizations such as Toshiba not just as collections of semiautonomous units, nor as organization charts that stress control and power, but as interactive networks of communications, which can overcome geographical dispersal and divisional specialization.
- The concreteness of the idea of the intelligent building as a product or a series of products, quite different from the American emphasis on marketing, and much more precise than European equivocation. Behind the obvious commercial motives, there seems to be for the Japanese a drive towards an aesthetic of complete electronic capability.
- A willingness to extend the idea of the intelligent building beyond the isolated site, beyond the particular organization to a much larger scale. A new kind of city planning is seen to be a logical extension of the intelligent building—hence plans for Tokyo Bay, for the Osaka Teleport, and for the competition for the city of Kawasaki: "Kawasaki as an Advanced Information City," in which electronics turns the city into a gigantic, continuous university-level seminar.

Given the close-knit structure of Japanese industry and the ability of the great trading houses to take ideas and turn them into products, it is not too fanciful to anticipate that the Japanese will succeed in exploiting building intelligence first to regenerate their decaying city fabrics, which are suffering from the relative decline of the old capital industries, and secondly to capture a vast potential market for a new generation of products based on building intelligence, such as superior elevators, air-conditioning units, and office furniture.

Building Intelligence in Europe

European offices, particularly those in Scandinavia, Germany, and Holland, have developed in a quite different way from those in North America and Japan. The difference, which is not so much technological as organizational, is due in particular to the enormous influence of widespread industrial democracy on the quality of working life.

Because Northern European offices tend to be custom-built and because consultation between employers and employees about the office environment is so common, the Northern European office has taken a dramatic step away from the big open plan towards highly individualized, cellular offices in which the need to give direct access to nature is the strongest determinant to form. Consequently the new generation of low-rise, cellular, finger-like offices in Northern Europe is quite unlike those found anywhere else in the world. In this the developer has played an insignificant role. The PTTs (national post, telephone, and telegraph systems) themselves are making such slow progress towards deregulation that the duopoly in the United Kingdom between British Telecom and Mercury is liberal by European standards.

The influence of the intelligent building in Europe is in three areas:

1. Building intelligence has been linked, as in Japan, very firmly to large-scale economic planning and redevelopment. Examples include the use of advanced telecommunications (wide area networks and the like) to provide a locational edge for developments like the Amsterdam and Koln teleports, for whole cities like Milton Keynes, and for areas of urban regeneration like London Docklands. Much more than in the United States and Japan, the teleport movement is itself a covert step towards deregulation of the PTTs, by providing for the first time on a large scale, competitive pricing for telecommunications services.

2. Building automation is used, not just at whole building level as in the design of energy efficient perimeter skin walls or all-comprehending security systems, but at the micro level of workstations, allowing each individual office worker to adjust lighting, air-conditioning, and access to data.

3. A significant contribution, at least as important as in the United States and far more advanced than in Japan, is the thinking about how buildings can be made more responsive to change. This contribution has largely been in inventing ways of measuring building performance on a rigorous comparative basis.

Building Evaluation

Measuring building performance is one aspect of the increasingly important software of facilities management. It depends upon powerful, well-organized users who are anxious to achieve buildings that meet their changing demands over time.

The ORBIT 1 study, carried out by DEGW, Building Use Studies, and EOSYS in the United Kingdom in 1982–1983, established design criteria for offices in the era of information technology. ORBIT 2 developed these criteria in the quite different context of North America into a technique to aid building users and developers assess changing demand for office space by different kinds of office organizations with different kinds of technology. In addition, the ORBIT 2 technique allows the same users and developers to measure supply in terms of the capacity to accommodate changing organizational and technological demands of any given building. The method can be applied at the level of an individual building, organization, or city and related to the needs of divisions, organizations, or whole sections of the office market (Harbinger et al. 1985).

In terms of building intelligence the most important task is linking supply with demand. No building, however automated, with whatever enhancement of office automation or advanced telecommunications, is intelligent unless it can cope with change. Such measurements as those in ORBIT 2 are the first real tests of that intelligence. ORBIT 2 completes the loop between building hardware and software and brings the four factors mentioned above—information technology, organization, building technology, and facilities management—into one complete system.

Impact of the New Office

In the course of the completion of ORBIT 1, a prediction was made, rather rashly it seemed at the time. This was that the introduction of information technology into office buildings built in the British office boom of the 1960s and 1970s would be so demanding and stressful that for many users their existing office stock would become prematurely obsolete. What premature obsolescence means is quite precise: the moment when the cost of bringing an office building up to date to meet the new demands of emerging information technology exceeds the cost of tearing the building down and beginning again.

This prediction has come true in London with a force that was not anticipated. Never before famous for architectural innovation, the City of London is today remarkable proof of how closely architectural form is linked to social and technological change. The ostensible cause is the "Big Bang," the deregulation on 27 October 1986 of the Stock Exchange. Underneath lie the internationalization of the financial services industry and the concentration in a limited number of world cities, of which London is one, of unprecedented telecommunications and computing power. The result is huge pressure on the existing office stock, rendered, as predicted, prematurely obsolete. The inevitable consequence has been a rapid program of construction of a new generation of office buildings, of a far superior order to those they replace. Office buildings of the 1960s are being torn down to make way for the new. The whole pattern of property values is shifting, as existing space in traditional locations is unable to compete with new space of the new quality.

The prototype of the new kind of office is Richard Rogers' new building for the Corporation of Lloyd's—a building that breaks most of the traditional rules of office development. Needless to say, it exhibits all four dimensions of building intelligence:

1. Office automation
2. Advanced telecommunications
3. Building automation
4. Responsiveness to change

Because of excellent briefing and the peculiar needs of the Corporation of Lloyd's (a marketplace in which shared information for member firms is critical) Lloyd's is London's first intelligent office building and it is, no doubt, the precursor of many more.

Tom Cross, author of *Intelligent Buildings* (1985), says that the intelligent building is one that is fully leased. To his basic definition the Japanese would add a dimension of technological completeness and the Europeans one of responsiveness to individual needs and organizational change.

We have a long way to go before the perfect building—whether in Japan, the United States, or Europe—meets the completely satisfied user. It should be clear that the challenge ahead is at least the equivalent to that posed by the invention of the office building in Chicago one hundred years ago, when a new technology of typewriters and telephones was necessary to open up the Midwest. What faces us today is not only the invention of a new kind of office but also new organizational forms that will transform the workplace as well as the city in the next century.

Chapter 5

The Office Can Be Anywhere

Two computers and two monitors, one set for data transmission and receiving and the other for video teleconferencing, can connect the user to the information world—from anywhere. The means now exist for dispersing offices geographically yet maintaining excellent coordination of activities.

Motivated by an opportunity to save labor costs, Citicorp has moved its credit card operations to Sioux Falls, South Dakota from New York City. Thousands of jobs traveled there with the move. West Publishing, the St. Paul, Minnesota firm that publishes Westlaw legal data bank, sends some entries to South Korea, where they are keypunched into its data bank.

In Barbados workers enter data into American Airlines' computers for $2.50 an hour. Previously the same work had been done in Tulsa for $6.00 per hour. The Barbados operation netted American at $3.5-million saving in its first full year of operation.

Satellite Data Corporation (SDC) is moving much of its work to various places in the Caribbean, attracted by having to pay wages of only about $1.50 to $2.50 an hour against about $9 an hour in New York. SDC is looking at India as a possible place to expand its activities. It is day in India when it is night in the United States, and much of SDC's business is handling information at night for delivery to its customers the next day. Also, India has a well-educated labor force with significant unemployment.

One reason SDC can consider almost anyplace to set up shop is that its work depends on satellites for communication. There is a further possibility that should be noted: Offices can be put in places where there are no telephone lines or even electric lines. A combination of technical advances provides the scenario for locating offices without the usual power and telecommunications sources. The chief advance has been the increasing ease and decreasing cost of satellite communication, which makes it possible for a dish with a receiver and transmitter to substitute for the usual phone and data lines. Ever more efficient photovoltaic cells generating electricity from sunlight can also play a part in divorcing office location from established electric power distribution networks.

The idea of moving clerical work offshore is not without its labor critics. A spokeswoman for "9 to 5," the National Association of Working

Women, calls this practice "telescabbing" and says that this union, which concentrates on organizing office workers, opposes moving office work offshore.

The Office As a System

A quote from CALUS sums up the revolution that has begun to take place now that the geographic dispersion of offices is becoming a reality. "Today an office is a *place* where an employee must be between specified *times* to suffer a variety of interruptions. . . . tomorrow an office will be a *system,* accessible via the terminal from *any place* at *any time.*" (1983)

The Office in a Car

While telephones have been in cars for quite a while, the advent of cellular radio has vastly increased the number of channels available and therefore the number of telephones in automobiles. Wang Laboratories even started a computerized car telephone answering service in the area around Boston. Of course, some portable computers can be used with car phones, and Tandon and others have introduced portable hard-disk drives. Portable facsimile machines used in cars piggyback on the cellular telephone's popularity. By the end of 1989 there were about 3 million cellular phones in use.

The Airborne Office

Some private aircraft with sophisticated communications equipment serve now as offices and TWA, American, Northwest, Eastern, Delta, United, and other airlines have installed Airfones on some of their planes. Airfones, a device from Goeken Communications and Western Union, allow passengers to make phone calls in flight. A wide variety of portable and pocket computer terminals are now available and now most airlines allow their use in flight; some airlines are considering carrying rentable portable terminals for passenger use.

The Office Away

According to *Frequent Flyer* magazine, about one of every seven of its readers needs temporary offices while traveling. This need is being filled in a variety of ways. First there are independent chains such as HQ who provide anything from an office with desk, table, chairs, and telephone to complete conference facilities; from just telephone answering to experienced secretarial and administrative staff plus computer equipment for word processing, telex, facsimile transmission, and reception as well as conference facilities complete with audio-visual equipment that can be used for video teleconferencing. HQ operates in more than 70 locations within the United States and is owned by United Technologies Building Systems. United Technologies, being very active in the intelligent buildings field, provides its HQ centers with its latest telecommunications equipment.

Another chain is World-Wide Business Centres, based in New York with 60 U.S. centers and several international ones. In addition to the services above, World-Wide offers translators in each of the countries where it is located.

Chicago-based EasyKeys rents temporary space and IBM personal computers, complete with business application programs. Each office is equipped with 7 to 10 IBM PCs and personnel are available to do the computer work if required. Access to several standard public databases is also offered.

These centers can be used for part of a day or longer; some can be rented for a year with the renter's name on the office door and listed in the building directory. Free-standing centers of this type are believed to appeal especially to businesswomen, since they allow the transaction of business in a location that is strictly business oriented, rather than in the somewhat ambiguous alternative of a hotel room.

Hotels and airlines are installing business centers around the world. While they do not all offer the same ranges of services, some are just as elaborate as the most sophisticated of the chain centers. It is now possible to book an office when you book your flight.

In that home-away-from-home, the motel or hotel room, computer devices utilizing the usual in-room TV set (see below) are beginning to appear. They offer electronic mail, airline reservations, stock market quotations, the purchase of flowers and gifts, lists of real estate agents, and many other services. Of course, the first thing you transmit is your credit card number. At least one hotel, the Sheraton Grand in Washington, D.C., rents portable computers to guests along with software that is compatible with Wang, IBM, and ITT computers.

Offices Apart

With state-of-the-art communications available to businesses, the accounting department no longer needs to be located next to the advertising department—they can be hundreds of even thousands of miles apart. Nor do executive offices necessarily have to be next to the research department.

Xerox has been experimenting with a collaboration of two groups of scientists with offices 500 miles apart, one group in Palo Alto, California and the other in Portland, Oregon. Each office is in constant communication with the other using cameras, computers, and microphones that are always in operation. The experiment involves a physicist, a psychologist, two architects, and assorted computer experts. While there have been some difficulties, Xerox believes that the experiment is worthwhile.

The "Electronic Cottage"

Toffler, in his book, *The Third Wave,* called the home the "electronic cottage," and it is becoming just that. Even though most homes are not well equipped to handle them, some of the activities that are carried on in homes now, including filling out various tax forms and preparing family budgets, are jobs that are at least a bit more knotty than some of those that are performed in offices. Some experts predict that by the time this book reaches print there will be more than 18 million computers in homes in the United States and these home tasks will become easier.

However, this may be just the tip of a growing iceberg.

Digital television is here. When 350 parts in a typical television set are replaced with eight semiconductor chips, the ubiquitous television set also becomes a computer. Right now digital TV is expensive, but its use will spread as the cost comes down.

At least three condominium developers in New York City have offered buyers more than the usual assortment of appliances. As a standard feature, apartments include a computer terminal, and some offer subscriptions and connections to data banks such as airline schedules, stock quotes, and other services.

Telecommuting

The beginnings of a strong trend that moves work out of the office and into the home are apparent. Data General Corporation has a number of terminals that can be used by workers at home. Digital Equipment Corporation has several hundred people who also prefer to work at home. The term "telecommuting" has been coined for the electronic connection between home and office. It is worth noting, however, that some home workers regularly make weekly luncheon dates and come into the office; the office is a social waterhole and many workers say they miss the interaction.

Telecommuting can be very well suited to the mother who has small children at home and wants to continue her career at the office while taking

This is a simple but effective height-adjustable shelf and pole system for offices in homes or elsewhere. (Courtesy of Rangine Corp.)

care of her children. It can also be attractive to handicapped people who find commuting onerous.

Evidence is beginning to appear that substantial increases in productivity can result from working in the home. A study of 16 clerical employees who work at home was done by Blue Cross & Blue Shield of South Carolina. Employees were 50 percent more productive than workers in the office who were doing identical work—keying insurance claims into the computer and coding other material. Some of these Blue Cross employees are earning $8,000 per year more than workers doing the same job on company premises. A possible reason for this increase is thought to be that home workers can set their own schedules and fit time available to the job; thus, they are more relaxed and free of the time constraints of regular office schedules. Mountain Bell in Denver has reported that some of its people who work at home have increased their productivity as much as 40 percent.

Another reason some companies like telecommuting workers is that they save on office space costs. A British authority estimates facilities cost of £14,000 (more than $26,000) per office worker per year in London. Also, office expansions using telecommuters can be accomplished without leasing additional space.

Rank Xerox found that facilities costs made up 31 percent of the bill for employing someone in Central London. The firm therefore established a separate computer network called Xanadu for 60 employees who work at home. They contract to work half-time at rates from £80 to £600 per day, depending upon the type of work they do.

As early as 1985, a report in *The Wall Street Journal* (1985c) estimated that there would be more than 7.2 million telecommuters before the end of the year, most of them being ''professional men with computer-related jobs and lots of autonomy.'' *WSJ* also reported that ''Self-employed telecommuters outnumber company-employed about 5-to-1.'' Writers,* researchers, consultants, software developers, computer programmers, and systems analysts are likely to be frequent telecommuters. This *WSJ* report, which was prepared by Electronic Services Unlimited, a New York consultant, also says that IBM alone has placed more than 8,000 computers in employees' homes. Other experts' estimates of the number of ''telecommuters'' in 1985 were consistently lower at less than one million.

The Chicago Tribune has reported that 10 million Americans give home addresses as their places of business on their tax returns, a 50 percent increase over 10 years ago. AT&T has estimated that 23 million people in the United States call home their principal place of work. Of course, while not all of these are telecommuters, this figure indicates that the increase in business done at home is quite substantial.

A survey by *Modern Office Technology (MOT)* revealed that more than 37 percent of its readers have specific home office areas for work in addition to what they do at their regular offices, and almost 77 percent of these people say that their companies pay for products and equipment that make it possible for them to work at home.

Some analysts say that the growing trend to telecommuting will lead to the need for more conference spaces in the office, since telecommuters will need to come into the office from time to time to discuss work completed and new assignments. They also note that the advent of more group work will add to this need.

*The manuscript of this book was put into a word processor and printed in an apartment where one of the authors lives.

The Portable Handheld Computer Terminal

A very important extension of the electronic office beyond its physical location is Motorola's 28-ounce portable handheld computer terminal that communicates with a mainframe via digital radio. It is battery operated and does not depend on phone lines. It enables the user to ask detailed questions and get answers quickly. Within a limited range, this allows salespeople, for instance, to communicate orders and to get delivery or special pricing information. Service representatives can enter information into the mainframe directly and instantly. In effect, this device extends the office into the community.

A Computer Community

A computerized community has been created in Ridgewood, New Jersey under the auspices of AT&T and CBS. Two hundred homes have been wired for computers of two types: one is a free-standing machine and the other attaches to an existing TV set using the TV screen as the screen for the computer. Services offered in this experiment, called Videotex, include news reports from CBS and *The Record* of Hackensack (the local newspaper), banking services, household hints and national and local advertising with the ability to buy items advertised through the computer.

Being able to have a computer at home has enabled brokers to start a few new securities trading firms that are run from the homes of the owners. Since the computer is enhancing the ability of people to work in the same places where they live, there is at least one architect in New York City, Peter Wheelwright, who has his office and home in a spacious loft and a booming business designing space for people who live and work in the same location.

Housing the New Office in Old Buildings

It is an inescapable fact that although the office of tomorrow can be "anywhere," it will often be housed in existing structures.

The value of the traditional office building in the city center is now questionable, however. Offices that have traditionally been concentrated in the cities have for some time been moving to the suburbs because it has become harder to get to and from city offices and too expensive to live near them in high-rent city apartments. These problems affect recruitment as well as length of employment.

The movement of the computer and office work performed with it into the home is an example of the greater freedom of work location now offered by the abilities of computers and improved communication devices that together allow office work to go on almost anywhere.

Duffy and Pye made a forecast ten years ago that freedom of work location would result in another change. They said that we may be "moving from an *employment* economy, in which most of us sell our time in blocks of eight hours, five days a week, to a *contractual* economy in which services rather than hours are sold." Some of the companies who have employees working in their homes pay employees for each job as it is finished, or in other words, as if each job were covered under a separate contract.

As part of their forecast they saw offices as smaller units that can occupy a wide variety of spaces, not necessarily in the central city core. They saw a future demand for many small units of space, of high but varying quality, dispersed throughout cities, such as old houses, old warehouses, "living rooms, the whole fabric of city and town."

Tax Credits for Renovation

According to the U.S. Department of Commerce, in 1979 the number of older buildings being rehabilitated for the first time exceeded the number of buildings being built. In 1985, the market share for commercial renovation was 55.4 percent, while new commercial construction accounted for 44.6 percent.

In picking a location for an office, older buildings may be attractive in a number of ways. The tax advantages are enticing because a wide range of renovation activities are eligible for tax credits which can be used directly to reduce federal income tax liability on a dollar-for-dollar basis.

Eligible projects include upgrading electrical, plumbing, and air-conditioning systems; adding acoustic materials; correcting building code violations; refurbishing wall and floor finishes; and redistributing interior spaces with new interior walls and doors.

There are conditions attached, however. The total renovation project cost must exceed $5,000 or the adjusted basis of the building, whichever is greater. For noncertified historic structures, at least 75 percent of the building's exterior walls must be retained, including 50 percent as external walls, and at least 75 percent of the building's internal structural frame work must remain.

How much are the credits? For U.S. residential buildings placed in service prior to 1936, a 10 percent credit of the sum spent for qualified renovation expenses is available. If the building is a listed, certified historical structure (either residential or nonresidential), a 20 percent credit is usable, no matter how old the building is. A certified historic structure is a qualified, rehabilitated building that includes any building (and its structural components) listed in the National Register or located in a registered historic district and certified by the Secretary of the Interior as having historic significance to a particular district.

Another condition that must be met to receive these credits in the United States is that straight-line depreciation (31.5 years for nonresidential and 27.5 years for residential) must be used for the renovation expenditures.

Because the amount of tax credits usable by each individual investor is limited to $7,000 per year (28 percent of the $25,000 passive load offset to nonpassive income), usefulness to a person with a large income is not great. Investors with an adjusted gross income (AGI) of more than $200,000 ($100,000 for marrieds filing separately), the credit is reduced by one-half of the taxpayer's AGI over $200,000. Thus, there is no credit if AGI exceeds $250,000 ($125,000 for marrieds filing separately).

Various types of grants for restoring historic buildings are available in Great Britain.

Two warnings:

1. Get detailed cost estimates before you decide to go ahead with a renovation. Renovation of an old building can cost more than building a new building.

2. Like most parts of the U.S. Internal Revenue Code, the regulations covering these credits are labyrinthine. It is essential to get qualified, professional tax advice *before* refurbishing, especially since there is the constant possibility that the federal tax laws may be changed.

A Checklist for Older Buildings

Some other things to check before buying and refurbishing an older building are the following:

1. Is the building in a location that is convenient for employees and customers? Is it near restaurants, shops, and public transportation lines? Is it in a ''safe'' part of town? Is it in a neighborhood that is on the way up or down? Is it zoned for all the uses you intend for the building?
2. Is ample parking available?
3. Is the interior circulation what you need? Or, does it have to be changed?
4. Is the interior area (usable square feet) adequate for your needs? Is it suitable for the type of offices you plan to have?
5. What is the condition of the structure? Can the existing walls be used? (Remember that to get a renovation tax credit, at least 75 percent of the existing walls must remain and be used.)
6. What is the condition of the floors, wall surfaces, windows, sills, foundation, plumbing, heating, air-conditioning, stairways, and roof? For instance, are the floors strong enough to carry the loads you intend to put on them? Careful estimates of each of these refurbishing costs need to be made by qualified people.
7. What about electric, telephone, and data lines? Is there sufficient floor-to-floor height for a dropped ceiling or an access floor to be used? Is there room for all the ducts that will be needed? Look for 12-foot distance from floor-to-floor; anything less is questionable for offices.
8. What about access to the building? Are the entrances of sufficient size for what has to be brought into the building? If it's a multi-story building, does it have elevators? If so, what condition are they in? Are their size and speed sufficient to handle the load?
9. Does the building meet fire, electrical, plumbing, and life safety codes? For instance, do existing fire alarms and suppression systems work? Will sprinklers be required?
10. How much will insurance on the building cost?
11. How much are professional fees for analysis and redesign?
12. How are improvements to be financed?

Chapter 6

Health Hazards and Worker Safety Issues

Two of the best recent books on office health hazards are the following:

Office Hazards: *How Your Job Can Make You Sick,* by Joel Makower (Washington, D.C.: Tilden Press, 1981)

Office Workers' Survival Handbook: A Guide to Fighting Health Hazards in the Office, by Marianne Craig (London: BSSRS Publications, 1983)

Published by trade unions, they explore worker safety issues in detail and make a strong case for office workers to form and join unions.

Ms. Craig says in her introduction:

> The book emphasizes repeatedly that you have a *right* to a safe and healthy job. But more than that, you have the right to work in a stress-free job, where there is flexibility and where you have control over what you are doing. You have a right to work in comfort with good facilities such as canteens, rest rooms and nurseries. In an age when they sent men to the moon there is no reason why these basic rights should not be ours.

Ms. Craig concludes the introduction by saying, ''Office work is dangerous to your health, but where you can trace the cause of ill-health and organise against it, it can be prevented.''

Distributed by the Trade Union Book Service in England, the *Office Workers' Survival Handbook* is well researched. It is worth noting that with a few exceptions, it uses a different database than the American book, *Office Hazards.*

Co-author Francis Duffy reviewed Craig's book for *The Architects' Journal.* Calling it ''a brilliant polemic,'' he says that

> what should concern architects most is the long catalog of deficiencies in the physical environment of the office. . . . Craig's clear and cleverly directed book is as valuable as most architectural guidance on office design. More significantly, it is evidence of an expanding and increasingly active client body.

> We architects will have to learn how to design not for but *with* these multiple and often fractious client bodies. It will be an interesting test for which neither our old professional arrogance nor some new and still hypocritical humility has prepared us. (Duffy 1981b)

Makower's *Office Hazards* has an introduction by Karen Nussbaum, President of Working Women, which is affiliated with Service Employees International Union as District 925 (read "9 to 5"). She argues that "the health of office workers is threatened daily by the machines we use, the chemicals in common office products, by the design of our offices and the structure of our work."

The press release for *Office Hazards* contains this statement by Makower:

> The nature of the problem is that the individual problems in offices are rather small, seemingly trivial things. An uncomfortable chair may not seem like a major calamity; neither does stuffy air or a few ringing telephones. But put an office worker in a bad chair in a noisy, stuffy office, require that worker to perform a deadend job for low pay on a video display terminal (VDT) with a dirty screen made worse by the glare from fluorescent lights; add a dash of pressure—a ruthless supervisor, for example, or economic or family problems—and you've got a potentially explosive situation.

These books zero in on real problems. Both include, for instance, extensive analyses of problems concerning lighting, seating, noise, stress, heating, ventilation and air-conditioning, and the myriad effects surrounding the use of VDTs.

The National Office Products Association assessed the situation in a study called "The Future of the Office Furniture Industry," which took a year and a half to produce with a research team from the University of Michigan. The study describes "the darker side of office automation" as "the potential decline in workers' health and well-being. Evidence is mounting that working in an automated office poses potential health hazards and job satisfaction in automated offices tends to be low." (National Office Products Association 1983) The research team compares the developing automated offices with automated factories and their dehumanizing atmospheres and goes on to predict that

> Union activity to organize white collar workers in automated offices is increasing. It is expected that by 1993 four times as many white collar workers will be unionized as are today. Government regulation of white-collar working conditions is on the increase, most noticeably at the state level.

And then there is a boost for participatory design: "A proven approach to these problems is to involve employees as much as possible in the decisions that affect them" (see Chapter 22).

Research Findings

Strain Injuries

Musculoskeletal complaints can be reduced or eradicated by the use of adjustable workstation furniture (see Chapter 8, Adjustability in Chairs and Worksurfaces). These complaints are important. Liberty Mutual Insurance, one of the largest underwriters of workers' compensation insurance, says that lower back pain is the number one industrial complaint and is responsible for $14 billion in claims per year. The Department of Health and Human Services says that lower back problems account for 93 million lost workdays each year in the United States. A lot of lower back pain in offices can be attributed to chairs and worksurfaces that are not fully adjustable.

Stephen Channer, Executive Director of The Business and Institutional Furniture Manufacturers Association, says, "Over the past two or three years, businesses have learned that you can't just buy a word processor, put it on a typewriter desk, and expect to get away without any worker health complaints (1983)."

One of the most serious groups of complaints comes from Australia. Dr. Peter Ellis reports in *Facilities* that there is an epidemic of repetitive strain injuries among electronic keyboard operators there affecting forearms, wrists, and hands. Ten thousand cases for industrial compensation have been filed in Australian courts and 20 percent of keyboard operators are off work at any one time (1986).

Radiation

Most authorities agree that both ionizing (X-rays) and nonionizing radiation from VDTs is so low that it is not a health or safety problem. Dr. Richard S. Hirsch, Human Factors Program Director for IBM, has said,

> Relative to the most stringent worldwide safety standards, the non-ionizing radiation levels measured from CRT's are: one one-thousandth of the least allowable exposure of ultraviolet, one one-thousandth visible, one one-thousandth infrared, one one-billionth microwave and two one-thousandth radio frequency. (1984)

Concerning ionizing radiation, Dr. Hirsch stated, "There is now a considerable body of literature on the subject of ionizing radiation in the office environment, and all of it indicates that VDT's are safe." The National Research Council has reviewed the available competent studies and has come to the same conclusion.

There is still, however, disagreement with these declarations that radiation from VDTs is not dangerous. There have been 15 alleged clusters of women operating VDTs around this country and in Canada where substantial proportions of each group have encountered difficulties with their pregnancies, including fetal abnormalities and miscarriages.

The National Institute of Occupational Safety and Health (NIOSH) and The March of Dimes Birth Defects Foundation have taken the position that VDTs cannot be responsible for these problem pregnancies because radiation levels from VDTs are so low. Further, the Birth Defects Branch of the Center for Disease Control in Atlanta concluded that 'the apparent clusters are statistically non-significant when compared with the national miscarriage rate," which they cited as 33 per cent of all pregnancies.

The Bureau of National Affairs has cited less optimistic findings:

> Epidemiological studies of the effect on humans of chronic exposure to low-level, non-ionizing radiation have not been carried out. . . . However, research at the University of Washington and at the U.S. Environmental Protection Agency in Las Vegas, Nevada radiation laboratory found that VDT's produce pulsed magnetic fields similar to those found previously to harm chick embryos (1989).

In 1988 an agreement was reached between management and labor in Sweden that had the effect of reducing the allowable amount of very low frequency radiation from VDTs; late in 1989 IBM announced terminals that meet the Swedish standards and said that it would continue to reduce radiation from future models. Digital Equipment Corporation also has a terminal that meets the Swedish standards, but says that there is little demand for it.

Professors William Butler and Kelley Brix, of the University of Michigan School of Public Health, reported on the first results of a survey of 4,215 clerical employees of the State of Michigan in September, 1986. They found that for women who work from 0 to 20 hours per week at VDTs the number of miscarriages was about as expected in the general population. However, for women who work at VDTs more than 20 hours per week, there were slightly more miscarriages reported than would be expected. Because of the small sample of more than 20-hour-per-week workers, the researchers called the results inconclusive (Butler and Brix 1986).

NIOSH started a large-scale epidemiological study of 6,000 married working women of childbearing age some years ago to try to find out whether or not working at a VDT can cause spontaneous abortions and birth defects. Three thousand of the sample will be women who work at VDTs and the other 3,000 will be women who work, but do not use a VDT. Results of this study have not been released at this writing.

Researchers at Mount Sinai Hospital's medical school in New York are planning to survey 10,000 VDT workers over a period of four years to assess health problems associated with VDT use. The study will focus particularly on the low level radiation issue described above. Volunteers from the Service Employees International Union will carry out the field work.

Stress

Stress symptoms such as insomnia, irritability, anxiety, and fatigue are common among office workers who use VDTs. A Harvard Medical School study found that "VDT users complain more about their job situation than any other type of employee."

Dr. Arthur Frank, a University of Kentucky scientist, studied more than 1,100 members of the Newspaper Guild to find out the effects of VDTs on their health. He found significantly more headaches; eye strain; deteriorated vision; and pain in the neck, back, and shoulders than he found in VDT nonusers. Perhaps more important, he said that "VDT users lost more time from work than did non-users. . . . VDT users were absent more than one-half day longer per month on average than non-users."

Back in 1981, NIOSH reported on what it called "the first comprehensive evaluation" of VDT operators' job stress problems in the United States. NIOSH studied 250 VDT operators and 150 non-VDT operators in the San Francisco area. NIOSH said,

> The major finding of the investigation is that working with VDT's is associated with high levels of job stress." The study also showed that "Significantly more clerical VDT operators reported job stress health problems than did professionals using VDTs or control subjects. (Bureau of National Affairs 1984)

However, another NIOSH-sponsored study executed by the University of Wisconsin Medical School covered 248 clerical VDT workers and 85 traditional clerical office workers. This study found that VDT workers are not generally subject to greater job stress than traditional clerical workers, but that the VDT workers in the survey were less satisfied with their jobs.

The authors believe that VDT job stress is associated with inadequate lighting design, inadequate noise control, the lack of adjustable workstation furniture, the intensity of VDT clerical work, and the lack of adequate rest breaks to relieve that intensity, plus one more factor, electronic monitoring of clerical VDT job performance.

NIOSH estimates that about two-thirds of the VDT operators in the United States are electronically monitored to determine their performance on the job in relation to speed, accuracy, and the amount of work completed. A monitored VDT worker testified before a House subcommittee that "Electronic monitoring is the most offensive and pernicious aspect of our jobs" (Bureau of National Affairs 1984). Union leaders despise the practice and it certainly is a major cause of job stress.

Visual Problems

Problems with vision have been widely reported among office workers who use VDTs; more than half of VDT operators complain about trouble with their eyes. Long, intensive work periods do cause eye strain, especially when workers have to shift their focus constantly from black characters on white paper to the typical computer screen with its light letters on a dark background. These continual shifts are quite a contrast to the typical non-VDT office job's steady gaze at black characters on white paper.

While the most common visual complaint is fatigue, there are others: irritation, blurred vision, and difficulty in focusing. Some of the known causes include glare and inadequate lighting design (see Chapter 13), as well as the degree of legibility of the message on the screen.

Distrust of Computers

Dr. Sanford B. Weinberg says that one-third of all workers distrust computers and 5 percent of those persons have cyberphobia—fear of computers—to such an extent that they have "severe, often physically disabling reactions, including dizziness, nausea and a rapid pulse rate," whenever they are asked to use a computer (1983). To overcome distrust and cyberphobia, he recommends involving users in the selection of the system and its layout, communicating fully about changes from management, and getting the new system up and fully running before closing out the old system.

U.S. Government Guidelines

The NIOSH guidelines follow. (The reader will find more detailed information from the authors in following sections of the book on the points covered in the guidelines.)

> Recognizing the state of knowledge regarding ergonomic, stress and radiation issues in VDT work, NIOSH recommends the following general guidelines, which may require modification in specific situations:
>
> (1) Workstation design: Maximum flexibility should be designed into VDT units, supporting tables and operator chairs. VDT's should have detachable keyboards, work tables should be height adjustable and chairs should be height adjustable and provide proper back support.
>
> (2) Illumination: Sources of glare should be controlled through VDT placement (i.e., parallel to windows as well as parallel to and between

lights), proper lighting and the use of glare control devices on the VDT screen surface.

Illumination levels should be lower for VDT tasks requiring screen-intensive work and increased as the need to use hard copy increases. In some cases, hard copy material may require local lighting in addition to the normal office lighting.

(3) Work regimens: Continuous work at VDT's should be interrupted periodically by rest breaks or other work activities that do not produce visual fatigue or muscular tension. As a minimum, a break should be taken after 2 hours of continuous VDT work and breaks should be more frequent as visual, mental and muscular burdens increase.

(4) Vision testing: VDT workers should have visual testing before beginning VDT work and periodically thereafter to ensure that they have adequately corrected vision to handle such work. (1984)

We emphasize that these are guidelines, not standards or regulations.

A voluntary VDT workstation standard has been developed by the Human Factors Society in conjunction with the American National Standards Institute. Human factors professionals formed the committee. Government agencies, labor unions, computer and furniture manufacturers, trade associations, and users were to review the proposed standard and make suggestions (see Chapter 19, on BIFMA and Other Standards).

Pressure for Regulation

The authors estimate that nationwide, more than half a million VDT workers are members of unions. Bills regulating the use of VDTs have been introduced in 23 state legislatures. Since what the unions are asking for and the content of the bills are quite similar, the list below is a summary of union demands in agreement with employers combined with the content of proposed bills. At this writing, none of the proposed bills (with one exception noted) have passed, but some of the items below are appearing in negotiated contracts between employers and unions. Other items below appear in model contracts proposed by unions.

The following items (some proposed and some in force in actual union contracts) govern VDT work:

1. *Eye tests and records at the employer's expense:* Not only are preliminary tests being asked for before the VDT worker starts work, but tests are also being requested at stated intervals, usually annually. One bill goes so far as to specify exactly what eye tests should be given. Record keeping up to 25 years after the employee has retired is being asked for so that analysis can be made of the visual effects of work with VDTs. Payment for employee glasses by the employer is being requested. The employer would be prohibited from using the results of an eye examination to screen employees for suitability for work at a VDT.
2. *Rest breaks:* Some bills and contracts follow the NIOSH guidelines. One proposed bill asks for a paid 15-minute break or 15 minutes of alternative work for every hour of work at a VDT. Another asks for a 30-minute break after two hours of intensive work with high visual demands. One bill would limit work at a terminal to five hours per day and another to four hours. Still another limits VDT work to three consecutive days.

3. *Individual monitoring:* Prohibition is requested.
4. *Lighting:* One bill asks for a light level no higher than 700 lux and elimination of glare with drapes and blinds, indirect lighting, or recessed lighting with louvers and installation of antiglare filters on VDT screens at the user's request. It also provides that no user or VDT screen shall face a window. Another bill calls for availability of a supplementary task light at user's request and adjustable general lighting levels plus screen hoods.
5. *Acoustics:* It is requested that no printer be in the same room with a computer unless the printer has an acoustic cover. One proposal would limit the noise level for the VDT operations area to 75 decibels, another to 85 decibels. Another calls for a detachable printer.
6. *Adjustable chairs:* One proposal specifies that VDT workers' chairs shall have user-activated adjustments for seat and backrest height plus backrest tension. Another requires one-half length armrests.
7. *Adjustable terminal tables:* Split-top, fully height-adjustable terminal tables are required with tops that can tilt and move horizontally to separate the screen from the keyboard by at least a foot. Some proposals even specify required vision angles and distances.
8. *Wrist rests:* Either built-in or separate wrist rests are specified.
9. *Foot rests:* Foot rests are asked for, to be available at the user's request.
10. *Adjustable document holders:* Adjustable holders are requested.
11. *Terminals:* A detachable keyboard is required, plus brightness and contrast controls adjustable by the user. Proposals specify that terminals be shielded with metal to prevent excess radiation and inspected for proper operation and excess radiation semiannually, with records kept of inspections. Terminal heat exhausts are required to be at least 4 feet from the nearest operator. All workstation and equipment finishes must be matte.
12. *Pregnancy:* It is proposed that, upon the employee's request, she shall be offered alternate employment to working at a VDT at the same location during the term of pregnancy without reduction of pay, benefits, or seniority. One bill extends this to males by defining persons affected as "reproductively active."
13. *New equipment:* Advance notice in writing to the VDT operator is required at least six months prior to installation of new equipment at his or her workstation.
14. *Temperature and air quality:* It is specified that the temperature be maintained at 65 degrees F or above and that air-conditioning be provided, along with air cleaning machines to get rid of any tobacco smoke in the air.

While none of the bills has passed at this writing, some of these points have begun to appear in state regulations. Procurement guidelines issued to all California state agencies by that state's Office of Information Technology say, among other things, that furniture specifications must require that chairs be adjustable with rolled or waffled edges; the bases shall have five prongs and casters. Moisture-absorbing material must be used in the seat, arms, and backrest. The user must be able to make all chair adjustments without the use of tools while seated with the chair in an upright position.

Tables and desks must be fully adjustable with matte surfaces to inhibit glare.

All employees of the state of New Mexico who use VDTs are affected by an Executive Order issued by Governor Toney Anaya in March, 1985. The order generally follows the union contract and state legislative proposals detailed above.

Suffolk County, New York put in force a bill regulating the use of VDTs. It required employers to pay 80 percent of the cost of eye examinations and glasses for employees who use VDTs, to provide 15-minute breaks every three hours, together with special lighting, adjustable chairs and worksurfaces, and VDTs with detachable keyboards. A state court overturned the regulations, saying among other things that the county did not have the authority to put them in force. New York Mayor Ed Koch vetoed a similar set of regulations.

The authors feel that present knowledge is not sufficiently comprehensive for strict laws and regulations to be enacted.

Chapter 7

Computer-Aided Office Design

"Computer-aided design," "computer-aided design and drafting," "computer-aided design/computer-aided manufacturing," "computer designed" and many other terms are used to describe similar ways of producing drawings for use by architectural, interior design, engineering, and manufacturing companies. Computer-aided design systems can be found in the smallest interior design firm as well as in large corporate facilities design and management departments. Though it is true that the uses of the computer for design purposes are varied, they are not as widespread as might be expected. To simplify terminology, it is perhaps easier to refer to each of these various computer systems as a "CADS" (computer-aided design system).

CADS for use in the interior design field has grown in a haphazard manner. The first developers of the software packages did not understand the needs of design professionals. Also, unfortunately, the design professionals had a limited understanding of the capabilities of the available computer systems. The first software packages and hardware were clumsy and slow and seldom fully utilized the true capabilities of the computer. Slowly the designers who became users began to understand what the computer can accomplish and they began to work with the software designers to develop more useful systems. Today these machine/software systems still do not fully meet the needs of the architect and interior designer, but there is more competition in the field and improvements seem to come more rapidly now.

CADS versus Creativity

It is reasonable to think that most large corporations would utilize computer-generated drawings in their architectural, interior design, and facility management departments, but there has been resistance to accepting proper

This chapter was contributed by Kirk P. Williams.

The computer monitor shows one of Steelcase's facilities management programs in use. (Courtesy of Steelcase Inc.)

CADS utilization. Many designers consider the computer a threat to their creativity, and the advantages of the use of the computer as a ''tool'' for creative innovation are often missed.

CADS does not remove or replace creativity. As far as creativity is concerned, the computer is neither more nor less than the drafting machine, pencil, and eraser. CADS is a tool and not a replacement for thinking. The computer allows the designer to sort through large amounts of data, search out pertinent information, and use that information to aid in making better and more timely decisions. The computer allows for greater precision than does the hand or pencil. The computer's ability to correlate information quickly allows for better understanding of a problem and the process is no longer tedious and time consuming. In this way the computer enhances creativity.

Unfortunately, not everyone adapts well to using the computer and professional people often view working on a computer as a demeaning task suited only for a draftsperson. This is a narrow-visioned idea. When the computer is also used as a design tool many problems can be solved long before the draftsperson puts the information into the final drawing; this tends to substantially decrease the volume of reworked drawings on a project.

The Speed of Computer-Aided Design

CADS is not always faster than the manual design system. Inputting a drawing of nonrepetitive parts may take as long or longer than manually producing a drawing of the same work. This depends on the system hardware and software plus the capabilities of the individual CADS operator. CADS can speed the process of preparing drawings by quick replication of parts of drawings used repetitively. Preparing a drawing of a second floor that is an exact duplicate of the first floor would take no more than ten minutes for the computer and printer to prepare. Even with some changes to the layout of the second floor, the process is shortened substantially.

CADS has the ability to produce drawings with exacting precision. This is of considerable advantage when working with open plan systems office furniture; panel creep (see Chapter 17, Panel Systems) can be automatically and instantly accounted for with no surprises on installation day. Locations are shown on the plan to very small tolerances as predetermined by the designer.

A Change in Thinking

Architects, engineers, and interior designers have been trained to produce drawings at particular scales—1/8 inch, 3/32 inch, or 1/4 inch. Our design skills and perceptions are generally based on "scale." Once the information for a drawing is entered into the computer, the drawing can be reproduced on paper at any scale and at infinite increments, because the computer takes information on proportion rather than at a particular scale.

CADS does not necessarily concern itself with the scale used as long as the information is entered in a consistent manner within the parameters the computer operator has given.

As an example, suppose you were standing a block away from a building. From that distance you can clearly see the design of the building, the entrances, the windows, and the building's general appearance. You cannot see the screw used to hold a window frame in place, even though it is there. As you walk up to one of the windows you can clearly see the screw and the slot in its head. You can only see a very small portion of the building, yet you can see the screw in exacting detail. The building has not changed in size and the proportions have remained the same. What has happened is that you brought the building's components closer to your eye and you are seeing the details. Nothing has physically changed; you have brought the details closer so that your eyes can see them. This is much like using binoculars; by bringing the binoculars to your eyes you see things far away as being much closer. If you reverse the binoculars, objects seem much farther away. The vision distance has changed while the elements you're looking at appear in the same proportions.

CADS allows you the same luxury. You can see a drawing on the CADS screen as being nothing more than a tiny geometric shape no bigger than a fly and as if it were a great distance away. Conversely, you could see only the wheel on the caster of a chair three times its life size, which would fill the CADS screen. The effect on the CADS operator is quite beneficial, yet seldom realized. No longer does the operator think in scale; now thinking is done in proportion. Where once the designer could draw a perfectly scaled desk at 1/8-inch scale without the aid of an architectural scale, he can now draw that desk in perfect proportion and not necessarily at any particular scale. In the daily performance of his profession the designer must constantly think in three dimensions and be able to translate designs into proportions. The CADS system encourages proportional thinking and the designer no longer must translate proportion into a scale he can work with.

An example may help to understand this better. Suppose that you have been using CADS for a year and have developed an excellent sense of proportion because you are a designer and CADS has reinforced this sense. You are in the process of designing an office for a vice-president of a prestigious corporation. One weekend you stop in at an antique shop and discover a beautifully designed table you think might be perfect for use as a conference table in the vice-president's office. It is of the same period as the other furniture you have selected for the office, but the carved detailing and the large size of the table might be out of scale when placed in the office with the other furniture. In order to obtain the table you must make your decision on the spot, since the shop owner has another interested buyer. If you are able to visualize the office you have designed with all its accoutrements within your mind, you can place the antique table in the room in proper proportion, which enables you to make the decision wisely. If you are unable to visualize properly in this way, you could end up with a table you cannot use and should not have bought. This is not to say that designers do not already think well in proportion. Using CADS may heighten and enhance that ability, however. Also, learning to use CADS is not the only way to achieve this ability, but through regular use of CADS your awareness of proportion is heightened and your skill in this area can be profitable in ways you would never have imagined.

CADS Capabilities and How They Differ

In the architectural and design world there are seemingly hundreds of computer salesmen grasping for the design businessperson's dollars. It would not be too bold to guess that the majority of those people in design businesses with purchase responsibilities and with power to make policies have little or no concept of what computers can do for them in positive and realistic ways.

CADS cannot provide a solution to a design business's design and production problems if that business does not already employ sound procedures in the management of production work. If little concern is given to standardization and procedure, then a computer will confound and complicate production.

Computers of course are only a part of the solution to the designer's problems. The software (programs) and hardware (machinery) combination is the key. The potential user must ask "What do I want this system to do for me?" Should the system be capable of storing massive amounts of information and be able to sort and recall it at the touch of a key? Should the system allow for additional information specific only to my business to be added to the software package? These questions seem to compound and the myriads of intermingled needs that are identified soon appear unmanageable. At this point the potential new computer system owner becomes frustrated and confused. Although there are many variations of systems, there are currently three basic types a design firm may consider: a Personal Computer (PC), a minicomputer, and a mainframe computer. Each type has different capabilities and there is some overlap among them.

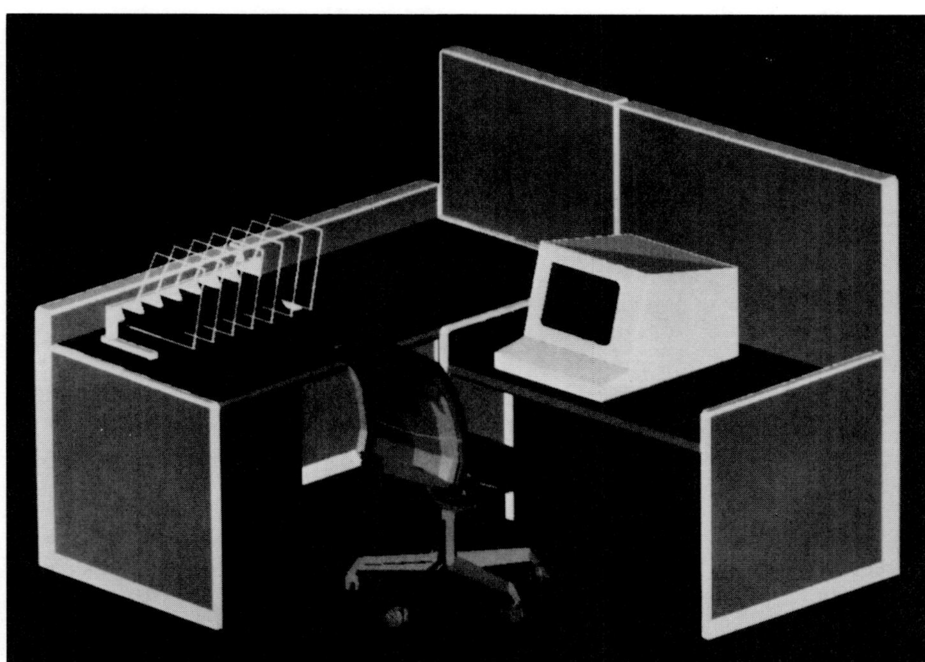

A drawing of an office workstation on the computer monitor. (Courtesy of Steelcase Inc.)

The Personal Computer

The PC is the most recently developed type for which usable architectural and interior design software packages have been created. These systems are limited in that great quantities of information in graphic form are not handled in the most convenient ways. Most PCs do not have the electronic or disk storage capabilities of their larger brethren. In addition, PCs are often limited in their ability to produce high-resolution screen graphic displays. With rapid advancements in computer technology, however, PCs may soon be quite capable of handling enormous amounts of data. For now it is probable that an entire large commercial building cannot be handled as a single drawing on a PC. Instead, large buildings may need to be divided into a number of smaller drawings, each representing one floor or segment of the building. These systems are also excellent for keeping inventories of interior components and preparation of purchase orders. PCs are easy to operate and affordable for most businesses, but their limitations should be realized and their applicability for future needs should be evaluated.

Many manufacturers of systems furniture have computer programs for designing with their furniture. Some provide everything from the computer program to the PC itself. Most have licensed this capability to independent computer software firms. Generally these packages allow for everything from drawing each component to providing listings of the components used to component pricing.

The Minicomputer

Minicomputers will generally handle much larger projects than PCs. Companies such as Intergraph produce minicomputer packages of hardware and

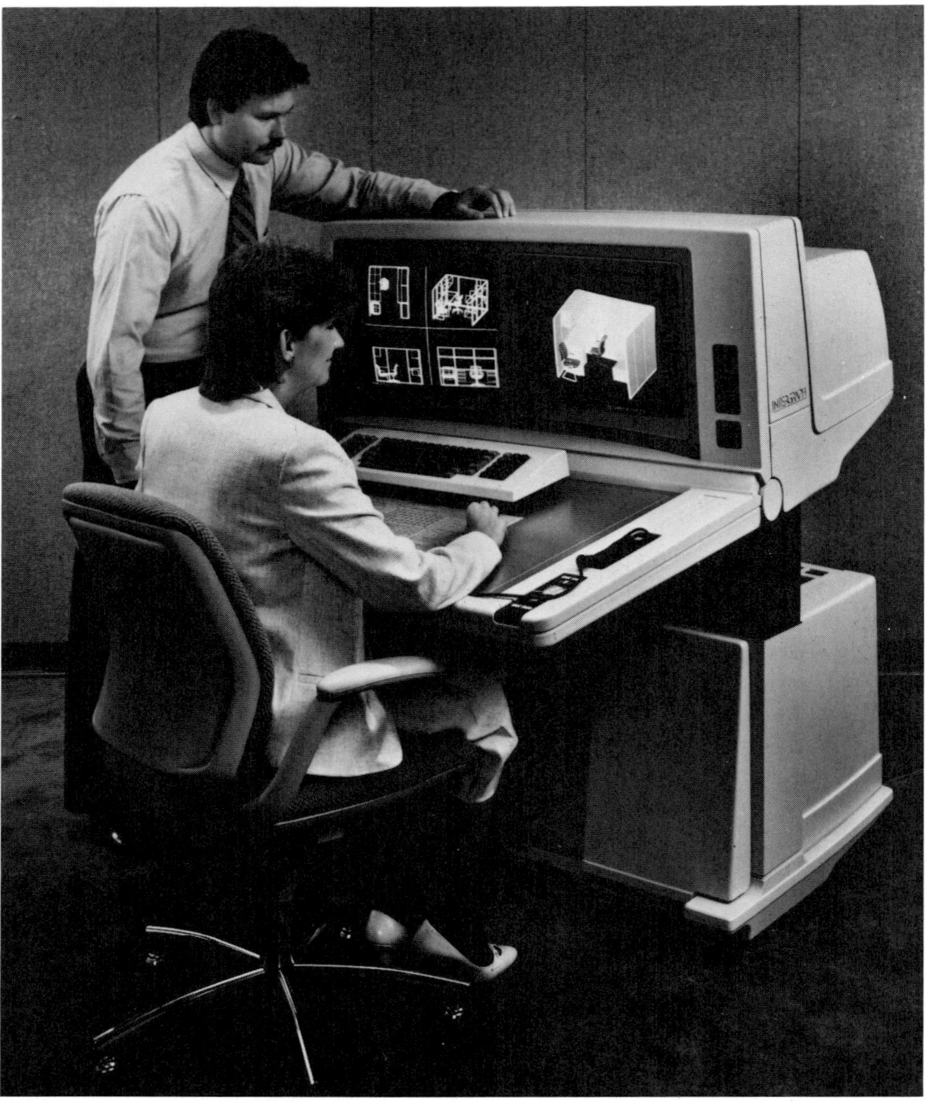

Workstation for computer-aided interior design. (Courtesy of Steelcase Inc.)

software for the architectural and interior design communities. In addition to their greater graphic capabilities, minicomputers can generate inventories and purchase orders.

Minicomputer systems often "stand-alone" just as PCs do (there is just one terminal for the central processing unit [CPU]), but they are also capable of having more than one terminal attached to share the common database. Each minicomputer terminal is able to utilize separate, unconnected information on its own diskettes or tapes in addition to being able to work with a common database shared by all terminals.

Mainframe Computers

Mainframe CADS computers have data-handling capacities far beyond the needs of most design firms or facilities departments. They are applicable for use by companies maintaining large amounts of data that must be referred to often. Examples are corporate facilities that move around large numbers of people and companies that maintain or design multi-floor and/or numerous buildings.

Mainframes utilize hard discs and tapes that are capable of storing and using immense amounts of information.

Mainframes, when used for CADS are, in the opinion of the authors, much better at handling three-dimensional information and thus are more appropriate for large-scale facilities management as well as for office interior design.

Perhaps their most important single advantage is their ability to allow for specific need programming. PC systems are more difficult to program; when you choose a smaller system, it is important to keep this in mind. Any size system should have the needed software readily available so that time and money are not spent on difficult programming.

For most smaller companies a mainframe computer used for CADS is impractical if only in terms of cost and maintenance.

Computer Linking

The new ability of computers to link and share data will allow a multitude of functions to occur in a time-efficient manner. It is now possible that some mainframes, some minicomputers, and some PCs can all share common information, thus giving the user the flexibility to utilize each type of system to its full advantage.

As an example, two-dimensional data can be extracted and transmitted to a mini from complicated three-dimensional information stored in a mainframe. Also, inventory information can be transferred among all three classes of computers. All three can work independently of each other while sharing common data. This means that a multi-story building requiring three-dimensional mainframe descriptions of conduits and other details can share data on two-dimensional aspects of the floor plan with a mini, while the furniture item listings (down to the ashtrays) can be shared with a PC.

A Typical CADS Installation

A CADS workstation might consist of a central processing unit (CPU), a console printer for alphanumeric printout, a stand-alone pen or electrostatic plotter, a display screen, and an electrosensitive design board with digitizing pen or puck, plus the computer programs to use the equipment for the design of buildings and interiors as well as for space planning and facility management functions. (All of the above will vary according to need.)

Many software packages allow the designer to view workstations in two- or three-dimensional diagrams in color. Two-dimensional floor plans of panels can be automatically translated to three-dimensional views. Three-dimensional designs can be rotated on the screen and viewed from any angle. Designs can be displayed as line drawings, as "wire frame" views

A close-up view of the screen and equipment for computer-aided office design. (Courtesy of Steelcase Inc.)

or in three-dimensional full color, with all surfaces shaded to show the contours of the furniture. The design can be panned from side to side, and the software has a zoom capability that allows the designer to bring the focus in for great detail or to "step back" for a broad view.

Most packages also include the capability to produce accurate drawings of floor plans, elevations, perspectives, and full-color renderings. They can also be used for typical facilities management functions such as listing the components of any design on file, the furniture and other inventories, depreciation schedules, space usage, and other varieties of facilities management reports.

An Example of a Software/Hardware Package

As a most important part of its E.S.S. System (see Chapter 22, A Case for Participatory Design), Steelcase, in association with Intergraph, offers the E.S.S. Design Program, an Intergraph package consisting of computerized equipment (hardware) including a minicomputer central processor, console printer, plotter and graphics workstation with twin display screens, and an electrosensitive design board. The package provides computer programs (software) to use with the equipment for the design of workstations and floor plans, as well as for space planning and facilities management functions.

Needs Analysis

The authors are not attempting here to describe in detail any specific system or suggest any specific route for action. What follows are some important points to consider in analyzing needs for a CADS system.

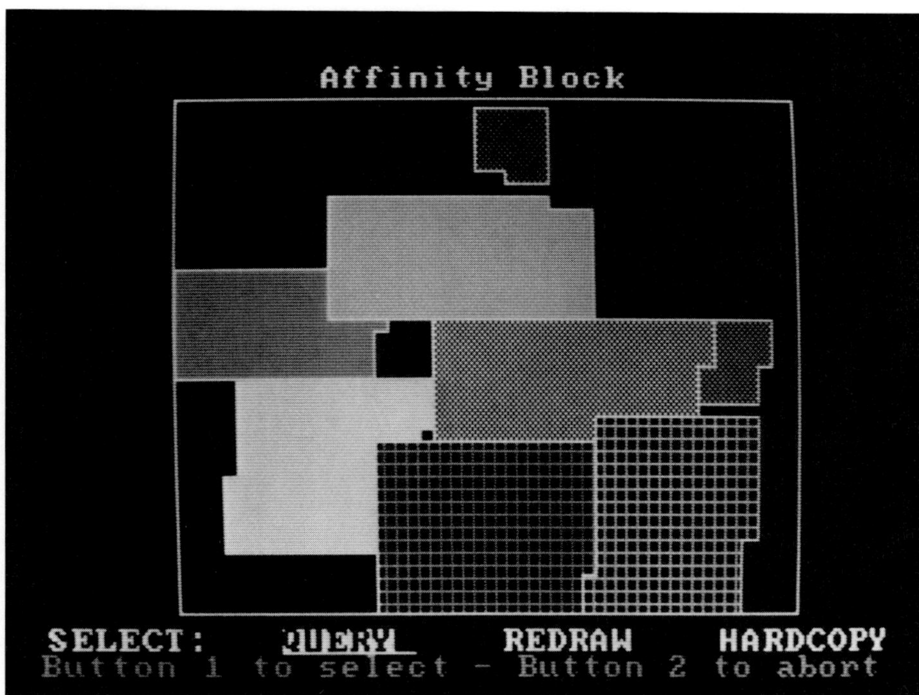

The computer screen shows department space requirements and relationships on an office floor plan using Steelcase-RDI/PC Facilities Management Software. (Courtesy of Steelcase Inc.)

1. Do you really need a computer? The cost of any system cannot be justified if it will not be fully utilized.
2. Are your current drafting procedures standardized and are your drafting procedures consistent?
3. What drafting tasks now being performed manually could be done better with a CADS system? Be aware that some information is better handled manually and even if your CAD system can handle massive amounts of data, you must still be able to manage its input and retrieval. Each firm must make a judgment based on its particular needs.
4. Could a service bureau satisfy your needs for CADS? Service bureaus allow you to have CADS capability without owning the hardware and software, but the process is much slower than when you own your equipment, since there is transportation time to and from the bureau. However, when the need for CADS capability is immediate, bureaus have the built-in expertise and sometimes can take projects on a moment's notice. Taking projects to a bureau can be a useful part of the learning curve for an uninitiated CADS user, especially if you just supply rough sketches to them. Use of a bureau may also help you decide which system you might eventually want to buy, since you will gain experience with various systems through your use of the bureau's setup. By doing it this way you may find out what you need as well as what you do not need—before you buy.
5. Do you need a project management (PM) program to go along with your CADS? There are a number of PM programs in the market, but some are not true PM programs, being geared more toward accounting and business applications. Many programs are so limited that their value is minimal for use in PM. There are quite adequate programs available for less than $500 that have useful applications with relatively broad capabilities: Apple's MacProject is an example. Of course, the cost of the hardware

required is an additional consideration. Packages with greater capabilities, such as Harvard Total Project Manager ™ and Primavera Project Manager ™, are available, but require a substantially higher investment; they also have more operational complexity. Visual presentation, program flexibility, program capacity and system complexity are basic factors to consider when choosing a computerized PM system. Caution and a thorough understanding of needs are necessary when considering the purchase of a PM system.

6. It is useful to organize an analysis team that includes a representative from each group of potential users, as well as from management, and an independent consultant who specializes in CADS selection.

The primary pitfall associated with CADS is not being prepared. Standards and procedures must be established by management before its introduction, since CADS will be no better than the management of the firm using it. The difference between doing the task manually and doing it with the computer is that the computer can organize and compare data much more quickly and in ways not easily attained by manual methods. Thus an immense amount of information becomes available to be used in an infinite number of ways. Management of this information requires good organizational techniques; if these techniques are not properly employed, no computer system in the world can help.

CADS Uses of the Future

In England, Robert Aish has been experimenting with a revolutionary approach to CADS that he calls "Intelligent Building Blocks." It was developed so that users could construct models of what they want in architecture; he had found that users understand models much better than they understand architectural drawings.

Center for training interior designers in computer-aided design. (Courtesy of Steelcase Inc.)

Aish's building blocks contain microprocessors; after the model is built, a computer reads the chips in the blocks and the way the blocks are connected and produces a drawing of the building in either two or three dimensions using a plotter. It also produces a picture of the model on the screen; this picture can be then rotated so that different aspects of the proposed building become visible.

The computer contains a database that allows it to simulate the performance the model building would attain, for example, average heat gain and loss over a year's time. In addition, the program allows the user to assign geometric, performance, and cost attributes to each block; these values can be printed out. This feature makes it possible to show untrained users the multiple consequences of a change in design—quickly.

The use of models in computer-aided design (CAD) may become very important because it allows users to participate in the design process in an unprecedented fashion. Dr. Alton J. DeLong found that whole dwellings can be designed by unsophisticated subjects in periods of from 4.5 to 9 hours, using one-inch to one-foot scale models.

Meanwhile, in the United States, large-scale animated presentations are currently being produced by several design corporations. Building on this technique, Hans Christian Lischewski, of the Pratt Institute's School of Architecture in New York, is working on a CADS program utilizing true three-dimensional holographic projections created from CADS drawings.

These innovative CADS uses may become commonplace in the future.

PART III

Interior Design Needs in Office Environments

Chapter 8

Adjustability in Chairs and Worksurfaces

Basically, office furniture needs to be adjustable to make people comfortable and lessen some of the postural and musculoskeletal complaints discussed in Chapter 6 (Health Hazards and Worker Safety Issues). Furniture must be able to fit people and must be adjustable because of the myriad differences in the sizes of human beings and their body parts. The science of measuring the human body is called anthropometry.

Body Measurements

The best single source of comparative date on human measurements is a three-volume work published by the National Aeronautics and Space Administration (NASA) called the *Anthropometry Source Book* (Webb Associates 1978). In it are summarized all the major studies from around the world (up to 1978) that conform to recognized anthropometric standards.

The source of this information is a group of nations and diverse races scattered around the world—Australia, Bolivia, Canada, Chile, Colombia, Czechoslovakia, Bantu (Africa), Ecuador, France, Great Britain, Greece, Iran, Italy, Japan, Korea, New Zealand, Panama, Peru, South Africa, Thailand, Turkey, the United States, Vietnam, and Venezuela.

Dr. K. H. E. Kroemer has extracted the following figures on ancestries claimed by groups of citizens in a U.S. Census poll in 1980. As you see, we have the most diverse ethnic and racial mix of any country in the world.

Nationality	Percent of U.S. Population	Nationality	Percent of U.S. Population
English	49.6	Japanese	0.8
German	49.2	French Canadian	0.8
Irish	40.2	Slovak	0.8
Afro-American	21.0	Lithuanian	0.7
French	12.9	Ukrainian	0.7
Italian	12.2	Finnish	0.6
Scottish	10.1	Cuban	0.6
Polish	8.2	Canadian	0.5
Mexican	7.7	Korean	0.4
American Indian	6.7	Belgian	0.4
Dutch	6.3	Yugoslavian	0.4
Swedish	4.4	Romanian	0.3
Norwegian	3.5	Asian Indian	0.3
Russian	2.8	Lebanese	0.3
Spanish-Hispanic	2.7	Jamaican	0.3
Czech	1.9	Croatian	0.3
Hungarian	1.8	Vietnamese	0.2
Welsh	1.7	Armenian	0.2
Danish	1.5	African	0.2
Puerto Rican	1.4	Hawaiian	0.2
Portuguese	1.0	Dominican	0.2
Swiss	1.0	Colombian	0.2
Greek	1.0	Slovenic	0.1
Austrian	1.0	Iranian	0.1
Chinese	0.9	Syrian	0.1
Filipino	0.8	Serbian	0.1

Note: The total is greater than 100 percent due to mixed ancestries of some respondents.

Since 1980, the number of smaller people in our population has increased because of increased immigration from Southeast Asia and Latin America. The United States has long had a substantial population of larger people, the descendents of immigrants from the countries of northern Europe, as shown above.

There are drawbacks to the NASA studies even though they are by far the best available. Because the population groups surveyed are small and many of the studies are not recent, it is quite possible that some of the differences might be larger than those shown. For instance, there is quite a bit of evidence from some U.S. Air Force anthropometric research that we, the American people, are growing larger (Randal et al. 1946). Because of better nutrition knowledge and practices, there may be similar differences in other countries and ethnic groups.

Also, a recent self-reported survey conducted by Dr. Maree Simmons-Forbes (1986) of 350 employees of The World Bank indicates that the first percentile in the NASA studies may be inaccurate, since 3.2 percent of the World Bank sample reported statures of less than 60 inches. The 99th NASA percentile may reflect a similar inaccuracy: 2 percent of the World Bank employees said that their statures were from 73 to 80 inches. Some of these taller people have statures greater than any of those in the 99th percentiles shown in the 88 studies included in the NASA report. These larger and smaller people are out there operating VDTs, and in Dr. Simmons-Forbes' sample they are probably among the 20 percent who found their work places "completely uncomfortable."

Body Dimensions and the Design of Furniture and Equipment

The NASA material mentioned above yields some differences in body dimensions that are important in the design of adjustable office furniture to fit people in all their dimensional diversity.

It is important to point out at this juncture that various parts of the body do not always correlate in size with height, for instance, or with weight.

The following sampling of figures from NASA's study shows that the differences in human dimensions can be quite large. Unfortunately most designers do not consider these differences properly in the design of office furniture or office workstations.

- Arm length (#32) can range from 25.3 to 34.0 inches (difference: 8.7 inches).
- Arm reach from wall (#80) can range from 27.1 to 38.5 inches (difference: 11.4 inches).
- Thumb-tip reach (#867) can range from 23.4 to 37.3 inches (difference: 13.9 inches).
- Maximum reach from wall (#572) can range from 29.4 to 43.1 inches (difference: 13.7 inches).

These arm reach dimensions are important in determining heights at which shelves can be mounted and the positions of drawers. Stature (height) combined with arm reach is also important. Similarly affected by these dimensions are appropriate depths of worksurfaces and the need for the horizontal adjustment of keyboard surfaces.

Seating and Posture

Dimensions that greatly affect the design of seating include the following:

- Buttock-to-knee length (#194) ranges from 18.2 inches to 26.9 inches (difference: 8.7 inches). This influences the depth of the seat itself.
- Buttock-to-popliteal (#200) (back part of the leg behind the knee) length can range from 14.8 inches to 22.8 inches (difference: 8 inches). This also affects the depth of seating.
- Popliteal height (#678), the distance from the bottom of the foot to the underside of the forward thigh, is probably the principal dimension affecting seat heights. It can range from 13.3 to 20.3 inches (difference: 7 inches).

This last figure difference shows that secretarial or operator chairs perhaps should be adjustable from about 12.5 to 19.5 inches, since many experts feel that the seat height should be adjustable to a point slightly under popliteal height. This roughly correlates with the figures from a massive study by Kroemer and Robinette showing a needed adjustability range of from 13⅔ to 20⅔ inches. (See Chapter 18, Chairs, for further corroboration of this range by Miller and Suther.)

There is recent evidence, however, from at least two studies by respected researchers that show that VDT operators adjust their seats to a

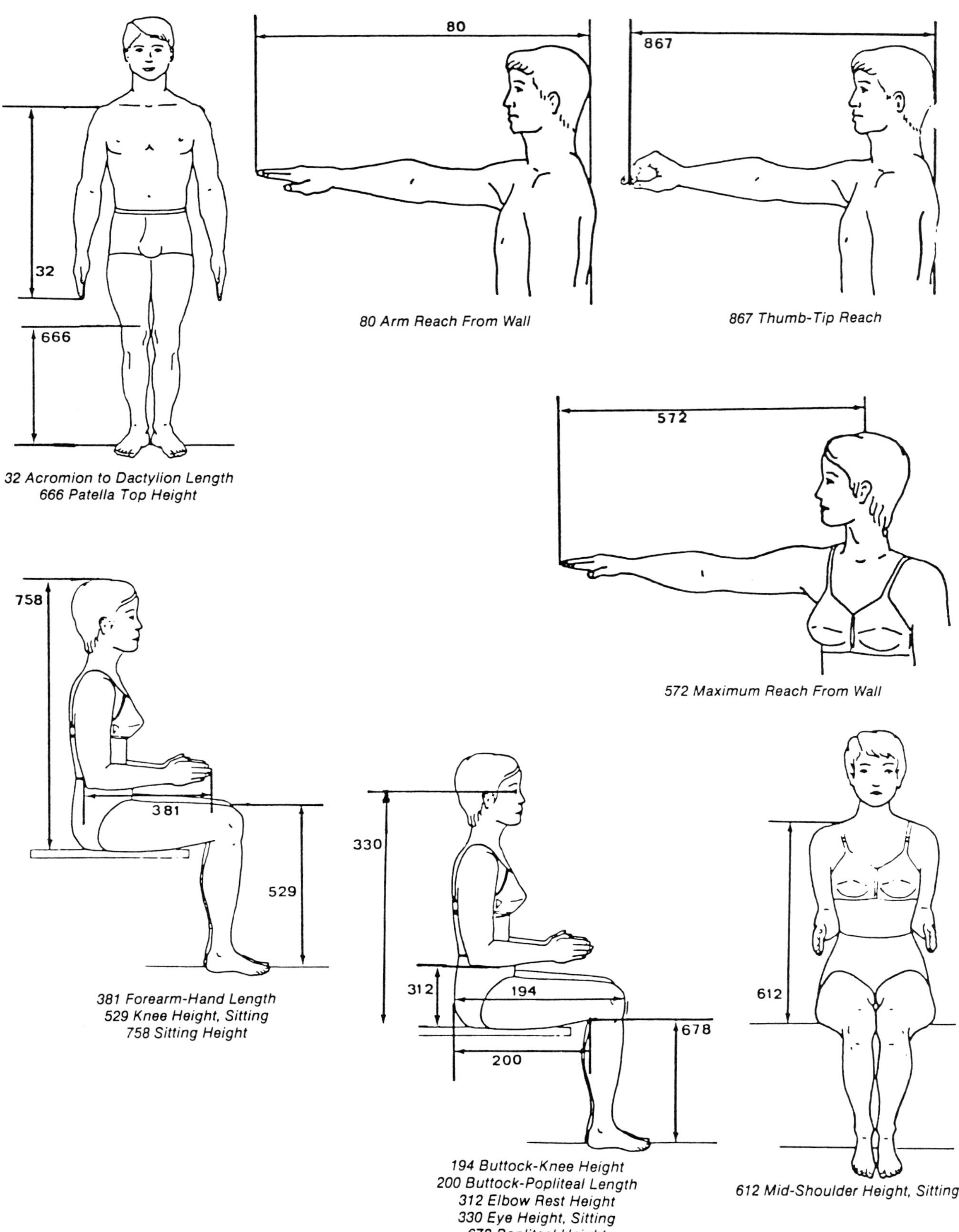

Key anthropometric dimensions for electronic office furniture design. (Courtesy of NASA.)

point appreciably higher than popliteal height, not just under it. People don't always do what we expect them to do.

Further, we should note here that just because a chair has an adjustability range of 7 inches does not mean that it will fit a majority of people; one chair on the market adjusts from 17 to 24 inches, but without the lower range (12.5 to 17 inches) will not fit most of the population. The part of its range from 19.5 to 24 inches may be useless.

There is no chair with this needed range of adjustability on the market at this time; the closest approximation is one with a range of 15 to 20 inches. The authors are convinced that the above dimensions are correct for many people and keep hoping that someone will introduce a chair with the lower range of seat height adjustment that is needed.

There are other indicators for seat height ranges:

- Patella top height (#666) ranges from 15.2 to 24 inches (difference: 8.8 inches).
- Knee height sitting (#529) ranges from 16.6 to 24.6 inches (difference: 8 inches).

These two measurements might indicate that the seat height adjustability range above might be extended by an inch or two. If fact, a study by Damon, Stoudt, and McFarland (1966) shows evidence for an adjustability range of 9.5 inches.

For the design of chair backs we might look at mid-shoulder height sitting (#612), which can vary from 20.6 to 28 inches (difference: 7.4 inches). This is a further clue to needed seat height adjustability and it also indicates that for full comfort and support the chair back should be at least 20 inches high. This kind of support is needed when many computer terminal operators adopt a relaxed position where they sit back in a postures similar to those associated with driving a car. Studies done here and in Europe confirm that substantial numbers of computer terminal operators like to do their work in this relaxed position; in fact, Rodney Cooper, FSIAD (1988) found that 90 percent of the programmers at one British computer maker adopted this laid-back position with their keyboards in their laps.

Grandjean says that ''the great majority of VDT operators adopt a very special seating posture: they lean the trunk backwards with angles of 105 to 120 degrees'' to the thighs (1982). In another study he observed that ''VDT operators exhibit a good instinct when they prefer a backward leaned trunk posture and ignore the recommended upright posture,'' citing several studies showing that when people lean back, their muscles relax and there is less pressure on the spinal discs (1983). This also means the chair must have the capability of expanding the angle between the seat and the back to at least 120 degrees, and some researchers think that this angle should be able to reach 135 degrees.

Sitting height (#758) and eye height sitting (#330) are indicators of where we should put something to be seen at best advantage by the sitter, like a computer terminal screen. Sitting height (#758) ranges from 29.6 to 40 inches (difference: 10.4 inches), while eye height sitting (#330) varies from 25.4 to 35.8 inches (difference: 10.4 inches). This measurement is a good reason computer terminal tables must have a height-adjustable surface for the computer terminal screen.

For the keyboard surface's adjustability, both for computers and typewriters, we can look at elbow rest height (#312) and forearm-to-hand length (#381). The former ranges from 5.8 to 12.6 inches (difference: 6.8 inches). This dimension is important in determining height adjustability for the keyboard surface, since many people are not comfortable while typing unless their forearms can be in a position close to a right angle with the upper arm; keyboard surface height adjustability allows this to happen.

Forearm-to-hand length ranges from 14.7 to 21.2 inches (difference: 6.5 inches). This suggests that the keyboard surface be able to move away from or toward the user; it is also important in determining how much of the depth of a worksurface can be used.

Adjustability Ranges for Keyboards and Screens

The keyboard surface should be able to be adjusted from 22.5 to 33 inches. The surface should be as thin as possible to leave room for the operator's knee and lower leg; it should also tilt as much as 10 degrees in addition to the usual 15-degree slope of most keyboards.

The keyboard surface should also be able to move horizontally toward or away from the operator in a range of about 7 to 8 inches; this is necessary because of differences in workers' body sizes, especially arm length, and differences in eye focus.

The screen surface should also adjust from 22.5 to 33 inches in height. There are at least two terminal tables on the market that adjust both keyboard and screen surfaces to a height of 42 inches; this enables the operator to work either standing up or sitting down. In addition, the screen surface should tilt at least plus or minus 7 degrees (one adjustable table on the market tilts −5 degrees to +25 degrees). Tilting is needed to eliminate glare from light sources. Adjustments for terminal tables can be by hand crank, gas cylinders or electric motors.

If the terminal is to be used by more than one operator, the terminal and keyboard are sometimes placed on a swiveling surface similar to a lazy Susan; although it revolves, it is not adjustable in height or tilt unless adjustability is built into the monitor and/or the keyboard.

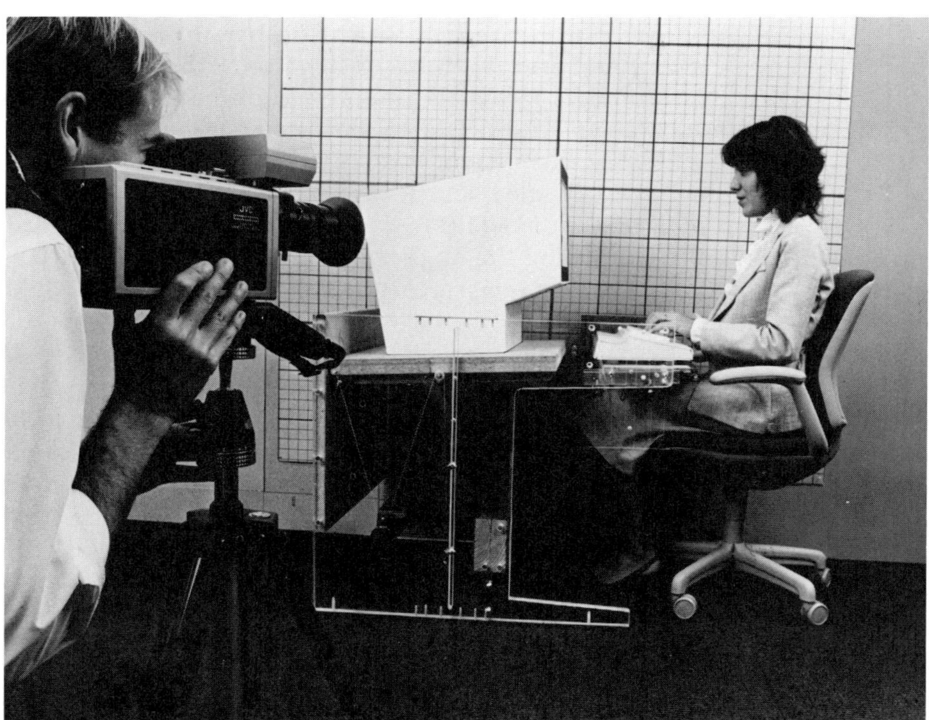

Video analysis of a worker at an adjustable terminal table mockup. By monitoring individual body sizes and changes in posture during the work day as well as the comfort of the operator, adjustment ranges can be evaluated. (Courtesy of Steelcase Inc.)

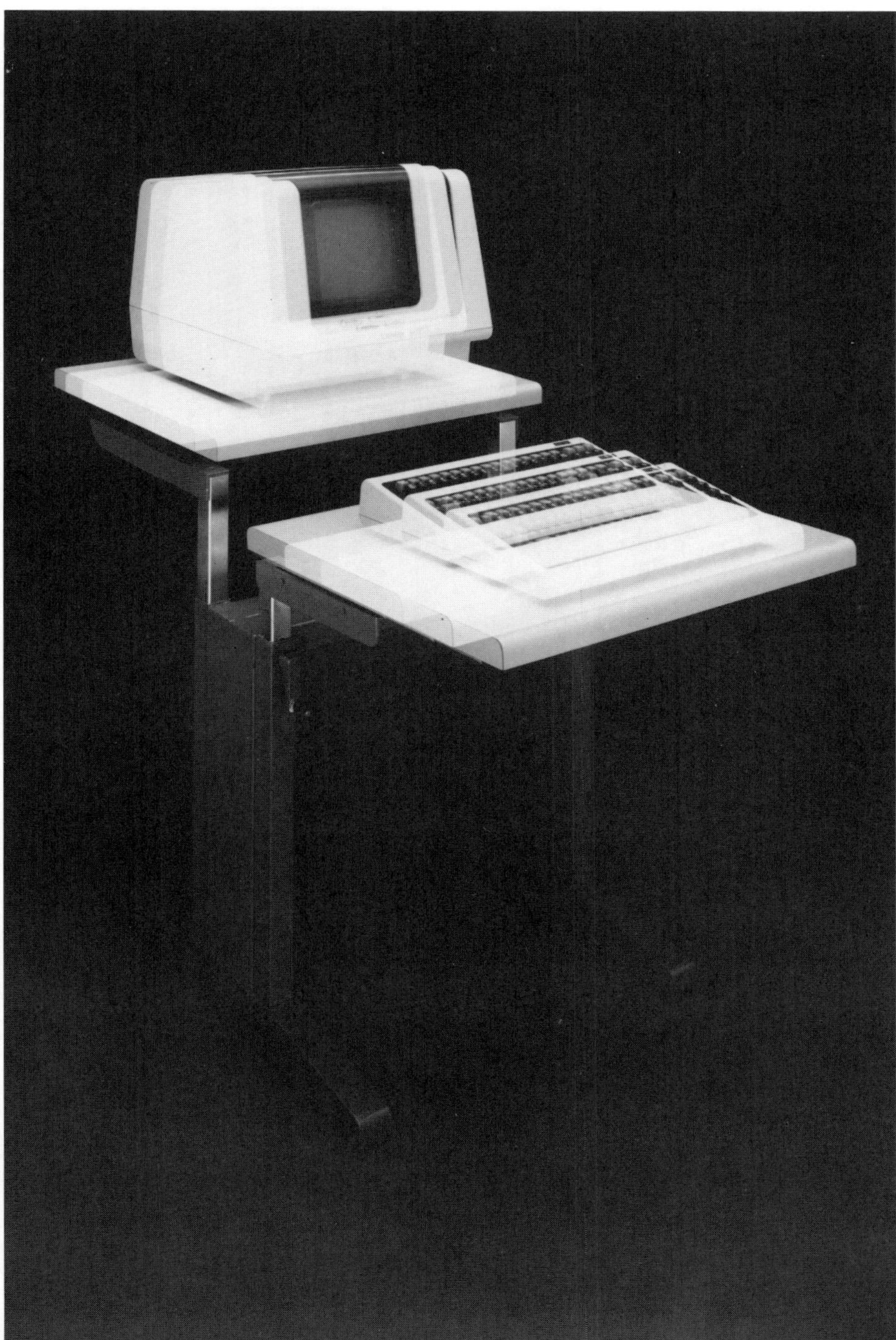

The in-and-out adjustment for differing arm lengths at a computer terminal workstation. (Courtesy of Allsteel, Inc.)

There are various devices that are less expensive than fully adjustable split-top terminal tables. Some manufacturers make small portable VDT stands that tilt and swivel. These stands can be used on standard desk and table tops, and while they adjust in a small range themselves, they are only a makeshift substitute for the fully adjustable terminal tables described above. There are also a very few adjustable roll-around stands on casters for those who only use terminals occasionally.

A somewhat better device for screens is a platform on an arm that can swivel. This appliance is either clamped to or set into a trough at the rear

An appliance that can be attached to any horizontal worksurface to adjust keyboard height and provide a document holder. (Courtesy of Watson Furniture Systems.)

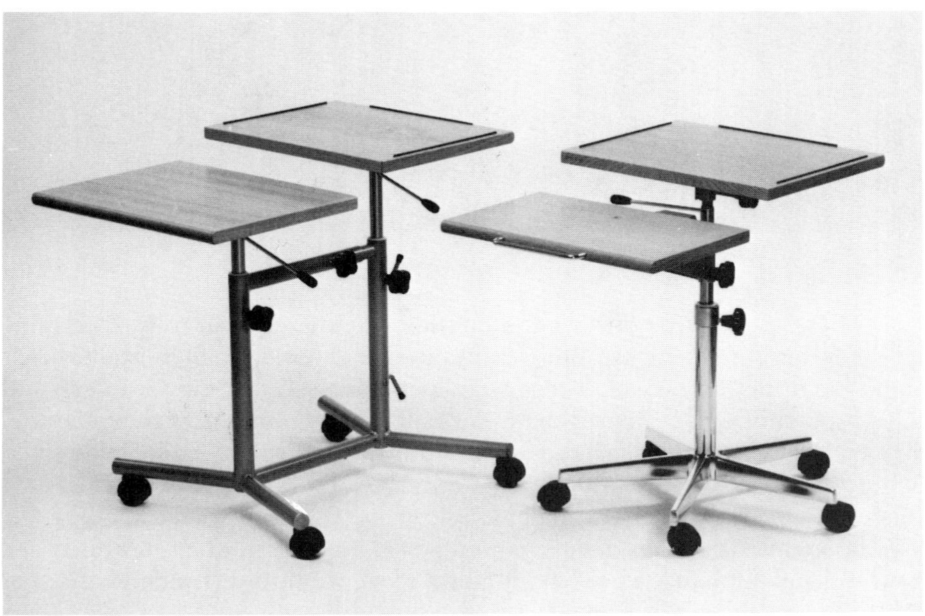

An early model of a movable, adjustable terminal table. (Courtesy of Human Factors Technologies.)

of the worksurface. There are at least three office furniture systems on the market that incorporate this trough into their worksurfaces.

Another device is a keyboard on an arm that attaches to the bottom of the worksurface. The arm swings out for use and stores underneath the worksurface that holds the screen. If the arm is adjustable in height and tilt, it is termed fully articulating. There are also keyboard shelves that attach to the bottom of the worksurface. The shelves are pulled out for use and pushed in to store the keyboard out of sight.

Several manufacturers make auxiliary writing surfaces that attach to the sides of their fully adjustable terminal tables. Some of these are adjustable in height in the same range as the keyboard and screen surfaces. Other tables have large enough surfaces that no extra tops are needed.

In addition to the furniture described above, a fully adjustable document holder for data entry tasks is becoming a necessity. In Europe particularly, adjustable wrist and palm rests are being required on the keyboard surface.

Another approach to the adjustability problem has been taken by the Swedish Telecommunications Administration (STA). Because the newer models of VDTs in Sweden come with tiltable, height-adjustable screens and thin, detachable keyboards, the STA does not believe that two separate adjustable platforms are necessary for the VDT workstation. In other words, the needed adjustments for the screen are added to the screen pedestal and therefore are not needed in a separate screen surface.

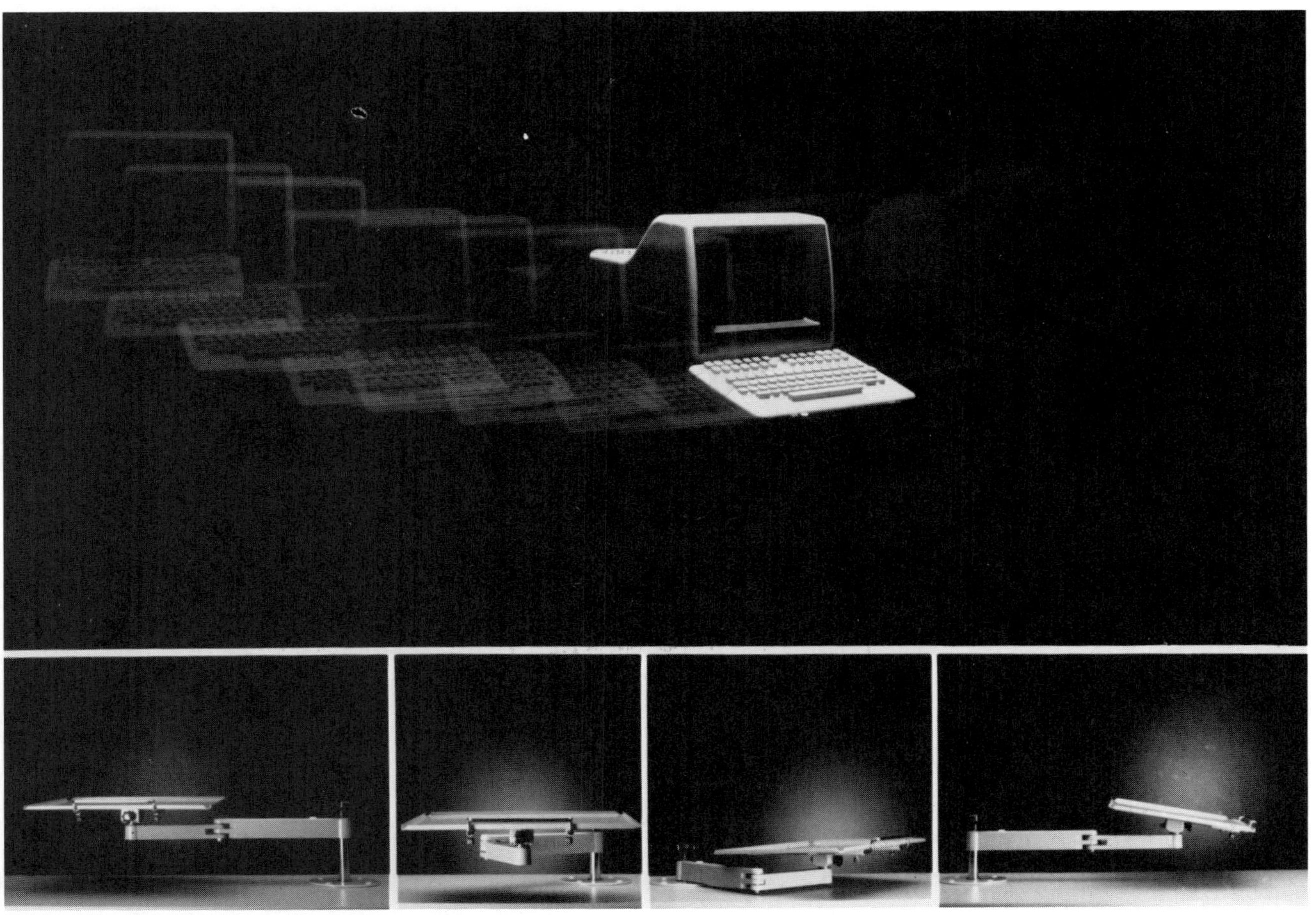

A swing-arm platform attached at the rear of the worksurface; it allows both screen and keyboard to be out of the way when not in use. (Courtesy of Westinghouse Furniture Systems.)

Wood panel system with printer housing and track at the rear of the worksurface. (Courtesy of Stow & Davis, a division of Steelcase Inc.)

STA has designed and is marketing ComforTable®, a single-surface, generic table with push-button electric height adjustment. There is also a digital readout which shows the height at which ComforTable is adjusted. All adjustments can be made easily from a sitting position, and STA says that the push-button-controlled adjustments are much easier to make than

Fully adjustable articulating keyboard platform attached under the worksurface. (Courtesy of Allsteel, Inc.)

those with the usual hand cranks. Further, ComforTable is designed to provide ample leg room. It has a solid top, sturdy leg design, and a disguised console for power, data, and telephone cables. Matte finishes are used.

The development of this worksurface was influenced by trends in the typical Swedish VDT work environment:

1. Because of strong union positions on long hours of unrelieved VDT work, much VDT work in Sweden is now part time rather than full time.
2. This and other factors make it likely that several persons will share one workstation, which increased the need for quick and easy adjustability.

Other Factors in Adjustability

There are other reasons for adjustability in chairs and worksurfaces:

1. The user of a particular workstation may change; office workers do move from job to job.
2. Many office employers are giving employees varied and diversified duties (some call this "job enrichment") to relieve the monotony of doing the same task over and over with no variation in activities. As duties change, and as workers move from one workstation to another, postures may change and both chair and worksurface may have to be adjusted for different tasks.
3. The need for adjustment changes with the age of the user. Even though body size may not change greatly as the user gets older (we do shrink a little), customary body postures are quite likely to change.
4. Adjustability in both seating and other office furniture is absolutely essential in order to accommodate the handicapped office worker. Example: The reach envelope of a person seated in a wheelchair can be vastly restricted compared to that of an able-bodied person.

A tall operator using a range of adjustments. (Courtesy of Watson Furniture Systems.)

All of the above material on adjustability needs assumes that we are talking about a workstation where the worker is seated and is using a computer terminal with a keyboard that can move independently from the screen. Keyboards on some American terminals are permanently attached to the screen and can be moved only as a whole unit. This attached type is preferred where keyboard and screen must be portable and where workers stand up to do the job, as in some laboratories and warehouses and on some factory floors. This type of equipment is not suitable for sit-down jobs in an office.

The recommendations discussed in this chapter should not be treated as an arbitrary set of rules, since much research in the area remains to be done. They are, however, based on some 42 studies conducted by respected scientists in the United States, Switzerland, Japan, England, Germany, Sweden, Finland, and Belgium and represent what is believed to be the best information available at the present time. We will explain some of these studies more fully in other sections of this book.

Chapter 9

Wiring and Networks, and Access Floors

Wiring is certainly one of the most important problems in the automated office, and the number of outlets needed for power, telephone, and data is still rising. One of the divested AT&T companies has recently raised the number of outlets provided per employee computer terminal workstation to 10. Of course, one of the reasons for this is the proliferation of computers and their assorted peripheral devices; it is not uncommon to see three or more screens, three or more keyboards, a printer, a telephone or two, and a calculator—all at one workstation.

Another problem is the increasing number of uses for data cables. As Kenneth Parkinson points out,

> Data cabling is not only used for computers: a data cable network is needed to carry all types of messages. It is now used for background music, signalling (queuing systems at shop counters and indicators in factories, warehouses and public transport), remote terminals, shared resources, internal and external telephones, telephone links, telex, facsimile transmission, access control, alarms, closed circuit TV, clock and timing systems, broadcast and cable radio and TV signals, control systems for production equipment, energy management and other aspects of building automation. (1984)

The clear message is that more wiring capacity is needed and it should be planned as far ahead as possible. According to Steelcase, ''Some organizations report having to budget as much as $100 per *foot* for relocating cable every time a change is needed''(1986).

Fiber Optic Cable

Fiber optic cable, which transmits light pulses rather than electromagnetic ones, is changing the way we wire the electronic office. According to Pacific Bell, a ½-inch fiber optic cable can transmit 240,000 conversations, full-motion videoteleconferencing, graphics, data, and videotex simultaneously at speeds up to 405 million bits per second. Put another way, the contents of a 24-volume encyclopedia can be transmitted in a single second, using digital fiber optic cable, with less than one error per billion bits. This speed will increase; an experimental device at Bell Laboratories has already transmitted light impulses through optical fibers at 20 billion bits per second.

Because of their small size and big carrying capacity, fiber optic cables need less space in relation to carrying capacity needed, thus lowering the cost of building it into office spaces.

Optical fiber has other advantages. It is immune to electromagnetic interference—shocks, sparks, lightning, electrostatic discharges, and radiated electrical interference from machines. This means that it does not demand the elaborate separations needed between copper power and copper data and telephone lines to avoid interference and corruption of data and voice transmissions (see Chapter 17, Panel Systems). These glass wires make signal theft, eavesdropping, and unauthorized tapping almost impossible and detection of intrusion easy, thus reducing the need to encrypt information. They are available in flat wire form so that they can be placed under carpet tiles, but more of that later. Because of its multi-transmitting abilities and relative thinness, fiber optic cable has great advantages over coaxial cable, which frequently causes ridges under carpet tiles and offers less variety and amounts of carrying capacity.

Thomas and Betts' regular fiber optic cable can be bent to a 3-inch radius, which enhances its usability for wiring offices. It is expensive, but according to Pacific Telesis, "On a per-foot basis, fiber costs one-sixth as much to install and one-fourth as much to operate." No wonder Corning Glass Works has spent $87 million on new facilities to produce optical fibers to achieve a capacity of more than 700,000 miles per year.

Placement of Wiring

The cost of fiber optic cable is coming down, but, meanwhile, where do we put the wires we have? There are several methods now in use.

Dropped Ceilings and Power Poles Some designers distribute power, data and telephone wires from the ceiling, especially where there is a dropped ceiling with enough space. Wires are then routed from the ceiling, usually through power poles. There are plenty of objections to power poles on an aesthetic basis, but some heavy computer users swear by them because wiring patterns can be changed so easily and quickly with them. Power poles can have plenty of capacity, too; there is one on the market that can handle thirty-two 25-pair cables plus six 20-ampere electrical circuits (See Panel Systems). One power pole manufacturer, Wiremold, makes a pole with three channels, one for power, one for telephone and one for data cables.

Preset Ducts Another method of wiring is through ducts preset in the concrete floor when it is poured. Some ducts are flush with the concrete floor and some are buried. Unless these ducts are set very close together and can be tapped at close intervals, they usually do not offer enough flexibility to handle the rapid changes in the electronic office. They are also limited to the capacity set at the time the building was constructed. Many buildings with these trench ducts do not have enough wiring space in them for the electronic office.

Wiring is brought out of the ducts through floor outlets and if carpet is used, metal rings are sometimes placed on top of the carpet, where it is cut out and replaced to allow the wiring to get through. If rings are not used, the carpet rapidly becomes a mess as wiring is changed. The floor outlets used most with this system are known as pedestals, "monuments," or "tombstones." People trip over them if furniture is not placed over them.

Flat Wire Flat wire under carpet tiles is now possible as a method for wiring the electronic office because of its thinness and flexibility. Power cable is about 1/30th of an inch thick; data transmission cable is less than 1/10th of an inch, and telephone cable is less than 1/25th of an inch. Its use will probably grow even faster now that optical flat wire is on the market. Regular flat wire under carpet squares is now accepted by most codes and can be used for power, telephones, and data. Flat optical wire can only be used for data and telephones.

Some of the advantages of flat wire are that it offers great flexibility in placing and changing the positions of workstations, installation is fast, and

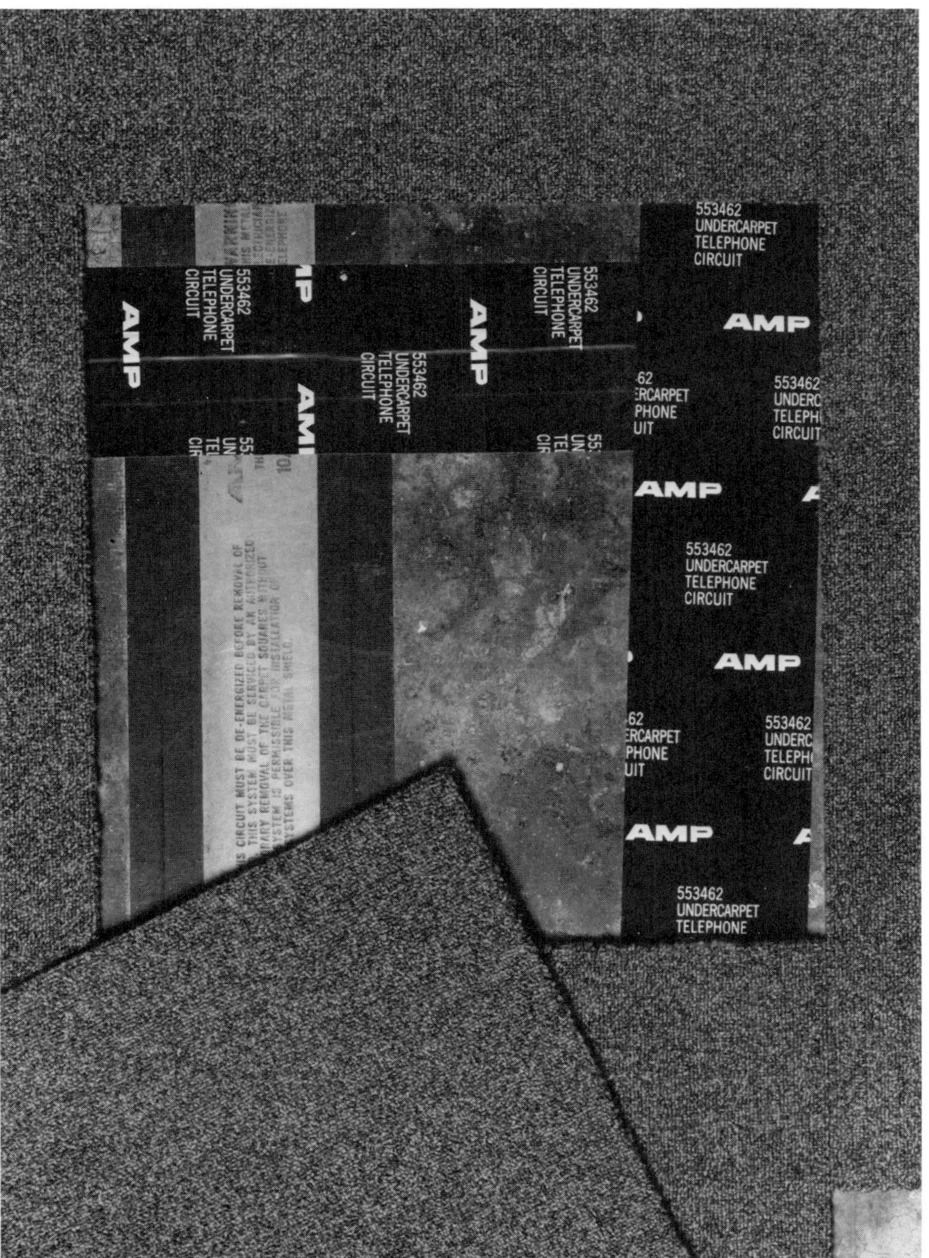

Flat wire laid under carpet tiles. (Courtesy of Interface Flooring Systems.)

no structural work is necessary. It has tax advantages, a tenant is not limited to landlord wiring patterns, and it is possible to buy only what is needed and add to it later. Flat wire is now available with an isolated ground, which is necessary for ''clean'' power for computers (see ''How To Avoid Electrical Surprises,'' below).

Some of the disadvantages are that without careful planning there could be a mess under the carpet tiles, which you should use to get full advantages of the system (carpet tiles are required to be used with flat wire by many codes). Carpet tiles are at least 25 percent more expensive than broadloom and you do have to buy extra tiles for cutouts where there are floor outlets, which are a part of most flat wire systems. You again must place furniture so that people do not trip over floor outlets. The wire entry point for flat wire, however, is a special wall box that poses no tripping problem.

Some office design experts point out that while the flexibility of flat wire is attractive, it is simply a method of distribution; it fails to remedy any fundamental lack of ducting capacity.

A six-wire, three-circuit electrical system is in this raceway; the receptacle marked 3G is isolated and dedicated for electronic data equipment, such as computers. (Courtesy of Westinghouse Furniture Systems).

Carpet tiles, flat wire, and connecting monument. (Courtesy of Interface Flooring Systems.)

It should be noted that some of the in-floor duct manufacturers are modifying their offerings so that they can be combined with flat wire in hybrid systems.

Access Floors Access floors are being more frequently used in the office as the growing numbers of electronic machines increase the demand for more wiring. Because access floors are available in different heights, capacity can be varied to suit needs. They are also attractive as plenums for air conditioning.

According to David B. Eakin, of the General Services Administration,

> The use of raised flooring throughout office space is seen as a basic requirement in new construction projects. The wire management problems of the future simply demand it. No other system offers the degree of flexibility and accessibility to cable, and no other system offers the capacity of handling the amount of cable that is expected to come into the office over the next decade. (1989)

A raceway with a high capacity for carrying wires and cables. (Courtesy of Knoll International.)

Wiring in Panels and Furniture Furniture panel systems are another route for wiring. Some types of wires have always been taken through conventional desks (see Chapter 17, Panel Systems). However, with the increasing availability of other ways to wire the electronic office, designers are beginning to question the expense of wired panels, which cost as much as 30 percent more than unwired panels. Some designers also feel that it may be quite difficult to rethread and reroute cabling through furniture when changes in panel configurations are made. When selecting a furniture or panel system, the wiring part of it should be checked for ease and convenience of changes. It is also important to know whether or not changes need the services of a licensed electrician.

It is necessary that any holes in furniture for wiring use be shaped, sized, and grommeted so that the cables and furniture are not damaged during threading. When panels or furniture carry wiring from one piece to another, the furniture connections must be strong and secure.

While most ducting inside furniture consists of raceways at floor level and/or worksurface level, there are at least four furniture systems on the market in the United States that have troughs at the back of the worksurface that not only carry wiring, but also allow the positioning of adjustable arms in the trough for computer screens, lamps, telephones, calculators, and other office appliances. All-Steel has Syntrax®, Stow & Davis uses troughs in Elective Elements 1™, and Sligh offers a similar system corridors for its 18th Century desks. The space under the troughs can be used to house the surplus coils of wire, which are frequently a problem. Several English and European systems have wiring troughs at the rear of desks and use the desk legs as channels for wiring. Some furniture companies furnish clip-on, three-channel cable trays for their desks and/or panel systems; Herman Miller's Action Office® is one example.

Be sure to check any channel or raceway in or on any furniture to be sure that it is large enough to handle not only the wires and cables but also the pin connectors used to join cabling for telephones, computers, and printers.

The Importance of Planning and Record Keeping

For any of these wiring methods, careful planning and even more careful record keeping are an absolute necessity to prevent accidental cutting and wrong connections. It is essential to know what each wire is carrying where; color coding the wires as well as the ducts helps. To assist in solving this problem, IBM now has a program for its Personal Computer specifically designed as "A tool to aid in the planning, installation and records maintenance for the cabling system." If good records are not kept, wires under the floor or above the ceiling can be an undecipherable muddle.

Hand-latched connector for a panel electrical power system. (Courtesy of Panel Concepts.)

Seven-inch high raceway at the base of a panel containing power, data and telephone wiring. (Courtesy of The Harter Group.)

Another way to help prevent tangles and confusion is to put wires in trays or conduits, which are required in some jurisdictions. Trays have a great advantage in that wires can be laid in rather than "fished" through and clips can be attached to the trays to hold the wires in position.

Local Area Networks (LANs)

Computers and their associated devices need to talk to each other just as people do in the office. Offices need to communicate with each other, too. Devices made by one manufacturer frequently cannot communicate with machines made by another manufacturer, however. There is a great need to make this communication possible; LANs are one way of doing this.

Perhaps the best known LAN is Xerox's Ethernet, backed also by Digital Equipment Corporation and Intel Corporation. Ethernet is "essentially a coaxial cable installed in walls and conduits much as standard electrical and telephone lines are installed." Machines that fit the system are simply plugged into the coaxial cable. General Electric has a competitive system called GEnet®, which also is designed to make it possible for dissimilar computers to communicate with each other.

A local area network (LAN) kit and cover panel houses LAN equipment and cables at the base of an office panel system. (Courtesy of Knoll International.)

Because IBM is one of the few computer makers that manufactures almost all of the electronic devices that need to be joined together by an operating system and a network, IBM's entry into this race has been long awaited.

Wiring Space for LANs

When a LAN is introduced into an existing office, wiring space may already be tight and it may be difficult to connect incompatible machines.

A British company, Case Plc, has come up with a fresh approach to these problems called Grapevine, which converts an existing telephone system into a LAN while retaining its voice capacity. Computers and peripherals can be connected to the phone system and phones as well as the other machines can be used independently.

To accomplish this, a Grapevine distribution unit is attached to the main telephone PABX (private automatic branch exchange) to filter off the computer data for the computers while voice traffic is routed in the usual way. One problem with Grapevine is that transmissions are limited to a maximum speed of 9,600 bits per second; as you can see from the discussions above on fiber optics, much higher speeds are required. Case can also add a system called DCX for communication outside the LAN; then Grapevine and DCX operate as a single system to connect the office to the world.

AT&T has a LAN called Starlan® and Northern Telecom has announced one called LANSTAR, both of which link personal computers using existing telephone lines.

Another solution to the wiring problems inherent in the introduction of LANS may come with the application of rapidly developing fiber optic technology. It may be possible to utilize its greater carrying capacity and smaller size in reducing the total amount of space for wiring, thus providing wiring space for LANs.

How to Avoid Electrical Surprises

Because the electronic office machines of today's office, especially computers, will malfunction and/or lose data if unprotected from variations from and interference with a steady power supply, precautions must be taken to insure that the power supply remains viable.

Basically there are three things that can adversely affect electronic machine operation:

1. A power outage or complete loss of power. One method of dealing with this kind of emergency is to have backup batteries and generators for large computers or groups of smaller ones. The batteries supply enough power to run the computers, light the area, and run the air-conditioning they need for operation temporarily until the generators get up to speed and take over. This is usually called an ''uninterruptible power supply.''
2. Variations in voltage, which may be either voltage surges, when the voltage is higher than normal, or voltage sags, when the voltage is lower than normal. If these variations get large enough, they can seriously affect electronic machine operations. Variations can be produced by the starting of a large motor, such as those for elevators or large air-conditioning compressors, or even a coffee dispenser. According to *Facilities,* 90 percent of the surges that interfere with office machine operation happen this way (1988, 8). Sags seem to be a much less important cause of trouble.
3. Power line noise, defined as any unwanted energy that enters a circuit. It may be the shocks, sparks, lightning, electrostatic discharges, and radiated electrical interference that optic fiber is immune to.

For the second and third the remedies are filters, suppressors, and two types of special circuits: (1) a designated circuit with a common ground wire, a common neutral wire, and a hot wire used for a specific purpose or machine; and (2) a dedicated circuit with a separate neutral wire, a separate ground wire, and a separate hot wire all of which are used for a specific purpose or machine.

Chapter 10

Security and Fire Safety

Security measures in the office are undertaken with one common goal: loss prevention. They fall under two general headings, physical personnel security and information security. However, since both are subject to the threat of fire, we shall first treat fire safety separately.

Fire Safety Equipment and Training

One of the principal threats to the office, its contents, its information, and its occupants is fire. Of primary importance is the need to know when there is a fire threat present. Smoke and heat detectors with alarms seem to be the present preferred first line of defense. One additional alarm is a signal attached to an automatic sprinkler system, a Halon® or carbon dioxide gas system (particularly useful for extinguishing fires in computer rooms) or any other automatic fire-extinguishing system to let you know that the system is in operation. Any of these alarms should also inform the fire department that a fire is in progress and start the operation of smoke control systems if they are in place.

The selection of the types of alarm signals used should take account of the fact that people who are sensorily impaired may be present. The signals should be both visible and audible.

Although the automatic systems described above are quite useful and earn reductions in insurance premiums, there are many organizations, especially in England, that place great reliance on hand extinguishers and hose reels plus the training of office workers to use them, even though they may have automatic fire suppression systems in place as well. Hand extinguishers should be carefully selected so that their contents will put out the types of fires that are likely to occur in the areas where they are placed. The importance of training office workers to prevent fires and to handle fire emergencies cannot be overemphasized. The old-fashioned fire drill is a good idea.

Escape paths should be clearly marked and planned so that people in wheelchairs can use them. Clear, easily readable signage is necessary for both escape paths and fire-extinguishing equipment. Emergency lighting should be in place, especially in the emergency escape path areas.

Making the Office Less Combustible

Careful selection of fire retardant office furnishings can reduce fire hazard. You can insist that upholstered office furniture meet the voluntary Business and Institutional Furniture Manufacturers Association (BIFMA) and Upholstered Furniture Action Council (UFAC) flammability requirements. You can go further by specifying various grades of fire-retardant foam, fire-retardant wood or metal frames, self-extinguishing waste baskets, fire-resistant upholstery barriers under the outer cover, and even fire-rated fabrics for either upholstery or draperies.

Effective December 16, 1989, a New York state regulation on drapery and wall fabrics requires fire gas toxicity tests; the information must be on file before fabrics can be installed (Smith 1989). It is expected that this sort of testing will spread across the United States (see Chapter 19, BIFMA and Other Standards).

Other fire-rated interior office furnishings include panel systems, doors, carpet, carpet underlays, melamine plastic laminates, resilient flooring, glass, and even stair treads. All of these choices can be made with fire hazards in mind.

There is a recently-introduced line of wallcoverings from B. F. Goodrich called Early Warning Effect (EWE), which can give an advance warning of fire before smoke or flames are visible. When even a small surface area reaches 300 degrees Fahrenheit, the wallcovering emits a colorless, odorless, and harmless gas that triggers ionization-type smoke detectors, which are the most common type in use today. A temperature of 300 degrees Fahrenheit is well below the ignition levels of most materials in the office. If EWE is used, workers must be told about it because usually no flame or smoke will be visible when the alarm is triggered.

Uniroyal makes Naugahyde 2–200 ™ Flame Blocker vinyl upholstery, which is designed to pass the Boston Full-Scale chair burn test by extinguishing the test flame in 3.5 minutes and to "prevent ignition and combustion of foam underpadding by blocking the flame."

Check any questions about fire prevention measures of any kind with your local fire marshal.

Physical and Personnel Security

To reduce the possibility of unauthorized entry to the office, entry doors should be at least 1¾ inches thick and should be of solid core construction. If a typical pin-tumbler lock is used, it should operate a minimum 1-inch throw deadbolt made of hardened steel. This is the minimum security requirement. More sophisticated locks such as those operated by button combinations or magnetically coded cards are available. Door frames should be strong and reinforced if necessary.

Who Gets Through?

For most offices, it is sufficient to have a receptionist who handles visitors. However, if greater control is needed, a variety of systems and devices are on the market. Employees may wear badges that identify the areas where they work and are permitted to be. Visitors may be asked to wear badges identifying them and their purpose on the premises. Some firms use electronic card readers that recognize only properly coded cards. Where high levels of security are required, devices that recognize individual voices and others that recognize palm and fingerprints are used by themselves or in combination with pushbutton numeric keypads. There is even a system that recognizes retinal blood vessel patterns, a stable characteristic that's virtually impossible to steal, duplicate, or forge. Closed-circuit television is also widely used.

Information Security

Paper shredders have been around for some time but after Iranian terrorists were able to reconstruct secret documents from the American Embassy in Teheran by putting together long strips from a shredder that only shredded in one direction, the cross-cut shredder that cuts paper into minute confetti less than 1/16 of an inch in any direction became more popular. At least one manufacturer advertises a shredder that can shred binders, including the steel rings, as well as paper. One good place to put a shredder is right next to the copier; ''waste'' paper could be valuable to a competitor. Some security experts insist that papers and carbon copies should be burned after being shredded. In any case, shredded and other waste paper should be removed regularly so that it does not become a fire hazard.

Locked files, some with combination locks, vaults, and various forms of safes are other ways of protecting valuable papers, money, and securities. For the storage of computer disks and tapes the files should be tamperproof, fireproof, and climatically controlled; an ordinary insulated file or safe won't do.

Recently, Meridian introduced a new file control system with an electronic lock/interlock through a liquid crystal display access panel in the top of the file. A series of numbers is assigned to those authorized to access the file and/or individual drawers, and that combination must be entered on an electronic keypad to open the file. The access panel can be wired to a computer which can register by whom and when the file has been entered. The device is electrically operated but if power goes out, a hand-held flashlight powered by batteries can be plugged in to open it.

Sotr-Wal International has a similar, but more elaborate system with an optional bar code reader for both files and identification badges, plus optional integration with personal computers for remote access.

Protecting Information Media

In the electronic office, access is a key word in the control of information inside computer and peripheral memories. Who is allowed to use the computer and to know what information is stored inside it?

In most small businesses, the answer is anyone, but that could be fatal to the enterprise; it is no secret that computer fraud is a growing business. No business is too small to make the effort to control access to its computer programs and records. Computer fraud costs to American business have been estimated at $8 billion per year.

Methods of restricting access vary, but most start with passwords and/or more complicated procedures identifying the operator as authorized. To gain access to some computers, the user must call the computer, give a password and then wait for the computer to return the call. Increasingly, locks are found not only on desks and files but also on computers and printers to control unauthorized use.

Caring for Tapes, Discs, and Diskettes

Temperature, humidity, dust, and access controls are prime necessities for storing electronic media. Since these factors are primary ones for the computer also, the media are frequently stored in the same room or area that contains the computer itself. A wide variety of racks and cabinets are on the market for ordinary storage.

For some important tapes and discs, however, more protection is needed. Gas and flame-proof locked filing cabinets are used for the highest degree of protection. Some firms store duplicate tapes of important records in a separate location to make sure that both sets of records are not destroyed. Usually the duplicates are updated every day (see Chapter 14, Information Storage).

Chapter 11

Acoustics

The importance of the acoustic environment in offices is reflected in the General Services Administration (GSA), Public Buildings Service (PBS) Guide Specification (PBS T 4-13500) for an Integrated Ceiling and Background (ICB) system. This guide specification recognizes that the acoustic atmosphere of any office is a product of several interrelated elements in it: the ceiling with its lighting (light fixtures can reflect and reverberate sound even though the other ceiling panels are sound absorbent), windows, draped or not, air-handling components (compressors, fans, and ducts), screens or panels, any office furniture and equipment in use or idle, and the floor surface for conventional floors as well as the special acoustical problems of raised floors (see Chapter 9, Wiring, Networks, and Access Floors and Chapter 16, Carpets). Proposed density of people and equipment is also a factor.

The interrelationships among all of these elements of the acoustic atmosphere are quite complex, and absolute quantitative measurements do not exist for evaluating the diverse qualities of the resulting environment (including the acoustics). PBS therefore uses an expert human jury to evaluate contractor proposals under this guide specification, and has developed the concept of a ''Speech Privacy Potential,'' which can be rated in a numerical way as an important part of the evaluation of the characteristics discussed below.

Requirements

Acoustical requirements in offices generally consist of:

1. Privacy of speech at both low and normal voice levels

2. The ability to perform normal office work with no distractions from the sound of another worker's normal speaking voice

3. A suitable general sound pressure level in the office with no distractions or vibrations from noisy machinery

The level of sound must not be too low; if it is too low the space becomes acoustically "dead" and everyone can hear everyone else's conversations. If this happens "white" or masking sound may be used; for this purpose, a generator produces mixed, unintelligible sounds across the sound spectrum used by the human voice. Because the use of masking sound is tricky, an acoustical expert should be employed.

The general sound level must not be too high and therefore, not too distracting. In the authors' experience any general noise level above 50 decibels can be troublesome in a typical office. One acoustical expert flatly states that the minimum level for open-plan offices is 42 decibels and that the maximum level is 48 decibels.

Requirements will vary outside the general office area for boardrooms and other conference areas. Please see Table 11-1 for an explanation of various noise levels in offices in terms of activities possible at each level. (Also see Chapter 15, Teleconferencing.)

TABLE 11-1. Noise Criteria for Offices and Workspaces

	Offices
NC[a] (or NCA[b]) Curve	**Communication Environment**
NC-20 to NC-30	Very quiet office; suitable for large conferences. Telephone use satisfactory
NC-30 to NC-35	"Quiet" office; satisfactory for conferences at a 15 ft. table; normal voice, 10 to 30 ft. Telephone use satisfactory
NC-35 to NC-40	Satisfactory for conferences at a 6 to 8 ft. table; normal voice, 6 to 12 ft. Telephone use satisfactory
NC-40 to NC-50	Satisfactory for conferences at a 4 to 5 ft. table; normal voice, 3 to 6 ft; raised voice 6 to 12 ft. Telephone use occasionally slightly difficult
NC-50 to NC-55	Unsatisfactory for conferences of more than two or three people; normal voice, 1 to 2 ft; raised voice 3 to 6 ft. Telephone use slightly difficult
Above NC-55	"Very noisy." Office environment unsatisfactory. Telephone use difficult.
	Workspaces, Shop Areas, Etc.
NC-60 to NC-70	Person-to-person communication with raised voice satisfactory, 1 to 2 ft; slightly difficult, 3 to 6 ft. Telephone use difficult
NC-70 to NC-80	Person-to-person communication slightly difficult with raised voice, 1 to 2 ft; slightly difficult with shouting, 3 to 6 ft. Telephone use very difficult
Above NC-80	Person-to-person communication extremely difficult. Telephone use unsatisfactory.

Source: NASA, *Habitability Data Handbook,* MSC-03909, P. 3-44.

[a] NC, noise criteria.

[b] NCA, noise criteria average

Note: Noise measurements made for the purpose of comparing the noise in an office with these criteria should be performed with the office in normal operation, but with no one talking at the particular desk or conference table where speech communication is desired, i.e., where the measurement is being made. Background noise with the office unoccupied should be lower, say by 5 to 10 dB.

Four Basic Ways to Control Unwanted Sound

We will be talking about some specifics of four basic ways to control noise:

1. Limiting noise at its source
2. Absorbing or blocking noise along its path from source to receiver (Remember that sound does not always travel in a direct path; it may be reflected off surfaces along its way.)
3. Absorbing or blocking noise at the receiver
4. Positioning sources, paths, and receivers

In satisfying the above four requirements, a major factor is the distance between workers in the office, or how crowded it is, since the effects of sound lessen as the distance from the source to the receiver increases. This

In this environmental laboratory different types and levels of office noises are simulated to determine the effect of background noise on speech intelligibility. Office lighting can also be simulated in this lab to show the brightness, intensity and distribution pattern of lighting produced by different configurations of fixtures. The room's ceiling can be raised or lowered, for tests of both ceiling fixtures and acoustics. (Courtesy of Steelcase Inc.)

distance varies with the amount of square feet provided for each worker. In typical open-plan offices it will be in the following ranges:

Square Feet Provided for Each Worker	Least Distance Between Workers (feet)
110	8
120	10
130	12
140	14

In these ranges and below, an acoustically absorbent barrier such as a screen or a system panel, is necessary to meet acoustic requirements, along with an acoustically absorbent ceiling and a sound-rated carpet. In fact, the choice of a ceiling and lighting system mounted on it is probably the most important decision in planning the acoustical environment. The ceiling is a major surface area and the acoustical absorbency of its panels as well as the sound-reflecting characteristics of the overhead lighting fixtures greatly affect the acoustical character of the space. Sometimes banners or sound-absorbent baffles are hung from the ceiling parts that are especially sound reflecting. The next most important decision is to choose the carpet.

Another major factor in controlling noise is the orientation of a speaker to those who can hear him or her. It might be ideal if all workers in open offices faced away from each other in opposite directions, but that usually is not possible in view of typical space standards. The most effective attainable goal is usually setting up a 90 degree orientation of workers to each other within the normally rectangular divisions of office spaces.

Patterns of sound-absorbing ceiling panels. (Courtesy of Armstrong World Industries, Inc.)

Screens and Panels

Acoustically efficient screens or panels about 82 inches high with no more than a 3/4-inch open air space between the bottom of the screen and the floor usually do the best job, short of demountable full-height partitions or stud and dry wall. If more than normal lessening of sound is needed the studs can be staggered so that they are attached to only one side of the dry wall. This type of wall will be thicker than a typical stud and dry wall partition.

Acoustical efficiency of screens and panels is usually measured in two ways. As a sound barrier, the material's sound transmission class (STC) is determined; office screens and panels should have a STC of from 22 to 25.

To evaluate sound absorbing qualities, the rule of thumb for acoustically efficient screens or panels is that they must be rated as having a noise reduction coefficient (NRC) of 0.85 or higher, meaning that the screen absorbs 85 percent of ambient sound hitting it. An NRC of 1 would mean that all of the ambient sound hitting the screen is absorbed. Since high frequency sounds are the most disturbing, it is useful to take a hard look at the distribution of the tests and make sure that there is ample absorption at the 4,000 3,000, and 2,000 cycles-per-second frequencies.

Enclosures

Ambient or general sound is not the only sound to worry about. Noisy office machinery sometimes produces high sound levels, which demand other remedies in addition to panels or screens. According to Corlin and Falluchi, writing in *Contract* magazine, "an increasing number and variety of sound

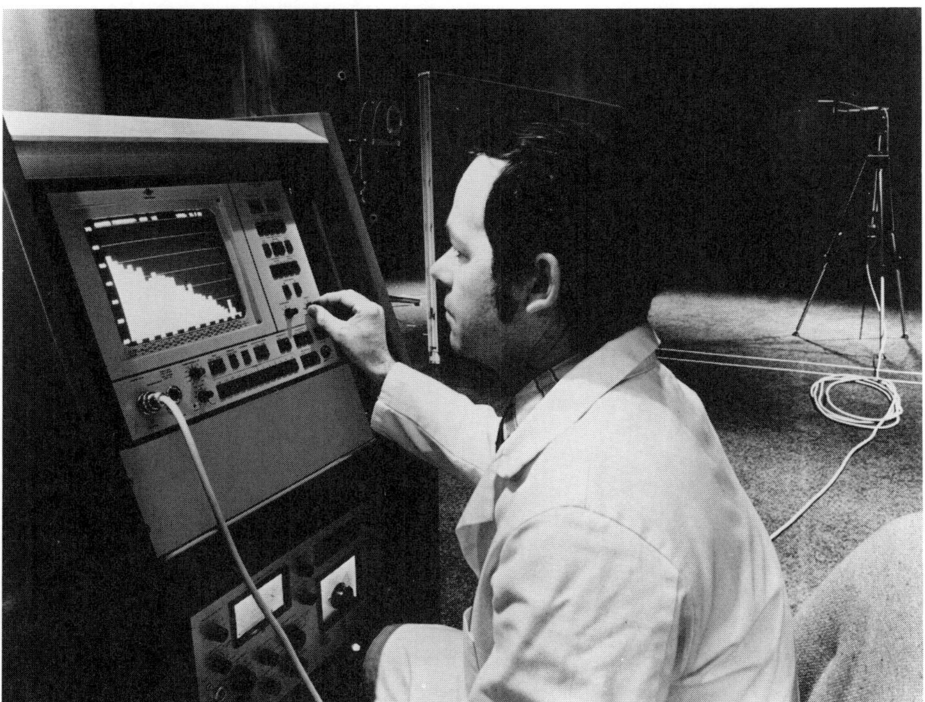

In this laboratory, office panel systems are tested to determine their acoustic characteristics. By monitoring the sound level emitted from the speaker on one side of the panel and the level picked up by the receiver on the other side, the technician can determine the efficiency of the panel in absorbing and blocking sound. (Courtesy of Steelcase Inc.)

shielding and attenuating enclosures are appearing on the market to fit individual pieces of office machinery; these are being used in many kinds of offices'' (1976).

The most common of these are printer enclosures. Sound reductions of as much as 90 percent are claimed for some of these cabinets. One insurance company says that putting acoustic covers on typewriters resulted in a reduction of 8.8 percent for the time needed to perform office tasks, a 13 percent decrease in absenteeism, and a 47 percent reduction in worker turnover. However, if an enclosure is used and the results are not satisfactory, a foam mat placed under the offending piece of machinery may be needed and if the machine is a computer terminal and keyboard, a mat with antistatic properties should be used. Noisy mechanical units such as air-conditioners can sometimes be quieted by using suppression mounts underneath them. Sound-absorbent panels that can be attached to desks, files, and walls are also on the market.

Carpet

The effects of carpet and carpet tiles as noise-reducing factors are well known. Thick-piled carpets laid over very heavy underlays can lessen ambient sound by as much as 70 percent, averaged over the audible sound frequencies, from 125 to 4,000 cycles per second, and are therefore evaluated as having an NRC of 0.70 after being rated on the basis of a standard test, ASTM-423-66, under laboratory conditions. Carpet and pad reduce impact noise and vibration noise as well. The NRC varies widely with the type of carpet and also with the various combinations of carpet and underlay. Either laying carpet without an underlay or using carpet tiles can lessen the amount of noise reduction by half. Specifications should be carefully checked before

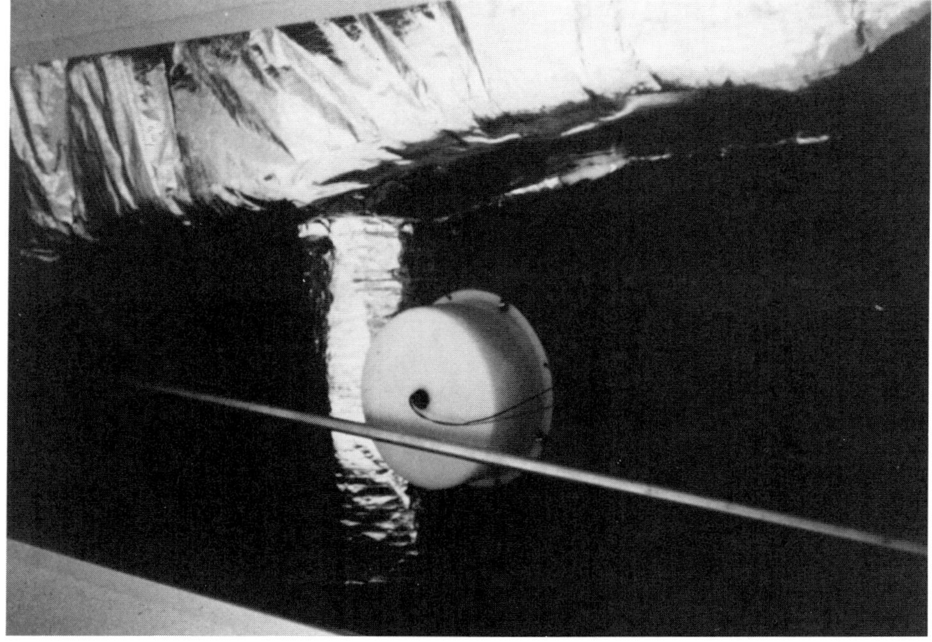

A white noise generator, used to create background sound in too-quiet offices or to mask sounds and give office workers a measure of privacy. (Courtesy of Sam Sloan, AIA.)

selection, because now most carpet mills have their carpets and carpet tiles tested and give the noise reduction coefficient as part of their specifications. Each individual carpet specification will also give the type of underlay used for the test if it includes underlay.

The acoustic ceiling, carpet, and tackable acoustic panels combine to hold down the sound level at Continental Western Life Insurance Co. in West Des Moines, Iowa. (Courtesy of Steelcase Inc.)

Draperies

Draperies can be quite efficient in reducing sound levels in two ways: absorbing sound and acting as a sound barrier. Robert Marshall (1970) credits certain types of draperies hung against walls with a 0.55 NRC, based primarily on the sound absorption qualities of the draperies. Eighteen-ounce-per-square-yard heavy velour draped on half the wall area is credited with a 0.60 NRC.

PPG Industries has developed a system for rating the sound absorption, heat insulation, and brightness control of draperies. They point out that

> Because of the 'fullness' created by pleating, draperies have a greater surface area in contact with the air. Therefore, they stay cooler than blinds or shades and do not *reradiate* as much energy toward people near windows. Light-colored fabrics stay cooler than dark-colored fabrics because they reflect, rather than absorb, much of the solar energy reaching them. . . . All fabrics have a beneficial effect in reducing noise, but the most effective are those which are tightly woven and relatively heavy in weight. (PPG 1976)

The amount of sound a drapery will absorb also depends on its degree of ''fullness,'' or the depth of each fold.

Draperies can also be sound barriers. The author's work in this area started some years ago when a client asked for ''acoustic'' draperies for a boardroom right beside a traffic light on a six-lane highway. The situation was complicated by the fact that the small-paned windows had rather loose-fitting steel frames reminiscent of 1920s construction, which let in sound like an open sieve.

After some rudimentary experimentation it was found that most light-blocking fabrics utilized as linings (usually selected for windows in audiovisual rooms) will block sound as well. The draperies were made long enough to extend up a foot into a valance at the top and to drag the sill slightly; by doing this an effective sound seal was formed with the light-blocking fabric. This client had 460 feet of office exposure to this highway; eventually 460 feet of sound-blocking draperies were installed.

Using this same technique, a successful drapery system was provided for a restaurant. The owner wanted to divide a large room into private dining rooms of varying sizes. A ceiling track grid system was installed and the draperies were made long enough to drag both the floor and the ceiling.

This kind of drapery has also been used to subdivide areas of a television station, to block computer noise in a factory office and to reduce noise in glass-enclosed offices.

This technique can be important because light-blocking linings on window draperies are often necessary to prevent veiling reflections on computer terminal screens and can serve as sound blockers as well.

A study of some remodeled U.S. Army offices in the Pentagon found that it was 54 percent less expensive to use draperies on walls than to use acoustical panels and that 200 percent more sound attenuation resulted (*Federal Design Matters* 1977).

However, one word of caution: if you are using draperies or any other device to block sound, make sure there are no spaces in or around the barrier where sound can leak through. Things to watch for include open spaces around pipes, air-conditioning ducts, electric and phone outlets, and joints where walls meet ceilings and floors.

Also, if you are hanging draperies on walls, leave at least an inch to as many as 4 inches space between the drapery and the wall or window; this will increase the drapery's effectiveness.

Other Factors

Draperies, carpets, and screens are not the only interior components that help reduce noise levels. Planning and close attention to interior finishing details are also important factors. These include the following:

- *Doors:* Most hollow-core doors transmit more sound than solid core doors. The tightness of door closure through careful fitting of the door to its frame is another important factor.
- *Wall coverings:* Some of these can absorb sound, especially if woven cloth or carpet is used on walls.
- *Walls:* If walls are hollow and have no insulating material in them—and sound reduction is needed—investigate putting some in.
- *Air-conditioning systems:* If there is noise from this source, baffles and insulating material can be put into or around the ducts (or wrapped around them), fans can be replaced with quieter ones, and compressors can be enclosed with sound-absorbing and/or sound-blocking material. Pipe or wire chases are often conduits for unwanted sound; sometimes they must be baffled and/or insulated.
- *Windows:* If the windows transmit too much noise from the outside, single panes can be replaced with double ones and window closures can be tightened. In severe situations, triple glazing can be used. Sometimes recaulking around windows and doors will greatly reduce the amount of outside noise transmitted to the interior.
- *Computers:* Noisy mainframe computers can be completely enclosed in special rooms (they often are because they have special power and air-conditioning needs).
- *Ceilings:* The open space or plenum above a dropped ceiling becomes a means of transmitting sound from one office area to another. To minimize noise from this source, sound-absorbent or sound-blocking baffles are sometimes installed vertically in the open space created by the dropped ceiling.

In evaluating most types of acoustical problems, a common-sense approach is often a viable way to solve them.

Chapter 12

Indoor Air Pollution

When the energy crisis hit in 1973, the trend toward sealing buildings to prevent heat loss soared. Not only were new office buildings designed with unopenable windows, increased insulation, tighter construction, and reduced ventilation, but also substantial efforts to seal existing buildings were made. Unfortunately when buildings are sealed this way, the amount of fresh air entering the building is sharply reduced. Because of this reduction and other factors, including some of the newer machines used in the office, indoor air pollution in the office has become a real problem.

The "Sick Building Syndrome"

There are several studies indicating that air pollution in office buildings is more dangerous than typical outdoor pollution. Although outdoor air pollution is tightly regulated, very little regulatory attention has been paid to the indoor variety. A spokesman for the Environmental Protection Agency (EPA) has denied that EPA has any legislated responsibility for indoor air pollution, which has been called the "sick building syndrome."

Some of the known pollutants are microorganisms, ammonia, carbon monoxide, nitrogen dioxide, sulfur dioxide, benzene, toluene, xylene, phenols, hydrocarbons, formaldehyde, asbestos, glass fibers, pesticides, ozone, chloroform, radon, methyl alcohol, nitropyrene, trinitrofluorene, trichloroethylene, and tobacco smoke. Sources of the substances include air fresheners, solvents, tobacco, construction adhesives, liquid erasers, cleaning fluids, fire retardant chemicals, photocopying machines, carbonless paper, duplicating machines, sound-dampening and insulating materials, and "outgassing" of chemicals from building products and furnishings. Asbestos is a widely recognized pollutant found in existing buildings and it is a cause of cancer. If found, it should be either sealed off or entirely removed.

Formaldehyde is a pervasive source of indoor pollution. Used as an inexpensive glue, it is found in insulation, particle board, plywood, and textiles. It may be released from these materials by moisture in the air for as long as four years after installation. Exposure to it may cause burning eyes, tears, and irritation of the respiratory system.

Other adhesives may cause trouble, too. Several thousand pounds of adhesives may be used in a high-rise office building, especially for carpet and upholstered panel systems as well as furniture and wall coverings.

Ozone from photocopying machines and some ''air ionizers'' can cause headaches, and tobacco smoke is a well-known and much discussed air pollutant.

Microorganisms in air-conditioning systems can be dangerous because they breed in duct insulation material, especially when that material is old newspapers. Under certain conditions, the starches in the paper can furnish a medium where microorganisms can flourish; they can also breed wherever moisture collects. The outbreak of legionnaires' disease in 1977 was traced to a microorganism concentration found in a ventilation duct.

Frequent complaints of office workers include headaches; eye irritation; and upper respiratory tract complaints such as sore throats, colds, and coughs. These problems have led to three notable research studies, an American effort by Turiel et al. and British studies by Alan Hedge and by Sheena Wilson, comparing the incidence of these complaints in open-plan air-conditioned offices compared to non-air-conditioned cellular offices.

The American study found that ''significantly more complaints of health problems (eye irritation/itching, nose/throat irritation, shortness of breath, chest tightness and eye inflammation/infection) were found among those working in the air-conditioned open-plan offices'' (Turiel et al. 1982).

Hedge did six surveys. His results indicate that

> Overall a significantly higher incidence of reported headaches was found among staff working in open-plan offices compared with those in conventional offices and this seems to be related to the incidence of problems of reflected glare. Problems of eye irritation and respiratory complaints (coughs, sore throats, etc.) are similarly found to be most common among staff in open-plan offices, but importantly, only when those are air-conditioned and have poor daylight penetration . . . (Hedge 1986)

Sheena Wilson has reported on a questionnaire survey of 4,373 workers in 46 buildings of varied ages and selected to cover a range of ventilation systems in Great Britain. The object of her project was to find out how widespread ''building sickness'' is and what types of buildings produce it. Building sickness is defined as ''general, non-specific symptoms of malaise, in particular lethargy and headache and irritation of the nose, throat and eyes . . . experienced by people during the time they are in the building and that cease shortly afterwards'' (1987b). The definition does not include infections mentioned above and there are no indications that specific pollutants are involved.

Among Wilson's findings are the following (1987b):

- 80 percent of the sample experienced symptoms of ill health that they associated with being in their place of work.
- 25 percent experienced one or two symptoms and 29 percent had five or more.
- 57 percent experienced lethargy, 47 percent had stuffy noses, and 43 percent suffered headaches.

- 34 percent described the air in their offices as slightly or very stale, and 45 percent said the air was slightly or very dry.
- Of the people with more than five symptoms, 50 percent rated their environment as reducing their productivity by more than 20 percent.
- Clerical/secretarial workers had 50 percent more symptoms than managers and 30 percent more than professionals.
- Women reported symptoms much more frequently than men.
- The relationship between computer use and building sickness was not strong, except where people worked more than six hours at a VDT.
- Air-conditioned buildings had consistently higher rates of sickness than buildings with either natural or just mechanical ventilation systems.
- Older buildings registered higher rates of complaint than new ones.

Coping with Pollutants

These problems are serious, so serious that the suggestion has been made that buildings be tested for pollutants after they are built, but before they are occupied. One troublesome aspect of the problem is the unknown properties of many building materials. It has been suggested that manufacturers of products used in buildings test their products for indoor air pollution potential and make those test results available to specifiers. If this problem continues to grow, products may be selected for their nonpolluting properties. A potentially even greater problem is presented by multiple pollutants. Although quite a bit has been discovered about the effects of various single pollutants, much less is known about what combinations of pollutants can do.

There are several ways to attack the problem of indoor air pollution. Filters of two general types can be installed. Electrostatic filters precipitate and remove airborne polluting particles, and passive filters do the same job; both need regular maintenance to be effective.

Studies have also shown that at least one air change per hour is needed and that probably two changes per hour are better. Rooftop intakes for fresh air are usually better than ground-level intakes that are nearer to the street and car exhausts. All air-conditioning ductwork, seals, and fans should be regularly checked and maintained.

Some of the newer variable air volume (VAV) systems are microprocessor, direct digitally controlled and may be installed in a new building or retrofitted. In some situations VAVs have improved air quality and used less installation space than conventional HVAC systems. Some users complain, however, that VAVs respond only to variations of temperature and cannot be regulated to affect air quality.

Remember that there are two basic ways to bring controlled air into the office, through the ceiling or through the floor. If it is brought in through the ceiling, the ducts should be part of an integrated ceiling system; through the floor, an access or raised floor should be used.

If the demand for individual air-conditioning at each workstation (with conditioned air coming through the furniture itself) becomes widespread, it may be better to bring the air through the floor because of the shorter distance of travel and because it looks better to most people than poles or pipes from the ceiling. Some advanced European systems bring the air in through a raised floor and then exhaust it through the ceiling light fixtures; in some situations drawing the exhaust air across the light fixtures may reduce the air-conditioning load by exhausting heat from the ceiling lighting at the same time. There is at least one American air-conditioning system available now that operates in conjunction with an access floor.

We should also mention that the air-conditioning system is related to other systems as well; it must properly control humidity, not only for human comfort, but also for machine wellbeing in terms of static electricity control.

The design and specification of the air-conditioning system is also related to the total load put upon it by the lighting system and the increase in electronic devices in the office. Air-conditioning systems used to be designed to compensate for heat loads (heat pollution) of 3 to 3.5 watts per square foot. These loads are growing to 4 to 4.5 watts per square foot with random groupings of office appliances that produce concentrations of heat. The new VAV systems do help in selectively combatting high heat conditions in these areas.

NASA has recently announced that research performed for the projected permanent manned space station indicates that there are plants that will clean up some indoor air pollution. The thin-leafed spider plant, the Chinese evergreen, the peace lily, philodendrons, and the golden pothos among others will significantly reduce the amounts of nitrogen dioxide, carbon monoxide, formaldehyde, and other toxic gasses indoors. Gerbera daisies, bamboo palms, and chrysanthemums are especially effective in removing benzene and formaldehyde from the air. Other good plant air purifiers include ficus, mother-in-law's tongue, and English ivy, according to B. C. Wolverton, a scientist at NASA's Stennis Space Center in Bay St. Louis, Mississippi, who conducted a two-year study for NASA (Wolverton 1988).

Sometimes indoor air pollution comes from inadequate ventilation caused by simple glitches. Cases abound where the air intake is blocked with debris or where there have been multiple rearrangements of offices without adjustments of the air-conditioning system. There is the famous case of an environmental control system that was installed with a complex computer and program to control it. When the system failed to work and employees loudly complained, somebody found that the computer had never been plugged in.

A new voluntary standard for indoor air quality, ''Ventilation for Acceptable Indoor Air Quality, 62-1989,'' has been approved by The American Society of Heating, Refrigerating and Air-Conditioning Engineers (ASHRAE). The standard has been sent to the American National Standards Institute for adoption.

Much research is being done on the problem of indoor air pollution, and it is hoped that new and more effective solutions will be developed.

Chapter 13

Lighting and Energy Conservation

We know that lighting design is important to productivity in the office. According to H. Richard Freidin,

> Shortly after the OPEC oil embargo of 1973–74, the General Services Administration cut back lighting levels from 100 foot-candles to 50 foot-candles in the keypunch area of a Social Security Administration office in Baltimore, Maryland. Immediately, productivity levels fell by 28 percent and were not restored until the lighting was restored as well. (Freidin 1982)

Important as lighting design is, there are no hard and fast rules for it because office workers are not all alike in their needs and preferences. In designing millions of square feet of electronic offices, the authors have found a wide variety of preferences among office workers as to the type of lighting they want, ranging from a spotlight effect within a dark cave to full bright sunlight.

Although there is no easy way to satisfy every individual preference, as studies are performed on how to light the electronic office, a few useful principles are beginning to emerge.

One principle that we must emphasize is that window light and cathode ray tubes (CRTs) are incompatible. Light from windows can hit the computer screen and reflect into the eyes of the operator; this is glare or veiling reflection, as it is called technically.

The troubles that come from windows in the electronic office are at war with what is evidently a fundamental human characteristic: People like windows and like to work where they have a window view.

The quality of the view is important, too. A nine-year study of hospital patients by Roger S. Ulrich found that

> Twenty-three surgical patients assigned to rooms with windows looking out on a natural scene had shorter postoperative hospital stays, received fewer negative evaluation comments in nurses' notes, and took fewer potent analgesics than 23 matched patients in similar rooms with windows facing a brick building wall. (Ulrich 1984)

All the patients had had the same operation.

Reducing Glare

Some experts say that when a computer is operated in a space with a window, light-blocking window coverings should be used so that as little light as possible enters.

If, however, glare is present, the source should be identified. A good way to do this is to cover the computer screen with a mirror for a moment to identify the origin of the glare. Then the source should be blocked, perhaps with a baffle, or removed. If that fails to work, there are several other ways to deal with the problem.

One way is to place a filter over the screen. There are several varieties on the market. If the glare is coming from above, which happens with some general lighting systems, sometimes a hood placed around the screen works. Then again getting rid of glare may be just a matter of adjusting the tilt of the screen and/or the tilt of the surface under the screen. Louvers or diffusers on the under side of ceiling lighting fixtures can be used when glare is coming from above. Another factor in reducing glare is the use of matte rather than shiny surfaces for everything around the computer, especially the screen housing, the keyboard, and the worksurfaces.

For glare originating from ceiling fixtures, there is a new modular lighting system that allows fixtures to be snapped in and out where needed as offices are moved or rearranged. This system also makes it possible to direct ceiling light more easily where workers want it.

Sharp contrasts in reflectance values cause distraction at the VDT workplace and should be avoided. Since most VDT work involves white paper, the reflectance value of everything around and in the workstation should be in the range of 30 to 50 percent. Manufacturers of melamine laminates can give you these percentages. If the values of other components are not available from their manufacturers, they can be judged from comparisons with laminate values.

The choice of the type of screen display can affect office workers' eye comfort. Most CRT screens show light letters on a dark or black background. Some computer makers use green letters on black and there are also amber and white letters on black, amber, or green backgrounds. A very few manufacturers use black letters on a white background which makes the text look almost like ordinary typing on white paper.

Arguments continue as to which combination is best, but at least one study (G. Radl 1980) presents hard evidence that black letters on a white background are the best combination for the computer screen.

Testing 24 males and females, Radl assigned the same VDT task first on screens with light characters on dark backgrounds and then on screens displaying dark characters on light backgrounds. Nineteen of the 24 subjects preferred the black letters on a white background, 2 said they had no preference, and the other 3 preferred the opposite combination. Visual comfort of black on white was rated by the 19 as more than twice as comfortable.

Radl also pointed out that less eye adaptation is necessary because of the similarity between black and white on the screen and black letters on white paper and that using black letters on a white background is an effective way to avoid veiling reflections on the screen.

A variable intensity task light. Adjustability is achieved with a plastic cylinder, patterned with a network of dark lines, which encases a fluorescent lamp. Light is blocked according to the density of the line patterns. Brightness levels are adjusted by rotating the cylinder. (Courtesy of Steelcase Inc.)

Indirect General Lighting Plus Task Lighting

Most present offices use general fluorescent lighting, and a large portion of them use parabolic baffled direct downlighting. This kind of lighting generally produces glare and does not conserve energy use, however. In the words of Dr. Arthur Rubin of the National Institute of Standards and Technology, ''Uniform lighting levels to accommodate the most visually demanding task are no longer considered to be an acceptable approach to lighting design'' (Rubin 1984).

Although there is much disagreement among lighting authorities about how the VDT office should be lit, there is a definite trend toward the use of indirect uplighting, sometimes incorporated into the systems furniture, along with adjustable separate lighting on the task with dimmers, also sometimes attached to furniture. This may be a lamp under a shelf or cabinet; it can also be a portable lamp, usually of the Luxo type or one that fits into a special track at the rear of the worksurface (Chapter 17, Panel Systems). These uplighters are often free-standing and portable so that they can easily be moved when offices are rearranged.

Indirect versus Direct Lighting

A major study performed at the University of Colorado at Boulder by D. L. DiLaura and R. G. Mistrick and sponsored by Peerless Electric Company compared a parabolic louvre direct lighting system with two indirect systems for the VDT workplace in terms of workers' subjective preferences.

They found a three-to-one preference for the two indirect systems over the direct parabolic because they produced less reflected glare on the VDT screen, walls, ceiling, and other workplace surfaces. Workers felt that the indirect lighting produced a more pleasant, higher quality visual environment; the indirect lighting also made the workers feel more productive (DiLaura and Mistrick 1985).

Other studies have indicated that workers perceive less light in an indirect lighting environment than they perceive in a direct light environment—even though the measured footcandles are identical in both. The result may be that some workers complain unless footcandle levels (and energy consumption) are substantially increased.

Energy Conservation

The use of an indirect system in conjunction with task lighting cuts office energy use by 30 percent or more. The major part of the savings comes from

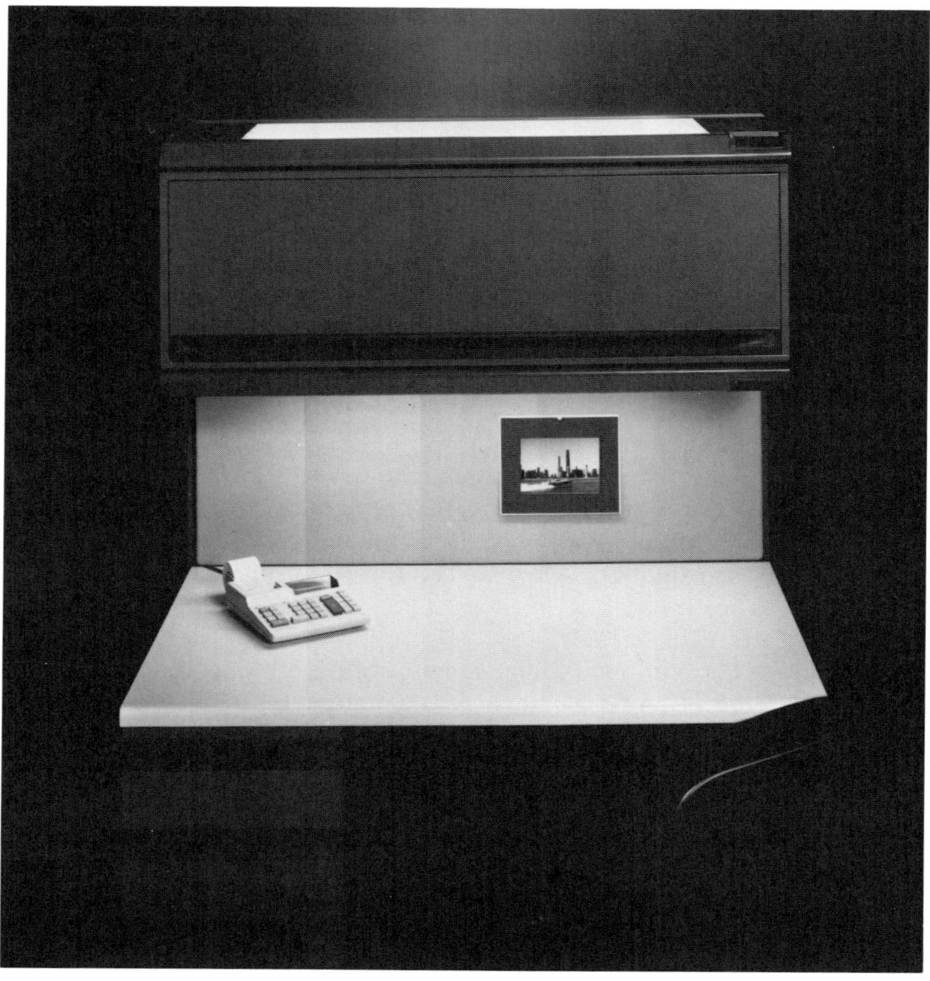

Ambient uplighting and task lighting combined with workstation furniture. The task light has a five-level dimming switch for adjusting the light to the needs of the worker. (Courtesy of Allsteel, Inc.)

the fact that while the light is better directed, less total light is used. The remainder of the savings comes from the reduced load on the air-conditioning system.

Gere Picasso, former environmental research manager at AT&T Communications, reported an even greater saving when 135 office workers were moved to a newly designed facility. The lighting load was reduced from 4 watts per square foot to 1.6 watts per square foot, a reduction of 60 percent. At the same time, employee satisfaction with the lighting increased significantly (Picasso 1985). (See also Chapter 22, A Case for Participatory Design.)

There are several other methods of cutting energy costs for lighting. Lighting expert Dr. David B. Goldstein estimates that better lighting design could save 75 percent or more in energy costs over present conventionally designed offices while improving the working environment and aesthetics. Some other ways to cut energy costs are discussed below.

Motion, Sound, and Heat Sensors

When spaces are not occupied by people, they do not need to be lighted. Three types of sensors, to detect heat, motion, and/or sound, are used to turn off the lights automatically, when people are not using a space. An

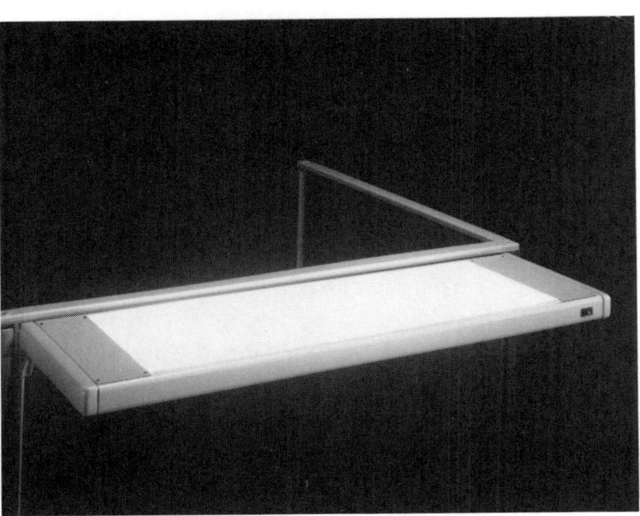

Clockwise from top left, task lighting, a combination up-and-down light and an ambient uplight. (Courtesy of Westinghouse Furniture Systems.)

example is Infracon®, a device developed by Tishman Research and United Technologies Building Systems. It is an automatic infrared sensor that turns lights on and off based on whether or not a space is occupied. Ceiling mounted Infracon senses both heat and body movement. These devices save a significant amount of energy because most office spaces are not occupied 24 hours a day. Savings of 56 percent were reported at New York's World Trade Center with the use of sensors of this type.

Paine Webber has installed 1,200 Infracon sensors in its 410,000-square-foot headquarters in New York City and, on the basis of first-year results, projects that they will pay for themselves in two years.

Scheduling

A simple automatic switching system can be used to turn lights on at times workers customarily are present and turn them off when workers customarily go home. Some scheduling systems perform a dual function by allowing a higher light setting for workers in the office during the day and turning on a lower setting during the times when maintenance people do their jobs at night. These are called zoning controls when applied to various buildings separately.

Daylighting

The use of daylight to reduce lighting loads involves a sensing and switching system that constantly adjusts lighting systems so that a constant light level is maintained as the amount of daylight rises and falls. The use of daylight can now extend deeper into buildings with the addition of "light trays," parabolic surfaces that reflect daylight into portions of a building that otherwise would not receive it. Where there is a lightwell or atrium, a method of optically reflecting focused sunlight from lenses and mirrors on the roof into the building interior is now being used in a few buildings.

Caution is advised when using daylighting in offices where there are computer screens; direct light often creates too many reflections on screens and, even with indirect daylighting, ambient light levels must not get too high. Photocell light sensors and dimmers in conjunction with a programmed computer are usually utilized in systems using daylight as a major component.

Glass that is coated to allow transmission of preset amounts of light is frequently used for daylighting designs. Some of these glass coatings allow transmission of the light portions of the spectrum while blocking the portion that produces heat.

Energy savings from daylighting alone have been reported in the range of 16 to 30 percent.

Where scheduling and daylighting have been combined savings have occurred at rates of 33 to 43 percent.

Tuning

Tuning is a method of adjusting the amount of light in a specific area to the activities going on there. It usually consists of either brightening or dimming all the lights in a specific space or turning off a portion of them. It is fairly inexpensive and if planned for, allows for maintaining the light level as older lamps lose capacity. It also allows simple and low-cost changes when spaces are rearranged.

Energy savings of as much as 30 percent have been reported when tuning is used by itself; when it is combined with scheduling and daylighting savings it can go as high as 51 percent.

More Efficient Ballasts

The development of the electronic ballast allows fluorescents to be run at a much higher frequency, for greater efficiency, and energy costs are reduced by an estimated 20 percent.

More Efficient Lamps

Once there was only incandescent lighting; then for a fairly long time there were only two types, incandescent and fluorescent. Now, however, there are many types and variations of types to be added to the list of possible solutions to light design problems. This particular technology is changing so fast that it would be folly for us to give you any pat solutions.

Lamps do not produce the same amount of light as they grow older; their light output lessens with age. Lighting engineers often set system initial output capability as much as 50 percent above the amount of light needed to compensate for lessened lamp output and dirt. This extra capacity allows desired lighting levels to be maintained while waiting for relamping time when all the lamps are replaced at once, thus saving labor.

Formerly, when this was done, lamps were replaced with the same lamp. Now relamping has a whole new look, basically because of two new developments:

1. Lamps are becoming much more efficient and are made to last much longer.
2. The number of types of lamps available is increasing.

Lighting technology is advancing rapidly and technological innovations will continue to change the scene.

The following are some of the newer choices on the market:

Philips makes the PL series of compact twin-tube fluorescent lamps that fit, for instance, into a swing arm desk lamp produced by Nessen for use with Steelcase's 9000 system furniture. There are three PL capacities. the 7-watt lamp, producing approximately as much light as incandescent bulbs rated at 25 to 40 watts; the 9-watt, producing about as much light as an incandescent bulb rated at 50 to 60 watts; and the most efficient model in this series, a 13-watt product that puts out as much light as incandescent tubes weighing in at 60 to 75 watts. The longest of these PL tubes is 7½ inches. This series will give good color rendition. It is rated as having a life of 10,000 hours as compared to the usual incandescent unit's 750- to 1,500-hour life. Philips has other lines of energy-saving lamps, plus an adapter that allows the PL series to be used in a standard incandescent socket.

Sylvania GTE's 100-watt Metalarc® metal halide lamp has attributes similar to Philips' PL line, with good color rendition and long life. It uses between 61 and 42 percent less electricity than a 300-watt incandescent or a 175-watt mercury lamp and delivers more light than either. It also fits into smaller ordinary fixtures, not only because it is just 5 inches long, but also because it fits an ordinary incandescent socket.

Some of the newer lamps fit into ordinary incandescent sockets and some do not; the latter may require special fixtures. This is true for fluorescents as well. When relamping it is important to check out fixture requirements before making a choice.

Another choice is the high-pressure sodium lamp, said by some experts to be the most efficient lamp, since it is as much as six times as efficient as fluorescents; however, its color rendition is rated as poor by some experts. Mercury vapor lamps are said to be out of the running because they are not that much more efficient than incandescent.

Lines of energy-saving lamps competitive with Philips and Sylvania

GTE are offered by General Electric, Duro-Test, and Voight Lighting Industries among others.

A technological advance for use in exit signs is a lamp offered by Diolight Technology, rated at 80,000 hours (more than 9 years). The typical exit sign lamp lasts about 1,000 hours, equivalent to two months' use.

Check with your local utility. Many power and light companies will help you conserve energy and make your lighting more comfortable for your office workers. A few utilities will subsidize the necessary changes.

Chapter 14

Information Storage

It is now possible to store information electronically on magnetic disks using almost any computer. With a combination of electronics and optics, information can be stored on laser disks. It has long been possible to store information photographically in various microforms.

Nevertheless, paper persists as our chief form of information storage for a very simple psychological reason: you can see it and feel it; it's tangible. You can retrieve information easily and quickly from these other media in visible form and even print it out, but people want the tangible piece of paper and they do not trust these other media to produce an image that can be touched and held in one's hand. They also fear that information will be lost in the imagined ''black hole'' of the computer memory.

Paper Storage

Even though information is stored electronically, we have an urge to print it out, and we do so. As a result we still have to sort and store the paper as well as the tapes and disks. For the most part, we still have to process paper by hand. Actually methods of storing paper have changed very little.

There have been some improvements, such as the separation of papers that you work with and need every day from those that are needed only occasionally. The papers needed for everyday work can be kept in or near the workstation and the rest can go to a central storage section, which you can walk to when necessary. Another improvement has been the retreat of paper storage into the walls, some of them full-height, not only providing the storage space itself, but also using the paper as a material for insulating one office from another acoustically.

Another increasingly popular method of reducing office square footage devoted to filing is to use any of the high-density mobile filing systems that

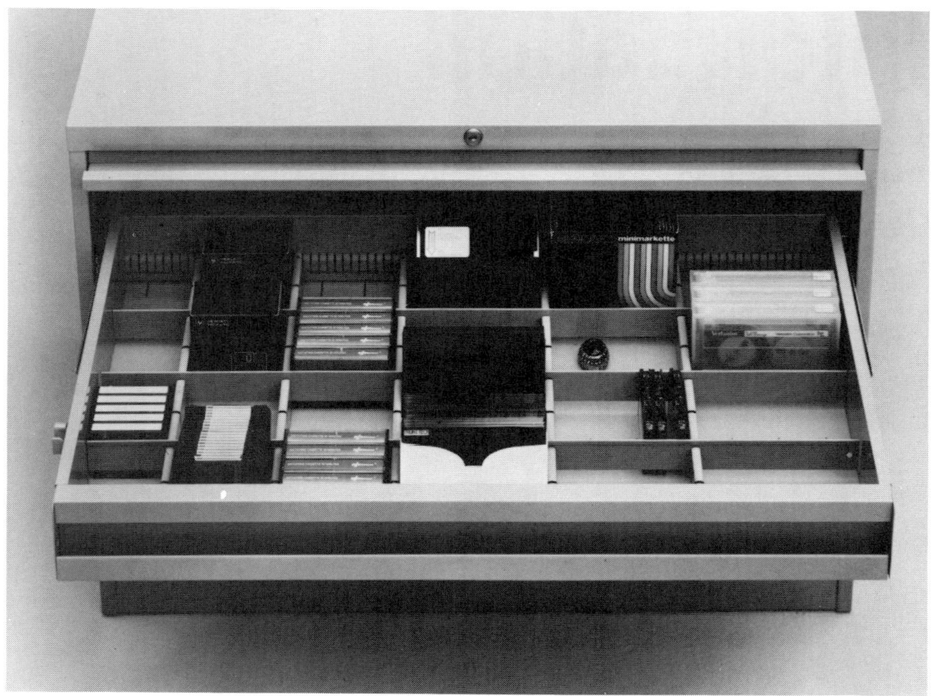

Roll-out lateral file drawer with a media compartment kit stores a variety of electronic media, such as cassettes, minicassettes, cartridges, microfiche, and floppy discs. (Courtesy of Steelcase Inc.)

have come onto the market in the past ten years. These consist of banks of shelves and/or filing drawers that move on tracks laid onto the floor. Instead of using square footage for an aisle between each filing bank, an aisle is created by the user manually, electrically, or mechanically in front of the specific file bank to be used.

While these systems can reduce the space needed for filing up to almost 50 percent, two cautions are in order. The floor load limit must be

How to save floor space with movable files and aisles. (Courtesy of Kardex Systems, Inc.)

thoroughly checked before installation, since the filing systems produce great concentrations of weight that the floor must be able to support. Also, safeguards must be installed to avoid a user's being trapped between the rows when they are pushed together.

Another alternative is an electronically operated, computer-controlled mechanical file, such as the Kardex Lektriever system, which puts the contents of 12 four-drawer vertical file cabinets on a 4-by-8-foot piece of floor space.

Paper Volume

The volume of paper produced by U.S. offices is huge. Xerox estimates that the U.S. market produced 850 billion pages of business documents in 1981 and that this figure rose to 1.4 trillion pages in 1985 (Wiggins 1987). Datapro Research has estimated that the figure was 2.5 trillion pages for 1986 and that by 1990 it would probably rise to 4 trillion.

May Maguire, writing in *The Office* (1989, 58), says, ''Consider that each day, U.S. companies generate 2.7 billion sheets of file-folder contents, 600 million pieces of computer printouts, 234 million photocopies and 21 million general paper documents.''

Still, we hear much about the coming ''paperless office.'' One answer to that dream is what a very large multinational told the CALUS survey: ''Within our organization, the paperless office is as far away as the paperless toilet.''

This concentration of filing cabinets becomes a social waterhole. (Courtesy of Sam Sloan, AIA.)

Compression Figures for Other Media

With the use of paper growing, we must look at the compression figures for other media, which say that we can save lots of paper and expensive storage space. Dr. Arthur I. Rubin, of the National Bureau of Standards, estimates the compression ratio of digital media (storage on magnetic disks) versus paper at 300 to 1 and for microform media versus paper at 1,500 to 1 (Rubin 1983).

To illustrate microform compression, a microfiche the size of an ordinary paperback book can contain the entire contents of the Queens Borough of New York City telephone directory. 3M advertises that 4,000 pages of information can be stored in a 4-by-4-by-1-inch space in a microfilm cartridge.

Also important is the marriage of computer-assisted retrieval techniques to microform technology, making it possible to store and then quickly recover and reproduce information from microfilm files. Systems such as the Eastman Kodak IMT-150 can replace 2,500 filing cabinets in one-eighth the space and retrieve wanted information in eight seconds.

It may be well to look at such solutions when some experts estimate that filing space costs anywhere from $8 to $45 per square foot per month. The compression figures above, however, may pale in comparison to those of the emerging technology of optical information storage and retrieval using lasers to record and read the data. Although optical information storage is commonly thought of in connection with home entertainment devices such as videodisc recorders and players, the technology is rapidly advancing to become a significant force in the storage of business information.

Credit card information provides an example of the power of compression. A magnetic strip on a typical credit card is about 1.5 by 7.5 centimeters and holds about 1,700 bits of information. Material capable of recording information optically can be laminated to the credit card and in the same 1.5 by 7.5 centimeters area 1.2 million bits of information could be held, a ratio of more than 700 to 1 over magnetic media and more than 200,000 to 1 over paper.

Optical media's powers of compression are increasing, and industry estimates place optical information storage costs at perhaps as little as one tenth the cost of storing the same information on typical magnetic media. A 14-inch Kodak optical disk can now store 8.2 billion bytes of digital data, and electrical-mechanical-optical files that can store 500 of these disks for immediate retrieval are available. IBM is marketing a 200-million-byte optical disk drive. Experts in the field estimate that the cost of storing a megabyte on an optical disk may soon be under 5 cents; this would be around half the cost of storing that same megabyte on magnetic tape and much less than the cost would be on an on-line magnetic disk.

Incidentally, several kinds of information can be stored on a video disk—printed matter, motion pictures, or graphics. Phillips has introduced a video disk machine called Megadoc that can store 3,465,000 pages of information in this one office machine.

There are presently available compact laser disks that have a 600-megabyte capacity per 3.25-inch diameter disk and that can be read by using a $1,000 compact disk (CD) reader plus a personal computer. These CDs have a clear plastic coating that makes them less susceptible to dust and grime.

At present, there is one disadvantage: many optical disks in the marketplace are not erasable. The NeXT™ computer system, however, is available with single read/write/erasable disks that store 256 megabytes each.

Maxell is selling 5.25-inch fully erasable, rewritable disks that can store 644 megabytes of data and/or images, a capacity equivalent to 1,700 conventional magnetic disks.

Another developing technology is digital paper, a thin, flexible, read-only film that uses laser beams to etch information into an infrared-sensitive dye on the film. It is estimated that a 2,900-foot reel will store data equivalent to that on 3 million conventional floppy disks or 1 billion sheets of paper. It also should be less expensive than erasable optic storage or microfilm.

Another Side of the Optical Revolution

Optical character recognition (OCR) has been around for some time, but recently the accuracy of OCR machines has improved to the point where there is one error or less per million characters read.

The use of an optical character reader (also OCR) allows the transmission of data from paper into the memory of a computer directly; the keyboard does not have to be used. A recurring *Wall Street Journal* advertisement for an OCR bears the headline, "Teach your computer to read." An OCR now on the market, made by Kurzweil Computer Products, a Xerox Company, optically scans any typeface, then converts the printed matter into spoken English so that the blind can hear what they cannot read. A leading computer scientist predicts that recognition of optically scanned hand-printed information should be possible soon in a range of applications.

There are two principal reasons why OCR use is increasing:

1. An OCR can put as much material into a computer memory in one day as a typical typist could in a week.

This Optical Character Reader transfers information directly into a computer's memory without keyboarding at a rate of one 8½-by-11-inch page every 20 to 25 seconds. (Courtesy of DEST Corporation.)

2. When an OCR is added to a computer system, no new personnel or terminals have to be added; thus more work can be done with the same people and terminals.

These devices have become smaller and less expensive; one desktop OCR now on the market sells for $500 and takes up about the same amount of room as a portable typewriter.

With these advances in mind, a Yankee Group research report foresees the development of "white collar robots" that, for instance, could open, read, enter, and acknowledge incoming orders for any enterprise with no humans entering the process. In a manufacturing business, these orders could be transmitted to numerically controlled machines that would manufacture parts to be assembled, packed, and shipped by robots; in short, this would be a completely automated factory. It may give you a slightly eerie feeling to learn that Fujitsu Fanuc, Japanese world leader in the manufacture of robots, is now using robots to make more robots.

As each one of these technological advances is assimilated into an existing office, changes in office design become necessary to accommodate them. There seems to be no end in sight for these processes of technological change and design change. Progress will continue in both fields.

Off-Site Information Storage

Where office space is tight and expensive, off-site information storage might be considered.

DataSafe, a San Francisco-based information storage firm, is an example of a full-service company in this rapidly growing field. DataSafe estimates that it costs $275 per year to have a typical four-drawer filing cabinet in an office: about $235 for square feet used, at the $35 per square foot current annual average rent for office space in the San Francisco area, and about $40 in depreciation per year on the file cabinet. DataSafe will store the same amount of records for $18 per year, a savings of $257, and 6.7 square feet of office space is freed up for other uses (Reis 1987).

The company has its own specially designed boxes for customers records; they even have a special box for architectural or engineering drawings, as well as any other items that should not be folded or creased. They will pick up records from customers within two hours and emergency service is available 24 hours a day.

Even though the records stored may be seldom used, when retrieval is necessary, DataSafe can deliver all requests made by noon in the afternoon of the same day, thanks to its computerized inventory system. Depending on the way the client sets up the service, the system can even locate records on an individual file or tape basis. It also delivers detailed inventory reports to clients. Most off-site storage customers are firms that use computers and routinely store duplicate or backup data off-site.

Security precautions at DataSafe are extensive, beginning with the use of subscriber code cards: Information can be retrieved only with a valid code card. The building in which vital records of this kind are stored is constructed of double-reinforced 8-inch-thick concrete and carries a four-hour, Class A, National Fire Protection Association rating. A comprehensive fire protection system is used, consisting of ionized smoke detectors, heat sensors, Halon 1301 fire suppressant, and dry-type sprinklers.

A delivery representative pulls a locked magnetic tape container from a mini-freighter. (Courtesy of DataSafe.)

Because a significant portion of the records stored are data-processing magnetic and microform media, special locked steel containers are used and the temperature of the storage space is maintained at a constant 65 degrees with relative humidity at 40 percent. DataSafe's trucks are also tightly environmentally controlled.

Ultrasonic devices are used for intrusion prevention, along with a steel vault door that deadlocks under mechanical or explosive attack. Employees are bonded and only bonded employees are permitted into the space. DataSafe also offers a Valuable Records Insurance policy that provides for the recreation of designated information in the event of loss, theft, or damage to stored records.

A record center attendant restoring a customer's carton to its place on the shelf. (Courtesy of DataSafe.)

The San Francisco area is also the home of Arcus, a firm that operates seven remote storage centers throughout the West.

In New York City, a firm called DataPort is utilizing a million cubic foot abandoned subway tunnel under the World Trade Towers for off-site business record storage. DataPort intends to offer electronic storage as well as business record storage. It is planning an optical fiber network so that clients can transmit what they want to store into DataPort's electronic storage devices.

Another player in this business is The Holding Company in Bryn Mawr, Pennsylvania, with electronic alarm systems featuring thermal, infrared, ultrasonic, audio, and shock sensors, as well as closed circuit television for monitoring its facility.

Even with the advancing technology and the availability of off-site storage, information storage demands constant attention from office managers, interior designers, and facility managers.

Chapter 15

Teleconferencing: Audio, Audiographic, Computer, and Video

Ability to conduct conferences by phone among several people at several locations has been around for some time. Since 1964, when AT&T introduced its Picturephone® system at the New York World's Fair, it has also been technically possible for people to communicate with each other at distant locations with movement shown on a video screen plus sound.

Teleconferencing is widespread, as shown in a reader poll taken by *Frequent Flyer* magazine, published by Official Airline Guides. To the question, "Have you ever participated in a meeting via teleconference?" 39.3 percent of 6,200 returned questionnaires (almost 2 out of 5) said yes (OAG 1982). (Incidentally, when these "frequent flyers" were teleconferencing they were not flying and spending money and time on travel and hotels. For instance, the Naval Underwater Systems Center in Newport, Rhode Island saved $589,314 in travel costs during the first year of videoteleconferencing.)

Several experts say that the necessary equipment for teleconferencing will be standard for all major corporate headquarters and that the equipment will also be found in many major executives' homes.

There are basically four kinds of teleconferencing:

1. Audio only
2. Audiographic
3. Video
4. Computer-to-computer teleconferencing (the environmental design implications for this type are covered in a general way elsewhere in this book).

There are many variations among the first three general categories.

Audio Only

The simplest and least expensive form of teleconferencing uses the telephone where speech-only communication is sufficient for the purpose.

Speaker phones are frequently used where there is more than one participant at a location.

Audiographic

Audiographic teleconferencing adds graphics to voice by the use of facsimile machines, viewgraphs, microfiche, or slide projectors, interactive writing devices and/or captured frame video devices, which transmit one graphics-only frame at a time.

For audio-only and audiographic teleconferences, AT&T Communications has the Alliance^{SM} system, which is able to connect up to 59 locations 24 hours a day, seven days a week using ordinary telephone lines. Alliance can be accessed without operator assistance from any push-button phone with ''asterisk'' and ''pound'' keys, and the originating location can be anywhere in the contiguous 48 states. Persons in the meeting can be called on either type of phone, push-button or rotary, and can be located in any of the 50 states, the U.S. Virgin Islands, Bermuda, Canada, Puerto Rico, or Mexico.

Monsanto uses audiographic teleconferencing in specially equipped rooms to communicate among six widely separated locations. Gulf Oil uses it to connect corporate headquarters in Pittsburgh with facilities in Houston and New Orleans. Gulf has one audiographics-equipped room in Pittsburgh, three in Houston, and one in New Orleans.

AT&T Communications has set up specially equipped access centers in White Plains, New York, Chicago, Dallas, and Los Angeles to handle Alliance teleconferences for either audio-only or audiographic meetings.

AT&T also employs Alliance for teletraining, the use of teleconferencing to connect students and instructors wherever they may be.

A variation of teletraining has been used by Jansen Pharmaceutical, a subsidiary of Johnson & Johnson, to introduce doctors to an advanced product. To reduce the expense of doing so, Jansen set up a special calling number with AT&T so that 20,000 doctors could call it and listen to a 30-minute segment of a seminar at their own convenience from their homes or offices. This procedure was much less expensive than having salesmen make individual calls on each doctor.

Video Teleconferencing

Video teleconferencing adds people to audio and graphics. The people who are involved in the conference can see each other in either less expensive slow-scan or freeze-frame video (where a complete frame is transmitted about every 30 seconds) or in more expensive completely interactive full-motion video.

There are mixed indications about the present success and future of video teleconferencing. On the positive side, Holiday Inns has started a joint venture with Comsat General to offer video teleconferencing by satellite in its 1,500 U.S. facilities. Many corporations are using video teleconferencing, and some are starting their own networks. Atlantic Richfield is planning its own $15 million satellite complex, and Federal Express has awarded a contract for a $16-million private satellite network.

Boeing started using videoconferencing in 1979, and its present facilities include dedicated conference rooms that can hold about 25 participants as well as portable systems usually used for 3 or 4 people. The number of Boeing locations connected is usually 3 to 5 but as many as 14 have been connected for a conference at one time.

The Pentagon has 42 videoconferencing studios in the continental United States. GTE has increased from 6 to 12 installations. Also, Aetna has established 15 video teleconferencing rooms.

An unfavorable indication is the closing of the 11 public teleconferencing facilities that AT&T had opened in cities across the country, even though the company had earlier announced plans for opening 16 of these. These closings occurred despite the fact that AT&T has announced the start of New York-London service (as have several other companies) and the fact that the cost of video teleconferencing has come down from around $2,400 per hour to about $625 per hour. AT&T has shifted the emphasis of its marketing efforts for this service to business people either in offices or at hotels. It is widely believed that video teleconferencing will show substantial growth in both markets.

With the advent of continuing technical advances, the cost of the equipment is coming down, too. For example, the cost of building a conference room for full-motion video has come down from about $700,000 to about $200,000 in the past two years. Still, AT&T has only sold two dozen of these during that period. Only about fifty major American corporations have built a total of about three hundred special-purpose rooms for video teleconferences. AT&T Communications, however, forecasts a sizable increase in the total of these rooms in the future.

The use of slow scan and freeze-frame machines reduces the cost even further; these devices send a picture every 30 seconds and can also send graphics. Portable machines that can be taken to the user's conference room have been introduced, and IBM is experimenting with equipment that will allow the user to dial for video teleconferencing using ordinary telephone lines, which will reduce the transmission cost even further. IBM has at least 30 plants around the world that now have video teleconferencing abilities.

Probably costs will continue to decrease. Dr. Lewis Branscomb of IBM says:

> Communications satellites offer a channel cost that is falling at 40% per year as demand rises. The information inside a computer runs at millions of characters per second, but can be accessed at only a few thousand characters per second over telephone lines. The satellite allows computers to communicate at the same speed at which they operate. Satellites are also making it possible to combine data-processing applications, such as facsimile and video applications, such as teleconferencing. (Branscomb 1982)

The trend toward more video teleconferencing will continue because of four major factors:

Savings

It is cheaper to hold a video teleconference than to spend money for airfares, hotels, entertainment, and valuable executive travel time. (Some experts, however, say that this is a minor factor.) Because of the falling costs of satellite transmissions and continuing technical advances the price of the service will continue to decline. For example, Crocker National Bank in California feels that it will save 20 percent of its travel costs by using video teleconferencing. Another example is a video teleconference with 3,800 participants convened by the Bank Administration Institute to tell bank managers how to set up market-rate bank accounts; a bank industry expert estimates that the conferees saved more than $2 million in expenses, travel, lodging, food, and entertainment.

Productivity

Pressure for more productivity from the use of managerial time is increasing. A Booz, Allen & Hamilton study reported by AT&T Communications found that ''executives, managers and professionals spend about 46% of their time in meetings and that this percentage is on the rise'' (1986). The pressure to cut the time and travel expense involved in face-to-face meetings through teleconferencing will increase. (This same study found that the other 54 percent of these people's time was split as follows: 21 percent for creating and analyzing documents, 8 percent for reading and 25 percent for less productive activities.)

Less Expensive Systems

Widcom has introduced a Personal Videoconferencing Station (PVS) for desk top use at $20,000. The PVS has five parts: two color monitors—one for incoming video, and the other for previewing, a color camera, a copy stand and camera for displaying graphic material, and slides and documents and keyboard for both control and drawing. The PVS can transmit and receive over telephone lines using a special coder/decoder or codec.

Compression Labs in San Jose, California is now selling a portable Mini Conferencing System that can be moved into the office so that executives can confer at their desks with others far away at theirs. One unit provides full motion video, audio, graphics, and system controls. These combined devices can be put into an office or conference room and the equipment can handle from one to four persons at each location, depending on which model is used. No doubt, competitive products from other makers will follow.

Effectiveness

There is some evidence that this medium is more effective than face-to-face meetings. British researchers Birell and White have reported on a study of video teleconferencing and its participants:

> The findings from this project . . . show that video teleconferences are in general more task oriented and are especially useful for the more competitive tasks. . . . We can, however, claim that, rather than always necessarily being a poor substitute, teleconferences do have some clear advantages over face-to-face meetings in terms of the quality of the discussions themselves and not simply in terms of their cost (Birell and White 1982).

Birell and White further comment that video teleconferences are ''shorter and more businesslike'' and that they could find no measurable loss in the communications process.

It should be mentioned, however, that Birell and White, as well as others, warn that certain meetings will not be successful without face-to-face contact and that video teleconferencing is often unsuitable for meetings among strangers or among people of markedly different rank.

For teleconferencing in general, research reported by AT&T Communications indicates that

> teleconferences tend to be shorter and better managed than in-person meetings. Participants tend to be better prepared and have clear objectives set. Discussions between speakers tend to be more focused. Negotiations tend to focus more on issues than on people and more movement toward resolving conflicting opinions is made in a teleconference than in in-person meetings. (AT&T 1986)

These findings are supported by a University of Wisconsin study of 149 North American organizations that were teleconferencing users, 85 percent of which rated the application of the medium as successful or very successful. This study also showed a very substantial and consistent pattern of growth among the subject organizations.

Whatever the future of video teleconferencing may be, an increasing number of firms are using or offering the service, including the following (in addition to those mentioned above): Aetna Life & Casualty, Satellite Business Systems, U.S. Sprint, American Satellite, Hilton Hotels, Marriott Hotels, and the National Broadcasting System (NBC).

Some experts estimate that video, in its various forms, makes up about 20 percent of the total teleconferencing market.

Design Issues

For audio and audio-graphics teleconferencing, sometimes only small modifications need to be made to existing conference areas to make them suitable for these two uses. Microphones should have a muting feature so that side conversations can be held without interfering with the conference itself.

External noise is a problem as are the acoustics of the video teleconference room itself. Any background noise (such as a ringing telephone) from within or without the room will be magnified by the sound system in such a way that speech may be unintelligible. The room must be acoustically insulated. The Sound Transmission Class (STC) of the ceiling should be in the region of 40 to 45, and the walls should have a similar STC. A two-door entrance with an air lock like those used for diving bells may be necessary to shut out background noise. All surfaces that can be should be acoustically treated. Sound baffles may have to be placed in the air-conditioning ducts to soften the noise of the system. Every possible source of unwanted noise should be eliminated, and there should be minimum echo within the room.

The configuration of the room itself is an acoustic factor. Because standard building materials are often used in 4 by 8 foot multiples, rooms tend to have a ratio of length to width to height of 3:3:1. This set of dimensions tends to have negative acoustic qualities, especially in relation to reverberation. A ratio of about 5:3:2 seems to work better.

Nonparallel walls and a few large pieces of upholstered furniture also seem to help.

Printers, clattering typewriters, and copying machines may have to be relocated well away from the video teleconference room, and the room itself may have to be located away from elevators and the street.

Another factor in the location of the room is that it should probably be in a neutral place, neither within the executive suite nor in the midst of general offices, so that every worker and executive will feel comfortable entering it.

Since teleconferencing requires good lighting, light may be high and

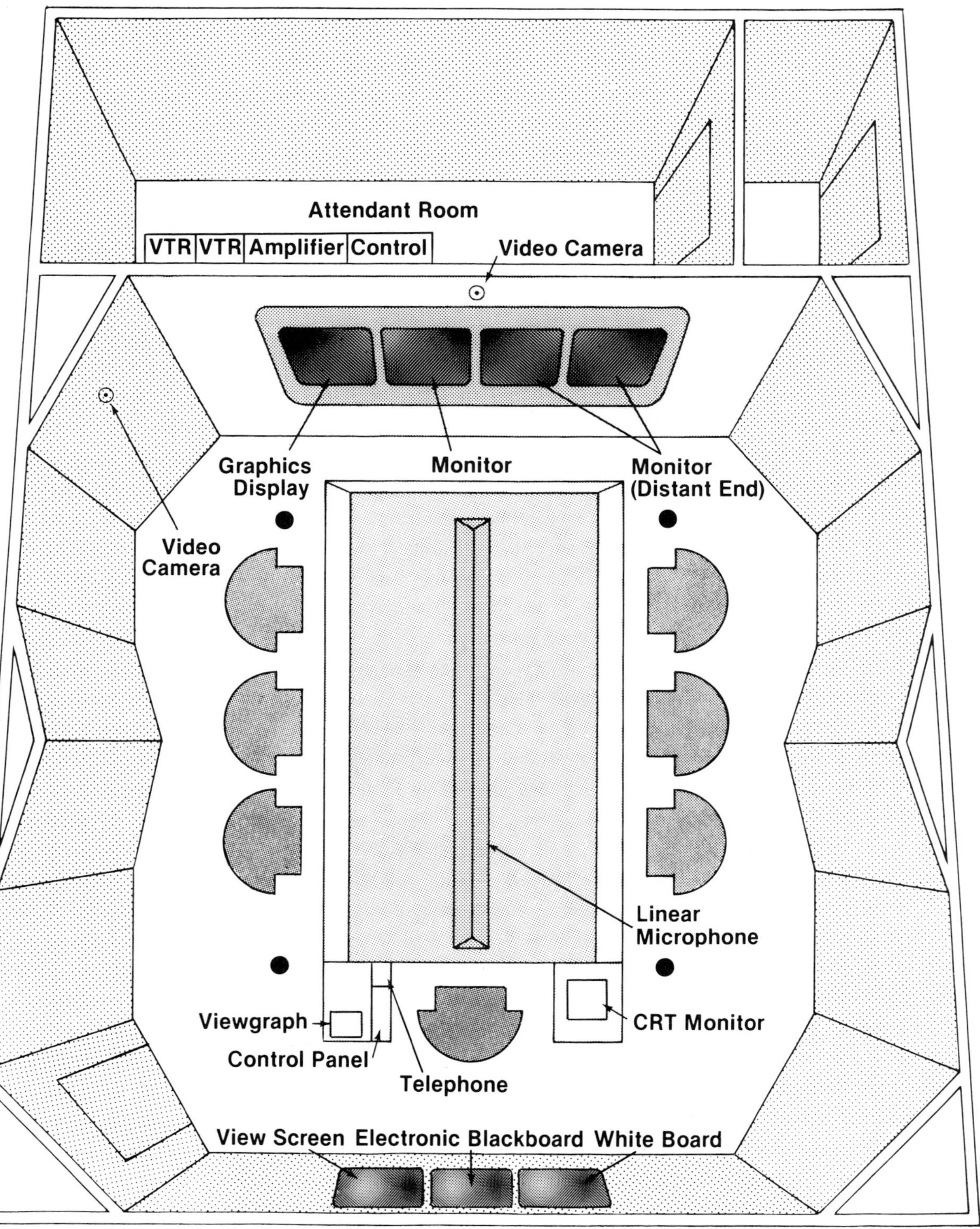

A schematic plan of a video teleconferencing room. (Courtesy of Cross Market Management Company.)

produce quite a bit of heat. Air-conditioning must be adequate to keep the room temperature at desired levels.

Because sharp contrasts of color and texture cause distractions, fairly neutral colors and matte finishes are best. These make it easier to focus on the participants.

In planning electrical capacity for a full-motion, interactive video room, remember that there will probably be five cameras, two to focus on conferees, one for zoom, pan, and tilt shots, one for freeze-frame images picked up from a slide projector, and one mounted on the ceiling to show graphic material placed on the conference table.

Of course, most of the above design suggestions apply to general conference areas as well.

Although the pace of acceptance of full-motion video teleconferencing has been slow, the medium continues to grow in acceptance.

PART IV

Office Interior Furnishings

Chapter 16

Carpets

Carpet is the floor covering of choice in the office. No other material gives the look and feel of luxury with the added benefits of sound absorption and thermal insulation. Although the initial cost is higher than most other flooring materials, when maintenance costs are factored in, carpet's life cycle costs are favorable.

Types of Carpets

There are six methods used for mass-producing carpet:

1. Weaving
2. Tufting
3. Knitting
4. Fusion Bonding
5. Needle Punching
6. Flocking

Woven and knitted carpets are made with the back being created simultaneously with the face in one manufacturing operation. Woven carpets provide better wear, better pattern definition and more dimensional stability than any other type of construction. Woven carpets are especially preferred when large areas of it are installed over pad because of their dimensional stability.

This chapter was contributed by Michele K. Williams.

A patterned cut and uncut loop pile woven carpet, Optimus with a 100 percent DuPont Antron XL face. (Courtesy of Karastan Bigelow.)

Woven wiltons, which have a tough, dense surface, are well known for their long-wearing qualities and are the most expensive type of carpet to manufacture. Velvets are somewhat less expensive to manufacture and wear almost as well as wiltons when woven of the same yarns and in the same density.

While wiltons and velvets are usually limited to five or less colors, another type of woven carpet, axminster, can be woven with an unlimited number of colors in intricate patterns. However, axminsters require very complex looms and undergo a complicated and expensive weaving process; a dwindling amount of carpet is woven with this method.

Very little knitted carpet is made today. Needle-punched or flocked carpet is rarely used in offices.

Tufted carpet with the same pile fiber and weight of pile as a woven carpet is usually less expensive to make; tufting is a quick and fairly inexpensive process when compared to weaving.

The manufacture of tufted carpet starts the way the old candlewick

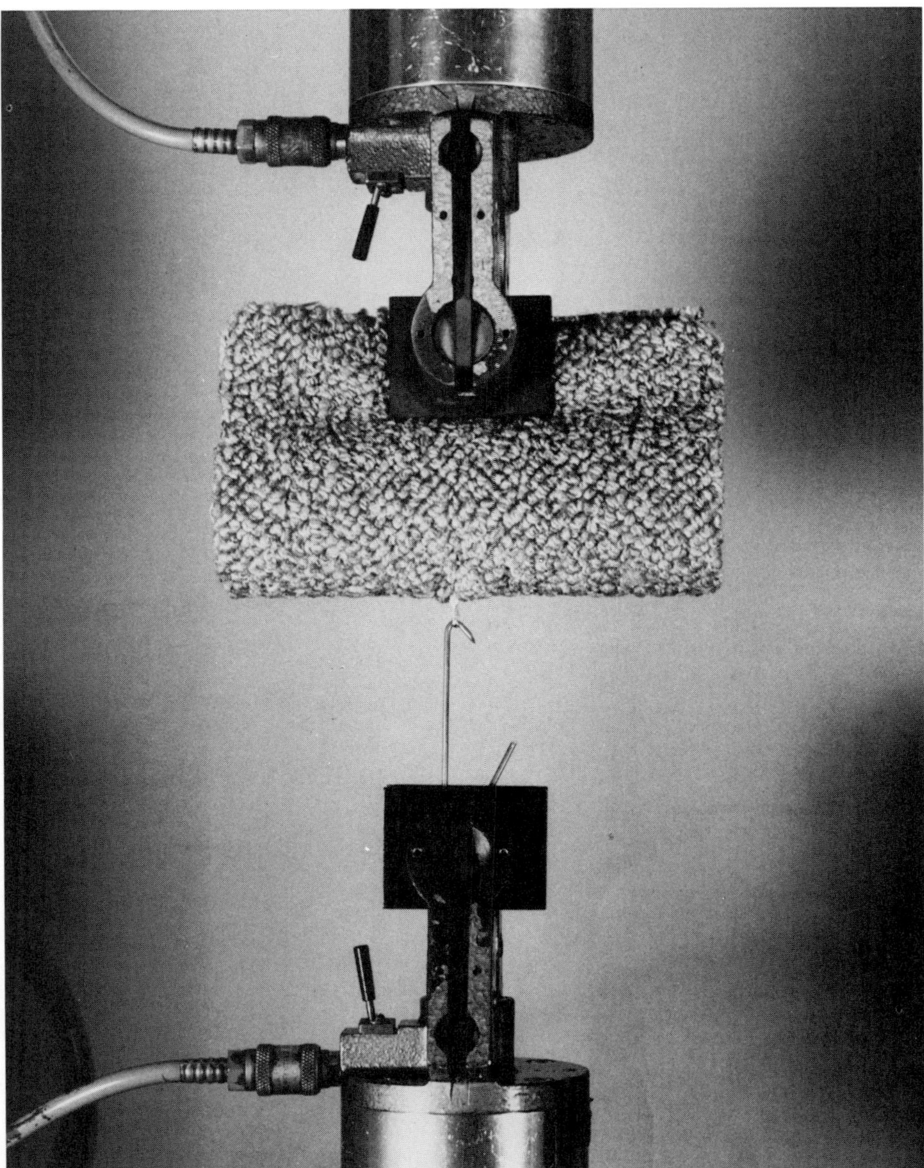

Mechanically testing the tuft bind of a carpet. (Courtesy of Lees Commercial Carpets.)

bedspreads were made, with a piece of cloth called a primary backing through which the face yarns are punched, leaving a loop on the top surface that may be sheared later. After the tufting process is completed, the result is not dimensionally stable. A secondary backing is therefore applied over the whole back to give the product the needed dimensional stability. Jute is still the preferred primary and secondary backing cloth for good quality carpet that is to be used indoors, except where moisture may be a problem. Polypropylene primary and secondary backs are widely used, especially where there are moisture problems.

Fusion-bonded carpet has its pile set in a thermoplastic, usually polyvinyl chloride (PVC). This construction makes tufts harder to pull out and gives greater resistance to edge ravel than other constructions.

Among carpets using the same face fiber, the denser and heavier the pile, generally the longer the carpet will wear. Looped or uncut pile will wear longer than cut pile. Looped pile will also maintain its appearance better than cut pile, which crushes and shows footprints and traffic paths.

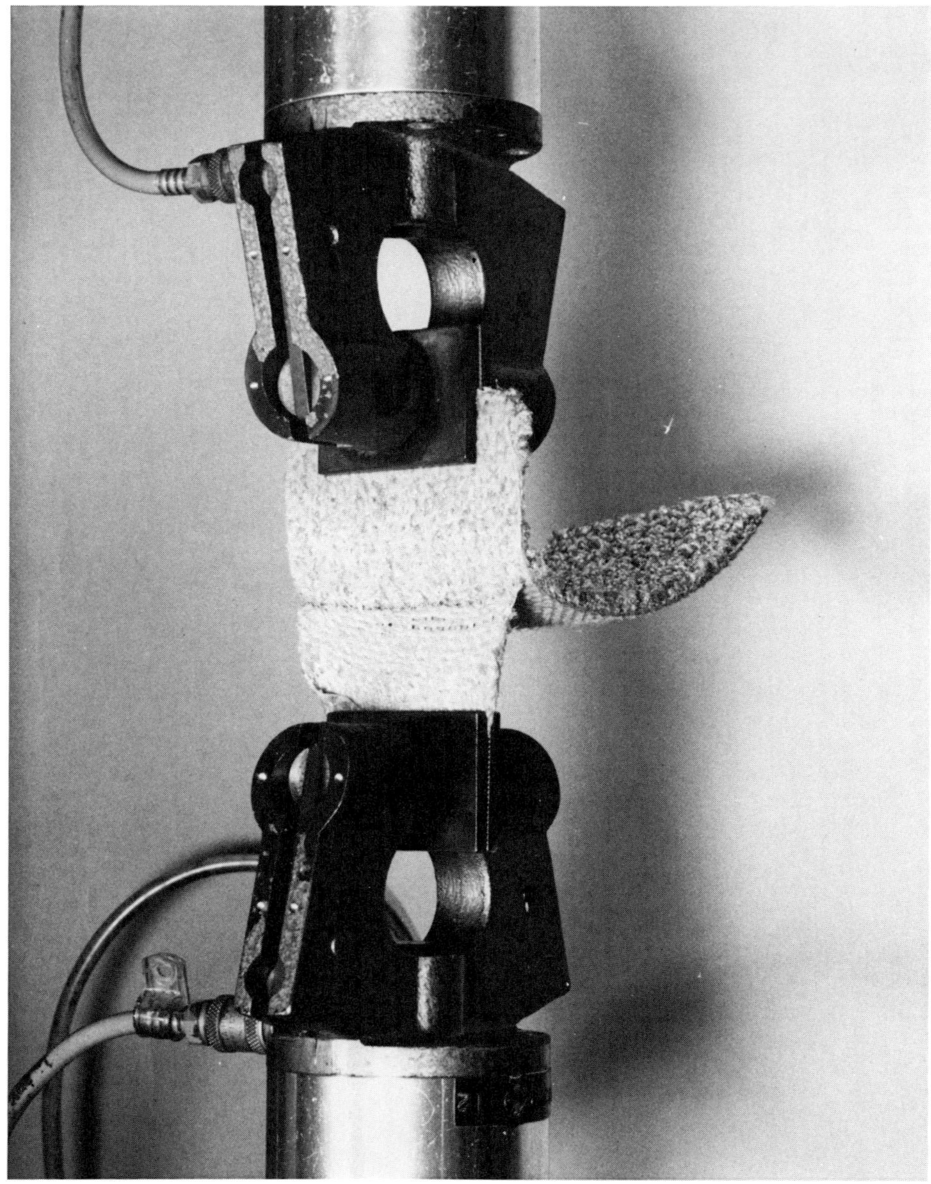

Testing for the secondary back adherence of a tufted carpet. (Courtesy of Lees Commercial Carpets.)

When pile is crushed, it appears that the carpet has changed its color; the apparent change results from looking at the pile from a different angle. Patterns may also be visually distorted by pile crush.

We should point out that it is no longer easy to distinguish woven carpet, for instance, from other carpet types, because the differences among the types are becoming blurred as new proprietary hybrid looms are developed that produce hybrid carpets that are truly none of the above six types.

Finishes and Widths

There are various finishes that can be applied to carpets. Fluorocarbon stain repellers are available, together with several antimicrobial, antifungal, and antiodor finishes. Many of these properties can be introduced into the solution from which fibers are formed—a more permanent method of imparting the desired characteristic to the carpet. Dyes may also be injected into the solution, and this is the most permanent method of dyeing. A variety of other methods are used. To avoid variations in color, the buyer must insist that the carpet for each area being carpeted comes from the same dye lot.

Most carpet is available as broadloom, which is defined as carpet manufactured in widths of 3 feet or more. The most common broadloom width is 12 feet; widths of 3, 6, 9, 15, and 18 feet are available in some lines.

Carpet Tiles

Some carpets are also available as carpet tiles (also called modular carpet or carpet squares), especially fusion-bonded types. If an office is in a state of

Carpet tiles laid to form a contrasting border. (Courtesy of Interface Flooring Systems.)

constant change, one advantage of tile over broadloom is that it can easily be picked up and moved. It can also be rotated or replaced as damage or wear occurs to extend total wear life. If a raised floor and/or flat wire is employed, then carpet tiles should be used. They are required with flat wire by most building codes. Broadlooms do not offer this same freedom and easy access without inconvenience and visible evidence of changes.

An important adjunct for carpet tile is the use of a release glue. Since all carpet tile systems require at least some tiles to be glued down to keep them in place, they should not be glued down permanently. A good pressure sensitive release glue will withstand many removals and replacements.

There are disadvantages to using carpet tiles. They cannot be installed over pad. If incorrectly manufactured or incorrectly installed, they may loosen or creep. A stock of spare tiles must be purchased and stored both to replace soiled tiles temporarily while they are being cleaned and to replace those that just plain wear out. Carpet tiles tend to cost 25 to 40 percent more than broadloom of equivalent quality. If you have an access floor, your choices will be limited to those lines that make the sizes that exactly fit your floor panels.

A low-voltage floor lighting system that is used in combination with carpet tile is Collins & Aikman's Safe-Lite™. The company has developed a low-voltage bulb, protected with a polycarbonate shield, that has a 100,000 hour life and that will withstand as much as 2,000 pounds of pressure per square inch. The bulbs are put in sockets on flat wire in the desired pattern; the tiles are prepunched at the mill to accept the bulbs.

These lights can be controlled by a timer switch, smoke detector, or fire alarm and can blink sequentially or remain constant. Safety uses include leading the way to fire exits with flashing arrows or words; lighting aisles in airplanes, buses, or trains; giving clear directions in smoke-filled corridors when wall- and ceiling-mounted lighting is obscured; and providing night lighting in hospitals and nursing homes.

Broadloom Installation Methods

Most people would choose carpet to be installed over pad because they like the way it feels; the use of pad makes it necessary to use a stretch-in installation method instead of direct glue-down. However, there are other considerations besides aesthetics in selecting an installation method.

In addition to feeling luxurious, carpet stretched in over pad will cover some unevenness in floor levels and is easier to replace than direct glue-down; aligning patterns is also easier. The use of pad increases acoustic absorption, insulative values, and wear life of the carpet.

There are disadvantages, however. In the office the biggest disadvantage of stretched-in carpet is its resistance to wheels on carts and castors on chairs. Rolling traffic can cause sewn or taped seams to pop, backing to delaminate and pad to break down.

Another disadvantage is that stretched-in carpet sometimes loosens and buckles when it is affected by changes in humidity and temperature. To combat this problem, a double glue-down technique is used: the pad is first glued to the floor and then the carpet is glued to the pad. It is claimed that this method also gives superior texture retention and makes carpet replacement easier. Seams in carpet directly glued to the floor are not as vulnerable to seam popping unless poor quality carpet or adhesive is used.

A further benefit is that the carpet goes down faster, thus requiring less labor and expense.

Using this method, however, means that the carpet feels harder and patterns are more difficult to align. Directly glued-down carpet will also wear out faster than carpet laid over pad. The Carpet Cushion Council cites independent tests that show that a properly specified pad will add from 17 to 50 percent to the life of the installation, depending on the type of carpet, the type of pad, and the area covered. Incidentally, not all carpets can be successfully glued directly to the floor. Before using any carpet in this way check with the carpet mill to see if the carpet's construction is suitable for direct glue-down. Some mills weave carpet in a special way for this use and will not guarantee their regular constructions for direct glue-down.

Some manufacturers make carpets with pre-attached foam backing that can be directly glued down, but the authors do not recommend the use of this type of carpet. Like the foam lining of your winter coat, the foam backings sometimes delaminate or break down before the carpet face does. If this happens, it is very difficult to remove the foam remains from the floor. In any case, if this type of carpet is installed, the edges must be glued together very carefully with a special glue formulated for this purpose.

Carpet Fibers

Nylon is still the longest wearing fiber. Fourth generation nylons with conductive fibers added are the unquestioned leaders as choices for carpet in the electronic office. This leadership is constantly being reinforced by technological advances in texturing nylon to look like wool and in dyeing techniques.

Wool is still the choice of many designers, however, because it looks luxurious, is springier under foot, takes dyes better for stronger colors, has superior fire resistance, and wears well, especially if 20 percent nylon is blended with it.

Acrylic fibers can be made to resemble wool in appearance, but wear longer, though not nearly so long as nylon. Acrylics are blended with modacrylics for resistance to fire.

Polyester fibers feel like wool, are less static-prone than other manmade fibers, are susceptible to stains and soils, and have about the same wear life as acrylics.

Polypropylene or olefin fibers have been used primarily for outdoor and kitchen carpets because they wear well and have great stain resistance. This fiber has had problems of a limited color range, poor resiliency, and a low melting point, but research is progressing to solve these problems so that polypropylene may be considered for office carpets; it is less expensive than nylon, and recently has become available with mill-applied soil-repellent treatments.

Static Electricity

A most desirable characteristic of carpet and carpet tile for the electronic office is the ability to handle static electricity successfully. Discharges of static electricity produce pulses that can disrupt the operations of electronic devices, particularly computers. There does not need to be a direct contact with the machine for this to happen; pulses of static electricity can travel through the air.

Disruptions can take the form of anything from false computer commands to the loss of vital information. Electronic machine operations are vulnerable and the electronic records they keep are equally so. Some industry estimates place the cost of static-related incidents at more than $6 billion per year.

The problem increases in scope as small computers become more powerful and more numerous in offices. Formerly most computers were mainframes that were put into special computer rooms where temperature, humidity, and static electricity were carefully controlled. Now that small computers are more powerful and constantly increasing in power, however, the problems caused by static electricity exist in most offices and must be dealt with no matter how few electronic devices are present.

Maintaining proper humidity levels is also important in preventing the buildup of static electric charges. Generally speaking, the higher the humidity in an office the less buildup there will be. The carpet, however, must have enough antistatic characteristics built into it to remain safe through a range of levels of humidity.

Walking and the friction of shoe soles with the carpet are probably the most important static electricity producers in the office. The amount varies with the size of the sole, the type of sole, and the heaviness of the step.

With the introduction of conductive fibers in carpet yarn, it was believed that the problem had been solved. These fibers reduced static electricity to a maximum of around 3.5 kilovolts (kV), worked at all humidity levels, and did not disturb colors or affect soiling. Shoe sole type made no difference in their performance.

A charge of 3.5 kV is below the threshold at which people feel static electric discharges. It was assumed that if people didn't feel them, the problem had been resolved.

Then, as the electronic machines proliferated, it was found that machines are much more sensitive than people where static electricity is concerned and that the consequences of machine disturbance are far more serious than the momentary discomfort people feel.

IBM, Honeywell, and Burroughs, among other manufacturers, have set the maximum safe charge level at 2 kV or lower to protect their machines. There is also a time factor involved; the static electric level must be reduced within 1.4 seconds, since this is normally the amount of time it takes for a person entering a room to reach a machine. If the charge is not reduced to an acceptable level within that short time interval, the machine can receive a shock. There is, moreover, a maintenance requirement; the carpet must continue to keep charges under 2 kV at all times after the initial entry of people into the room.

Conductive fibers in the carpet yarn alone could not enable the carpet to meet the requirements; higher performance was needed to protect the machines properly. To make carpets that will pass the more stringent tests, a new conductive backing material has been added to highly conductive face fibers to form a discharge system that solves the problem well enough that 220 volt electricity can be used.

These antistatic properties must be built into the face fibers and/or integrated into the construction of the carpet or carpet tiles. Although there are antistatic sprays on the market, their use does not usually prove to be nearly as satisfactory as properly specified carpet. They are messy to use, do not last long, and are at best a bandaid treatment. (For a further discussion of static electricity control, see Chapter 18, Chairs.)

Flammability

At this point, flammability standards for carpet are in a state of rapid change. We urge that in comparing carpets you find out from the supplier what tests the carpet has passed, in order to determine how flammable a particular carpet is. The carpet industry and the code authorities are moving away from earlier tests and toward the use of the radiant panel test ASTM E-648 (ASTM stands for the American Society for Testing Materials).

Wool is the most fire retardant fiber, nylon melts instead of burning, and acrylics are least fire retardant; acrylics are blended with modacrylics to increase their fire retardency. In considering flammability, remember that there may be local code requirements. If a pad or cushion is used under broadloom, its flammability rating should be verified. Similarly, if the floor covering is glued directly to the floor, the flammability rating of the adhesive should be checked.

Tests

Tests have been developed by the American Society for Testing Materials (ASTM), Underwriters' Laboratories, and various U.S. government agencies, especially the National Institute of Standards and Technology (formerly the National Bureau of Standards) in the Department of Commerce, to evaluate the ability of carpet to perform under specific conditions. The results of these tests are often listed as part of the specifications for nonresidential carpets.

Carpet is a sound-absorbent material. There is a rating test that measures its acoustical properties (see Chapter 11, Acoustics). Carpet may also be tested for colorfastness to light; thermal properties; tuft bind; and resistance to rolling loads, shrinkage, stains, pilling, abrasion, and matting.

Be sure to determine what tests have been performed for all of the properties discussed above, as well as who performed them. The number of tests done by independent testing laboratories often indicates the manufacturer's commitment to carpet performance.

Chapter 17

Panel Systems

"Shell" versus "Scenery"

To understand the attractions of panel systems in office design it is first necessary to examine the distinction between the building "shell" and the "scenery," as defined by Duffy, Cave, and Worthington in their book, *Planning Office Space* (1976).

Their basic concept is that the "shell" is the building itself, which cannot be easily altered, and that the "scenery," consists of the furniture and other interior furnishings, including panel systems, which are not permanently attached to the "shell." They feel very strongly that these should be considered *separately* in the office design process.

They caution that when "shell" and "scenery" are considered together as a design problem, it is likely that future changes will be more

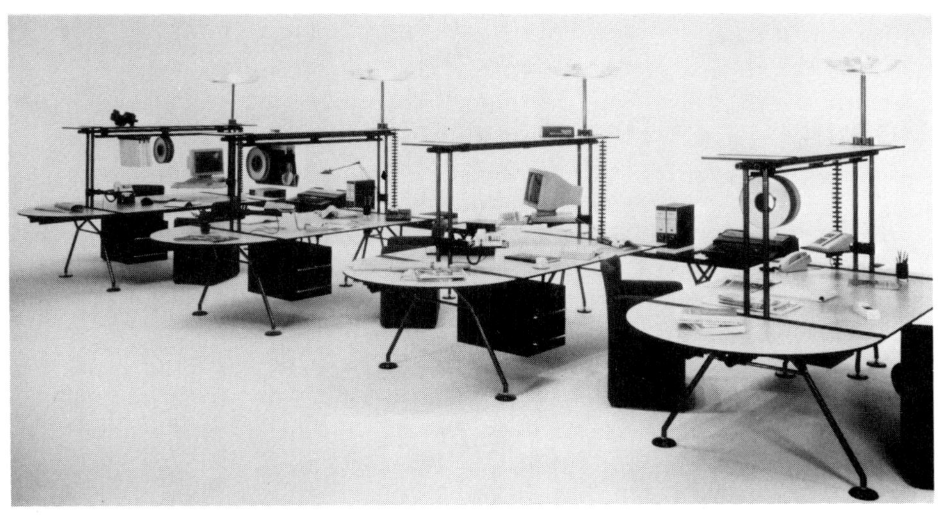

Designed by Foster Associates (architects), the Nomos system is very flexible for office design and has a high-tech look to fit the high-tech devices in the electronic office. (Courtesy of Tecno (UK) LTD.)

A panel system in use on the trading floor of the Vancouver, B. C. Stock Exchange. (Courtesy of Steelcase Inc.)

difficult to accomplish. (For a further explanation, see Chapter 4, Intelligent Office Buildings on Three Continents.)

These authors treat office planning and design as a continuing dynamic process, because the technology used in offices is continually changing and job descriptions are changing as a result. With continuing technological innovation, workplaces and overall office design must have the ability to be changed quickly and easily. Users should be able to make changes and adjustments in the scenery to fit their needs; user adjustments ''create the 'sets' for the office scene.'' There is an element of theater here.

The authors also feel that the uses of a ''shell'' will change over its life-span. The simpler its design and the less it is planned for a specific use or a specific organization, the more flexibly it can be used and the more different kinds of uses it can support. This means that it can not only be changed for diverse uses by the original tenant, but also it can be used by different successive tenants for different purposes.

Popularity of Panel Systems

Both designers and manufacturers have responded to these theories, whether they know of their existence or not, by making panel systems the stars of the American office furniture industry. According to the National Office Products Association (NOPA), manufacturers' shipments of systems furniture, both panel and modular, increased from 18 percent of total office furniture shipments in 1977 to 35 percent in 1982, when they amounted to \$1.4 billion. By 1988 the percentage was 47 percent and the amount was \$2.9 billion, more than double the 1982 dollar total (National Office Products Association 1983).

One big customer for panel systems is AT&T, which estimates that these systems are in use in 80 percent of their roughly 70 million square feet of office space.

NOPA defines two different types of systems furniture:

1. *Modular systems furniture:* Modular furniture made up of independent worksurface and storage units with panels used as end panels or space dividers
2. *Panel systems furniture:* Individually connected panels and worksurface, filing, storage, and shelving components and accessories that receive their support from the panels and that, when combined, form complete workstations.

The term *panel systems* generally includes both types.

Savings in Moving Costs

One leading panel system manufacturer claims that users will save up to 97 percent of moving costs by using a panel system as against stud and drywall construction: 35 cents per square foot as against $15.00 per square foot for tearing down the drywall and rebuilding it in a new configuration. Figures from other sources tend to support this cost estimate. One reason is that if the system is simple enough to take down and re-erect, user maintenance personnel can be trained to move systems in-house; for drywall, carpenters must be used.

These moving savings are important for most offices, since figures from the Business and Institutional Furniture Manufacturers indicate that the

In this Hannah desk system, desks are placed back-to-back, 8 inches apart, and wires and cables are stored in a track in the space between the desks. (Courtesy of Knoll International.)

''annual relocation rate'' or ''churn'' for U.S. workstations is somewhere between 15 and 30 percent. They become very important, especially for those few firms, and there are some, who change individual workstations, either by location or configuration or both, as many as ten times per year. It is much easier to change the configuration of a workstation with a panel system, which is essentially a kit of parts; you pick the parts to fit the job needs.

Space Economy

Another aspect of using systems furniture is saving space. A few years ago General Services Administration (GSA) reports indicated that by using systems furniture and open landscape planning a 10 percent saving in space was realized: workstation size was reduced from 150 to 135 square feet per workstation. One systems manufacturer claims a 20 percent space savings if you use his system. The savings come principally from two sources: (1) Furniture system walls are usually much thinner than stud walls, and (2) panel systems make much greater use of vertical space than do typical desks (see below).

In some offices, space saving has been taken to extremes. Many office workers are being squeezed by panel systems into workstations of less than 40 square feet. Making the workstations too small is a misuse of a valuable design tool.

One recent trend is to use panels for wedge-shaped cluster or pod workstations grouped around a central core that houses the wiring and in some cases, air-conditioning. There can be up to six workstations in a circle facing inward and the size of the individual stations can vary. Advantages claimed include:

- Up to 26 percent savings in space used per workstation and up to 43 percent increase in worksurface area
- The greater visual and acoustic privacy compared to desks in a ''bull pen''
- Adjustable keyboard surfaces, which are available from some manufacturers.

Industry experts estimate that by 1992 cluster workstation volume should top $500 million.

Panel systems are liked for other reasons. They utilize vertical space that goes to waste when only desks are used. The space above the worksurface can become a file bin or can be used for shelving when these items are hung on the panels. This kind of panel use does reduce the amount of floor space required for an office.

While we have mentioned elsewhere that the open plan with a panel system in it does not provide enough privacy for some people, this combination does supply more privacy than bullpen offices do.

The demand for privacy in the office has led to the growing popularity of another type of panel system, full-height movable walls that can be moved and reconfigured just as the other systems can. At least one manufacturer has designed a full-height wall system with special connecting devices that allow its use with its regular lower-height panels.

Tax Savings

One of the most attractive features of panel systems is the tax savings realized by using them instead of permanent attached-to-the building partitions or permanent interior walls. Panel systems—along with carpet tiles, flat wire, power poles, demountable full-wall partitions, furniture integrated task and/or ambient lighting fixtures, access floors, and anything else that

CenterCore's "penta pod," part of the company's circular concept for open plan office systems, is said to save as much as 40 percent of floor space needed for workstations. (Courtesy of CenterCore.)

is not permanently attached to the building—qualify as personal property rather than real estate or real property. There is a great difference in the way these two classifications are treated from a tax and depreciation point of view.

KnollWall is a modular, steel-framed, movable full-height wall system that can be reconfigured when changes are needed. (Courtesy of Knoll International.)

Real property or real estate (and anything permanently attached to it) must be depreciated over as long a period as 50 years at a rate of as little as 2 percent per year; this rule applies to any permanent interior construction. There are some faster ways of depreciating real estate but none are as fast as those that can be used for panel systems. It is also true that many state and local taxes take a lesser bite for personal property than for real estate.

Energy Savings

One further saving is energy costs. One leading panel systems manufacturer claims 50 percent energy savings if their system is used. While it may not be possible to save that much, the use of task/ambient lighting incorporated into the panel system will save 15 percent or more for lighting energy costs over the general lighting systems that most offices use.

The above observations are of course very general. Before you spend money on office design, it is essential to get qualified professional advice on tax matters to find what applies to your specific plans.

Specifying a Panel System

The following procedure was developed in working with a client who needed a panel system and task-management chairs for more than 1,000 office workstations in a new building with open floors. The client is a major aerospace electronics manufacturer. (See also ''Specifying a Task-Management Chair'' in Chapter 18.)

To choose a panel system, it is necessary to go through catalogs and select the leading systems for consideration. It is useful to see presentations of systems that are new or unfamiliar. Using the following design questions, the authors were able to obtain detailed comparative information to assist the client in making a well-informed decision.

1. What choice do we have as far as panel heights and widths are concerned?

The leader in this competition makes panel sizes in 1 inch increments from 30 to 80 inches high and from 12 to 72 inches wide and will make any dimensioned straight panel the client wants within those limits. Most of the systems we examined offered a good variety of panel sizes, but no other was this flexible.

2. Are both acoustical and nonacoustical panels available? What panel finishes are available?

The leader offers acoustical panels with Fiberglas® blankets covered with cloth and nonacoustical panels of cloth-covered honeycomb, Plexiglas® glazed panels, or panels half-glazed and half-fabric finished. Some of the competition have melamine laminate or vinyl surfaces available, but these did not seem particularly attractive in comparison with fabric. The fabric-covered acoustical panels are tackable. The leader also offers ten standard enamel colors for its one-piece steel frames.

3. Do you have curved panels?

The leader makes curved panels with cloth sides, Plexiglas see-through and half-Plexiglas, half-fabric covered panels. We wanted to use curved panels for some workstations to relieve the monotony that rectangular spaces and rectangular workstations create.

4. Is your system free-standing and does it have hang-on components? If so, what hang-on components are available?

It is necessary to determine whether or not the manufacturer offers a sufficient range of worksurface shapes and sizes, types of shelves and cabinets, and kinds of drawers and drawer pedestals. The leader made an excellent showing for these hang-on components with a wide variety of shelves, cabinets, and pedestals. Hang-on components are height-adjustable for every system we looked at, usually in 1-inch increments. This feature is very important in preserving height adjustability so that the surfaces can be adjusted to the differing needs of different sized workers.

5. Are any drawer combinations available as mobile pedestals?

The leader has an excellent variety of drawer combinations that are made as mobile pedestals. The importance of these movable sets of drawers lies in the fact that they make workstation location changes much easier; often, when inside office moves occur, the mobile pedestals can be rolled to the new location without emptying those drawers and filling others.

6. How are the panels connected? Is any angle possible? Is the system easy to set up and take down? Can it easily be reconfigured and reused?

This set of questions covers some of the key features of any system. The connection hardware should be simple so that the client's maintenance personnel can deal with it easily. It should therefore not consist of too many parts but permit a variety of angles so that different kinds of space configurations are possible.

The ease of setting up, taking down, reconfiguring, and reusing is one of the major reasons why clients buy panel systems. As mentioned above, it is much quicker and cheaper to redo workstations using a panel system.

We found one major system, however, that essentially could be used only *once.* We watched a very experienced installation team take components down and put them back in use again in a differently shaped series of workstations. The problem was that there was no apparent way to get this system's panels into a straight line again, even though the team drilled plenty of new holes.

The leader scored well on this set of features. Only one tool—an Allen wrench—is necessary for set-up and take-down. The manufacturer's hardware is quite simple and easy to work with and a good variety of connecting angles is possible.

Mobile pedestals permit workers to change workstations without emptying and refilling file drawers. (Courtesy of Steelcase Inc.)

The simplicity of the leader's set-up procedure paid off when we timed how long it took each system to be set up. The time necessary to set up the leader's was less than any other system tested and it was less than half the time necessary to set up the nearest competitor.

7. What is the system's wiring capacity for electrical power, data, and telephone cables? What kind of electrical system do you have available?

As it turned out, we asked the first question in the wrong words, but we learned fast: it should have been *How many raceways can you put into a panel and how big are they?* Most of the factory representatives that we talked to had to call the factory (and some of the factory people were not sure) when we asked this question. Getting this piece of needed information was like pulling wisdom teeth.

Another thing we didn't know about when we started this exercise was that at least two major electronic companies now have a rule that cables carrying data must be separated from electrical and telephone cables by a distance of at least 1 meter (39.37 inches) to prevent electrical interference (''crosstalk'') with the data cables; this interference can cause corruption of data and therefore computer errors. In this case there is definite need for two raceways, one at the base of the panel and one at about worksurface height, since this particular client is a heavy computer user. The leader could not only put two raceways into each panel, but could also put them at the exact heights wanted at no extra charge.

(After this study was completed, optical fiber wiring was introduced that can be bent around a 3-inch radius, and optical flat wire for use under carpet tiles was also announced. Since optical fiber wire is immune to electromagnetic interference, it can be used for data transmissions and does not have to be separated from power wiring as noted above. It may alleviate the need for a second raceway in some situations.

After the study was completed at least two major panel system makers introduced an additional raceway located on the top of the panel.

The question of wiring capacity in the raceways is becoming more important by the minute. Six months ago the informal standard for a computer terminal user's workstation was six wiring outlets. Recently, however, one of the major U.S. regional telephone companies set a standard of ten outlets for each computer terminal workstation.

The leader's raceway capacity allowed for sixteen 25-pair cables per raceway with the electrical system already in place in the raceway. There can be another one in each panel, doubling the wiring capacity of the panel.

Telephone data and power cables in a raceway panel system. (Courtesy of Knoll International.)

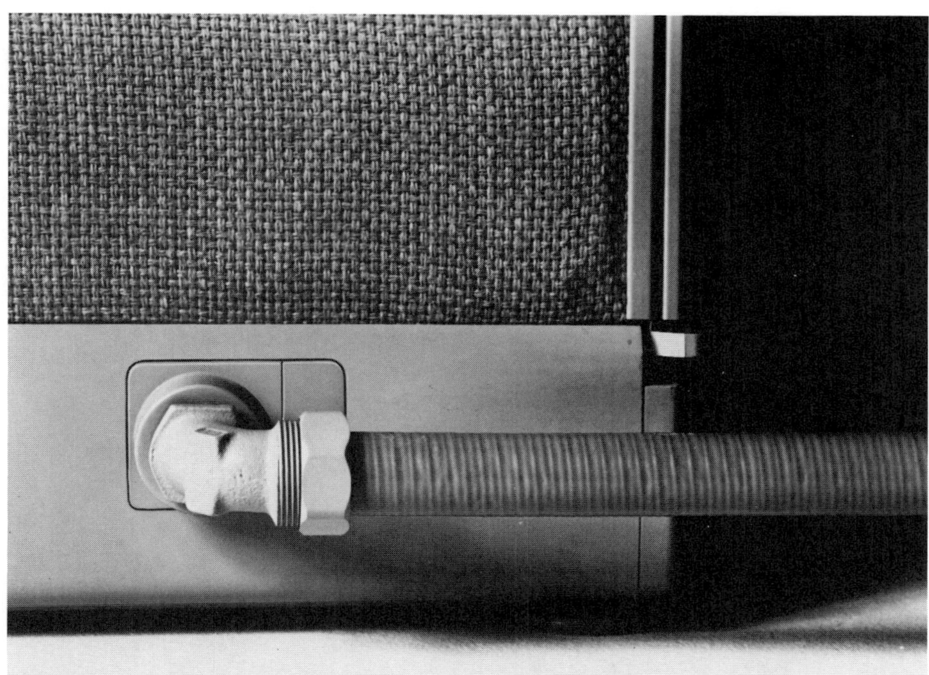

Power feed to a panel from the building's permanent wiring. (Courtesy of Haworth, Inc.)

8. How is the wiring brought to the panel?

The leader offered a power pole that can handle thirty-two 25-pair cables plus six 20-ampere electrical circuits, which, incidentally, matched the most amperes offered by any system we examined. The pole allows wiring to be brought to the panel systems from the ceiling.

The leader's electrical system was also the best at the time: a 3-circuit system, each circuit with 20-ampere capacity. One of those circuits was separately grounded to furnish "clean power" for computer use. The system allowed four electrical outlets to be installed on each panel from each raceway for a total of eight outlets per panel. Importantly, the system could be connected or reconnected with a safety, hand-latched connector that does not require the services of a licensed electrician.

One feature the leader's electrical system did not have was a provision for 220-volt power from the raceway. This feature is becoming a needed option in the United States because of the increasing numbers of printers and copying machines that use this kind of power; in Britain, this would not be a problem. The 220-volt option is now being offered by three of the seventeen systems examined.

(After this study was completed, the available options in panel electrical systems increased. One manufacturer now offers an eight-wire electrical system with multiple dedicated and isolated circuits with a 220-volt option; other makers provide seven-wire systems.)

9. Are hang-on paper management shelves available in your system?

These shelves, which are usually hung diagonally on the panel, act as visible paper files for current work. They are hung above the worksurface. The leader has a good paper management system.

10. Are lighting fixtures available as a part of the panel system?

This question was asked primarily to determine the state-of-the-art in panel systems lighting, both task lighting to focus on the work and ambient lighting for general light. The client purchased light fixtures directly from fixture manufacturers separately from the panel system. The leader does offer undershelf task lighting.

11. How thick is the panel? Does "panel creep" occur?

If a panel system is connected by a separate connector or pole, the thickness of that connector has to be added at the end of every panel in a run. This "panel

Paper handling devices on a panel. (Courtesy of Knoll International.)

creep'' results in a significant loss of precious square footage in a large office. While the leader's connecting system did not produce this problem, one system had panels 4³/₈ inches thick, the use of which, with its connectors, would have resulted in a space loss of more than 6½ inches per workstation in a row of them.

12. Is the panel fire-rated? Is the electrical system U.L. listed?
Almost all of the systems, including that of the leader, had a Class A fire rating and were U.L. listed.

13. What are the price and discount?
There were quite a few variations.

14. How fast can you deliver?
Again, lots of variations.

15. Will you train my client's maintenance crews to reconfigure the system?
Every manufacturer said it would.

16. Will you charge my client for that training?

Remarkably, one manufacturer's representative said the client would be charged—on an order projected to be for more than $1,500,000!

17. One question should have been asked: How strong is your panel?

One promising system was thrown out because its panels were too thin and that people just leaning against them were punching holes in the panels. Another was eliminated because it used a 1¼-inch lauan wood panel frame that we thought much too weak for a supposedly sturdy panel system. We also found systems with no divider or septum between the layers of Fiberglas® usually used as sound absorbent material on both surfaces of the panel. These septums, which can be metal, hardboard, fiberboard, or plywood, add greatly to the strength and stability of the panel.

The leader's system had one unique feature. To replace worn or torn panel cloth surfaces, the manufacturer sends a precisely sized piece of cloth for the panel. With a very simple and inexpensive tool, anybody, no matter how unskilled, can pressure fit the new piece over the old piece in minutes.

New Developments

A recent trend in office panel systems is to introduce interesting design details. Haworth has added what it calls Architectural Elements® to its Unigroup™. It has geometric glazed panels, some in combination with fabric,

In some panel systems, covers can be easily removed for cleaning, repairs, or color change. (Courtesy of The Harter Group.)

Architectural Elements™ from Haworth, Inc. permit the creation of interior architecture within the office. (Courtesy of Haworth, Inc.)

fanlights, and single and French doors. There are also slanted-top and gabled panels as well as several types and patterns for the window-pane portions of these components.

More recently, Haworth introduced a supplemental system called Places® containing 15 more gabled panels and 12 oblique panels with a variety of muntin options.

The Ethospace® panel system features walls of varying heights coordinated with full-height, floor-to-ceiling movable wall panels that can be customized. (Courtesy of Herman Miller.)

While they do not improve function, these additions do increase visual interest and give office designers more ways to individualize workstations.

Another contributor to this trend is Alma, with its ultimate anachronism, the Devonshire eighteenth-century-styled office panel system. Herman Miller, with Ethospace™, Knoll with Morrision, Modern Mode with Stratus, and both Teknion and Scandiline as well as JG have systems that show horizontal lines as the panels build up from the floor, allowing designers to vary color and texture on these smaller individual panels.

Haworth and Harter have both developed an office panel that becomes clear or cloudy at the touch of a button. Haworth describes the active portion as

> a light control film, a flexible plastic with a coating that scatters light, creating a frosted or translucent look. When low voltage electricity is applied to the film, the molecules in the coating instantly align, allowing light to pass through without obstruction, turning the window transparent.

Transpaque panels, an experimental product from Haworth, Inc., incorporate a plastic film sandwiched between glass. Push a button and the panel becomes transparent; push it again and the wall returns to translucency. (Courtesy of Haworth, Inc.)

The film is sandwiched between glass panels in a frame and all electrical connections are hidden in the standard raceway. Haworth calls it Transpaque™ and Harter named theirs F r o s t lucent™.

This system gives the office occupant the option of visual privacy at an instant's notice for such occasions as an employee review, a strategy session, or any sensitive meeting. The translucent condition also signals that the space is in use. This product can provide an island of visual privacy in an open plan office.

Software Innovations

Because panel systems have hundreds of parts and thousands of finish combinations and because facility managers need to keep track of what elements are in use and in stock, panel systems manufacturers such as Haworth and Herman Miller have developed computer programs for this purpose, as part of a strong industry trend in this direction. The use of bar codes to identify pieces of furniture and system parts is also beginning.

Steelcase has introduced what is believed to the most comprehensive set of programs for use with its Context™ system. To help designers working with Context, an information program contains a statement of the line that includes product descriptions, application tips, finish options, a reference index, and keys to planning with Context.

A second program automates specification, while preventing inadvertent specifying of configurations that will not work. Workstations can be stretched or compressed to fit specific spaces and visualized as three-dimensional isometrics. In addition, this program allows designers to rotate product groupings, experiment with positive or negative space, and place other elements such as seating and filing where they are needed.

According to Steelcase, these software packages will reduce error rates, reduce the amount of design time spent on repetitive specifications, and increase order accuracy.

For productivity increases due to the introduction of panel systems, see Chapter 23.

Context™ is a freestanding system that can be configured to support highly interactive, collaborative work processes. (Courtesy of Steelcase Inc.)

Chapter 18

Chairs

The Largest Survey on Seating Comfort

In the largest known survey of seating comfort, author Kleeman and Thomas Prunier of the National Furniture Center, Federal Supply Service, General Services Administration, analyzed material from 1,967 questionnaires with 90 pieces of information on each one. The information came from 1,967 air traffic controllers working for the Federal Aviation Administration (FAA).

The chairs the controllers used at that time had several adjustabilities in the following modes: The seat height could possibly be adjusted with

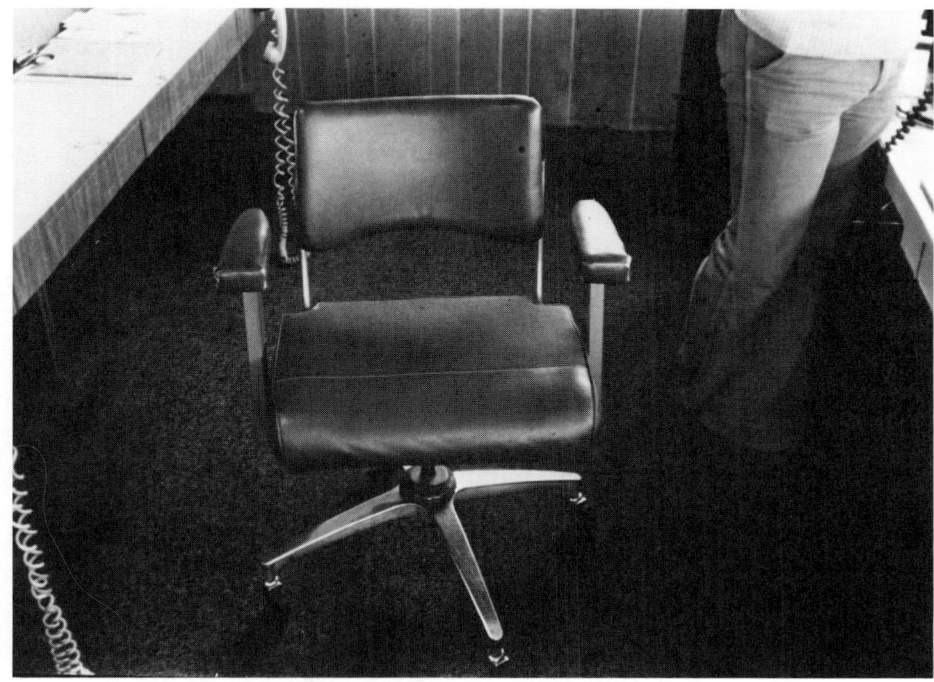

The hard-to-adjust FAA air traffic controller's chair.

bare hands, but might also need a wrench. Backrest height was adjusted the same way as seat height with a different wrench. Seat depth needed still another type of wrench. Armrest depth and armrest width needed a wrench so that the seat could be removed, then a wrench to adjust, and then a wrench to reinstall the seat. Only two positions were possible for each of these adjustments. Backrest tension was adjusted—after removing the seat—with a special key that came with the chair. The back rest pivot adjusted automatically. In total, these adjustments required three types of wrenches and most of them could not be done while sitting in the chair. Difficult! Contrast this with chairs that have gas cylinder adjustments that can be operated while sitting in a chair.

Remember that these chairs are task intensive: they are heavily used on three eight-hour shifts seven days per week. An FAA spokesman said,

> On a given shift change at our Center, sometimes it looks like a game of musical chairs—the controllers exchange chairs until they get one they can use, rather than go through the laborious task of adjusting. The current chairs in use are not very easily adjusted.

The major findings were summarized as follows:

1. When chairs are hard to adjust, users do not adjust them. Only one out of eight controllers adjusted their hard-to-adjust chairs at any time during their shifts. Easier adjustments were recommended, specifically gas cylinders.

Reinforcing this finding is a study by Tom Stewart (1980), analyzing 17 different workplaces with computer terminals. He found that 27 percent of them had no chair adjustability and that 95 percent of them had poor chair adjustability. Stewart said,

> The majority of the chairs had some adjustability but it was usually difficult to use. Typically it involved getting off the chair and exerting considerable force on a knurled knob. As a consequence, these chairs were seldom adjusted. Only one type of workplace had gas-lift chair actions and these were fully exploited by the users. (1980)

He also found that 94 percent of the workplaces he examined had no adjustability in other workstation furniture, particularly the worksurface heights and inclinations of desks and tables (Stewart 1980).

2. It is absolutely necessary that users be told and shown how to adjust their chairs. More than half the controllers did not use their back height adjustments because they did not know that their chairs had one.

3. The controllers preferred a chair with upholstered arms and a back; a stool would not meet their needs.

4. Woven fabric (not vinyl) was overwhelmingly preferred as the upholstery material. (Just as it is preferred by many computer terminal operators.)

5. The controllers prefer that the back should tilt and that it should reach shoulder height.

6. A chair's fit/comfort is of first importance to the controllers. Here is the complete ranking from the study:

Rank	Attribute	Percentage Agreeing with This Ranking or Higher
1	Fit/comfort	75.2
2	Safety	57.3
3	Adjustability	59.1
4	Durability (mechanical)	65.3
5	Durability (of upholstery)	67.7
6	Repairability	61.9
6	Appearance	51.9
6	Interface with other equipment	51.6

An FAA spokesman said, ''We would rank fit/comfort and adjustability as one and the same, or at least equally important. With the number of different-sized people who use these chairs during a 24-hour day, we do not believe that the desired degree of fit/comfort can be obtained without satisfactory adjustability.''

7. A not unexpected finding of this study was that as time spent sitting increased, people were less and less comfortable. A few of the controllers spent almost all of their working time on an eight-hour shift sitting. This heavy use, which is similar to work at a computer terminal in the office, reinforced our belief that the findings from this study would be useful in selecting chairs for the electronic office.

8. Some controllers are concerned about the stability of their chairs. We suggested that FAA consider a five-prong base instead of the four-prong one they were using so that the controllers would perceive their chairs as more stable.

9. Seat height adjustment was ranked first among wanted adjustment features. Here is the complete ranking of adjustments:

Rank	Adjustment	Percentage Agreeing with This Ranking or Higher
1	Seat height	73.3
2	Back height	59
3	Back tilt	64.4
4	Seat depth	63.8
4	Seat pitch	57.7
4	Arm height	57.9
4	Seat width	50
5	Back width	56.7
5	Back lateral	51
6	Arm length	63.6

10. You may remember that we felt that a seat height adjustment range of 12.5 to 19.5 inches was needed. The chair the controllers were using had a seat height adjustment range of 17 to 21 inches, which meant that the range from 12.5 to 17 inches was missing.

(On the basis of information supplied to us by the U.S. Air Force Aerospace Medical Research Laboratories' Anthropometric Data Bank, we learned that we could expect popliteal heights—the distance from the bottom of the forward thigh to the bottom of the heel—of from 13.3 inches to 20.2 inches.

Their figures calculated expected popliteal heights based on reported statures since the questionnaires had not reported popliteal heights. This makes what follows somewhat speculative.

Then again, it may not be so speculative. A study by Irwin Miller and Thomas W. Suther III of IBM showed a 90.8 percent correlation between stature and preferred seat heights in a research project involving 37 VDT operators. The operators were divided into two groups, a U.S. sample of 27 Caucasians and 2 Blacks, and an Oriental sample consisting of 3 persons of Japanese ethnic origin and 5 persons of Chinese ethnic origin. Ten of these operators were approximately in the group of lowest statures in both U.S. and Japanese populations; 11 were of about average stature; and 16 were of the tallest statures in both populations.

A finding in Miller and Suther's study supports our recommendation for a chair with seat height adjustable from 12.5 inches to 19.5 inches. They found that their subjects preferred seat heights of from 12.6 inches to 19.3 inches. This was the only known reported study that gave the subjects the choice of that low a seat height adjustment.

A bit of mathematical analysis revealed that air traffic controllers who had popliteal heights of 17.4 inches or more would be comfortable and people with popliteal heights of less than that would be uncomfortable. The resultant calculations predicted that 943 people would be comfortable and that 1,024 would be uncomfortable.

Actual survey results showed that 987 people, 50.2 percent of the sample said that they were uncomfortable or worse and 980, 49.8 percent said that they were comfortable or better. These figures are not conclusive but not far from the prediction.

Next, an analysis of comfort among the shorter people in the sample was performed. The greatest percentage of discomfort was found among those from 5 feet to 5 feet 2 inches tall: 77.8 percent of this shortest group were uncomfortable in varying degrees, and 73.7 percent of them found their chairs unsatisfactory. It was surmised that because these shorter people had shorter popliteal heights they were uncomfortable in chairs that would not adjust below 17 inches in seat height.

At that time 4.6 percent of the controllers were women and many of them were in this shortest group. Just as more women are appearing in offices everywhere, the number of women air traffic controllers is increasing.

11. Field investigations were conducted primarily because 21 percent said that their chairs interfered with other equipment. We went to towers, air traffic control centers, and flight service centers at John F. Kennedy Airport in Jamaica, New York; Bradley at Hartford-Springfield, Connecticut; the Nashville Metropolitan; the Washington, D.C. National; Causey at Bowling Green, Kentucky; and Kloten at Zurich, Switzerland.

12. Chairs bumping into radar consoles are a prime cause of damage to the chair arm fronts. Not much could be done to correct this because the heights of the consoles are not uniform. We have recommended adjustable-height radar consoles and adjustable-height chair arms to the FAA when they get their new computers and consoles. Similar problems exist in other types of offices.

The visit to Kloten in Zurich was very educational. Even a dozen years ago every chair in the tower was gas-cylinder adjusted. Their chairs had one-piece shells for the seat and back and the cushions (essentially one piece, with no zippers) were attached to the shell with Velcro®, making replacement and cleaning quick and easy.

Swiss towers are in operation 24 hours a day and their chairs get heavy use. Although they have some mechanical failures, they send their chairs back to the factory every two years to be completely remanufactured—not expecting chairs to last forever as we seem to do.

Specifying a Task-Management Chair

A task-management chair is defined as a chair used by either an operator or a supervisor in the office; it has arms. To choose chairs for a client who was looking into panel systems (see Chapter 17), the design firm looked at the largest survey on seating comfort, went through catalogs, and picked out chairs that seemed to meet the client's requirements. Those model numbers were given to factory representatives, together with the approximate size of the possible order. (Four of them sent the wrong chairs, which did not have one or more of the features we asked for.) These requirements were as follows.

1. Speedy delivery. The best bid promised 250 chairs every 10 days.
2. Warranty. The designers asked for the longest and most complete manufacturer's warranty obtainable. The winner gave a five-year warranty on all parts of the chair. (One of the losers made it much too complicated by splitting up the warranty; lifetime on the irons, 3 years on the gas cylinder and the fabric, 10 years on the casters and 5 years on the shell.)
3. A price limit. Eighteen of the 19 competitors came in under it.
4. Delivery set-up in cartons. Three companies could not meet that requirement.
5. The lowest possible starting seat height in order to seat short people comfortably. Although one chair went down as far as 15 inches in seat height, it did not win in the comfort tests. The winning chair adjusted from 16 to 22 inches. It is important to measure the compressed seat heights, since manufacturers evidently do not do this in any standard manner, or maybe they just estimate. (The bad-measurement prize went to a chair that arrived too late for the competition: This manufacturer's literature states that seat height on this chair adjusts from 18 inches to 22 inches; the actual seat height range turned out to be from 14 to 18 inches.) The highest range started at 18 inches and went to 22 inches; the lowest range among the 19 was from 15 inches to 19 inches.
6. Gas-cylinder-activated action on all adjustments so that the chair can be adjusted while the user is sitting in it. Although there have been service problems with some gas cylinder adjustments, warranties would be compared to weed out the weak ones. Gas cylinder adjustments were required because studies both here and in Europe show that chairs that are hard to adjust do not get adjusted and if chairs do not get adjusted, workers are uncomfortable, less productive, and more prone to aches and pains. As mentioned above, one European study of 17 offices found that only one had chairs adjustable using gas cylinders. That was the only one of 17 offices where chairs got adjusted. The winner guaranteed their gas cylinders for 5 years and to top that, their cylinders can be changed in 15 minutes or less.

One veteran office productivity researcher felt that 40 percent of the substantial productivity gains he found with adjustable workstations can be attributed to the adjustable chair with gas cylinder controls he used and 60 percent to the adjustable worksurfaces.

7. A back height of at least 20 inches to accommodate the relaxed, laid-back postures now being assumed, especially for those office workers who use a computer terminal. A height of 17½ inches, was the best that could be obtained; it should work fairly well.

8. Easily removable chair arms, so that if a worker wanted to take them off, it could be done quickly. The winner did not have that feature.

9. A seat that could tilt forward and backward. The degree of tilt was to be specified. A feature variously named Biotilt®, Free Flow® or Syncrotilt® was specified. This refers to the ability of the chair back and the chair seat to move independently and yet in a coordinated way to accommodate body postures from a right angle (90 degrees) of the trunk and thighs to an angle of as much as 135 degrees. Several chairs had this feature, including the winner.

10. Antistatic properties. Manufacturers were asked about this feature but it was not made a requirement. This feature is sometimes also referred to as ESD, electro-static discharge. The reason for this question is that the standards for the control of static electricity in the office are more stringent now than they used to be. As mentioned above, the old standard for carpet was a maximum 3.5 kilovolt charge; now the standard is down to 2 kilovolts. While the old standard was based on shocks to people, the new standard reflects the hazards of shocks to computers.

Some computer manufacturers have found that electrostatic charges were being passed directly from chairs to the machines and are therefore putting the antistatic chair requirement into their user manuals as a necessity for smooth computer operation.

One manufacturer (Comforto, a Haworth Company.) described the features of its anti-static chair:

The Motion chair, designed by Burkhard Vogtherr, to move with the user's body. It has just three adjustments: seat height, tension, and locking position. (Courtesy of Davis Furniture Industries, Inc.)

> To produce an anti-static chair a dissipative cover is needed. This type of fabric has a metallic yarn woven into it which dissipates static electricity.
>
> However, any static which does build up needs to be discharged further, i.e., ultimately into an anti-static carpet. We accomplish this through the following process: A copper wire is connected to the back dissipative cover running the current from the fabric to the steel posture control and the back height adjustment. The current travels down the posture control in the back to the seat where a copper wire connects the seat cover to the posture control. The current then travels down the steel gas lift to the steel base and exits through the anti-static caster into the anti-static carpet. (Welsch 1988)

A conductive vinyl upholstery called NaugaStat U® which also must be grounded, is available from Uniroyal.

The office has to have antistatic carpet or another antistatic floor finish for the antistatic chair to work, but that requirement is becoming standard for offices where there are computers and other electronic devices. If a chair mat is used, it must be able to conduct static electricity from the chair to the finished floor.

While this ESD capability was not a requirement for this competition, we feel that it will soon be a requirement, with the leadership in this area exhibited by IBM and Burroughs to keep their computers free of electrostatic discharges.

11. Information on standards and testing. Only three of the nineteen manufacturers said that their chairs passed the American National Standards Institute/Business and Institutional Furniture Manufacturers Association (ANSI/BIFMA) Standard X5.1-1985 for General Office Chairs (see Chapter 19). This standard is important and has begun to appear as a sales argument.

Two chairs were eliminated from the competition because they collapsed, one before the comfort testing, the other during the comfort testing. Neither maker of the collapsed chairs had said that their chairs met the ANSI/BIFMA Standard. It seems clear that not enough companies are using this standard or properly testing their chairs.

12. A 100 percent nylon fabric treated with a stain repeller. Only one manufacturer could not furnish this fabric. The reason for asking for it was twofold: Nylon is the longest wearing fiber and it does not promote pooling of perspiration in the buttocks region as most vinyls do. Du Pont now has a new, longer-wearing nylon called Cordura.

The authors believe that comfort is the most important benefit that the worker can get from an office chair and that comfort means more productivity as well as less physical aches and pains because these workers spend most of their working day seated.

Although there is no universally accepted way to measure seating comfort, it is possible to test simply by having workers sit in chairs.

Workers with an appropriate range of body types should be chosen. Since more than 1,000 chairs would be bought for more than 1,000 workers, body size variations would be large. Testers of both sexes with wide differences in weight, height, and age were included. Body weights ranged from 103 pounds to 250 pounds, heights from 4 feet 11 inches to 6 feet 3½ inches. Ages were from 19 to 63 years.

Because of time considerations, the test was carried out by only 15 people who tried out each of the 19 chairs, a total of 285 tests, each lasting from one to two hours with each tester doing his normal work. The chairs were identified with a tag giving a letter of the alphabet; all other tags were removed so that the testers did not know who made the chair they tested.

None of the 19 chairs tested met all of the requirements, although several of them had enough of the features to be seriously considered.

The winner was finally chosen on the basis of the comfort testing. When the results of the tests were carefully examined, it was found that the winner had most of the features asked for: the comfort tests showed that these features are essential for office chair comfort. One particular feature—arms—showed up in the tests as absolutely essential for comfort. Some manufacturers lost in the competition because, although specifically asked for chairs with arms, they shipped their chairs without them.

Chairs of the Future

Although cloth with metallic fibers is now used for the ESD chair, it may be possible that further development of the conductive fibers now used in carpet could make these fibers available for use in conductive upholstery fabrics. In any case the selection of all chair materials, not just the cover, will depend on the electrostatic properties of each material. In addition, each material will have to be pretested for these properties by itself and in combination with all the other materials to be used in an office chair.

The variety of options available on office chairs will also increase. Heat and vibration, for instance, will probably be offered, as they are now in some domestic recliners. Cooling may be available for work in very hot environments, or it is possible that air from the heating, ventilating, and air-conditioning system may be routed through the chair with a flexible hose, just as it is brought to the workstation in a few furniture systems now on the market.

Height-adjustable arms are available as an option on a few chairs in the marketplace. One Danish model with a readout attached allows the user to adjust it for comfort and make a record of the position of the arms in order to reset it. This chair also provides a readout for seat height.

There is also an innovative chair, Omnific, designed by Marta Tornero and Bruce Adams and made by Panel Concepts, that sports articulating arms on pivots that allow conversion of the chair with arms up in the normal position to arms down and out of the way in just two seconds by slightly raising the back while sitting in the chair. Each arm can also be raised or lowered independently to give unobstructed access to each part of an L-shaped desk.

Omnific can be upholstered but it does not have to be. The seat and back are made of self-skinned polyurethane foam in five finishes. Additionally, the foam can be specially formulated to meet ESD and a variety of fire code requirements or for custom colors.

We are also beginning to see the integration of personal computers into the chair. The Jefferson chair, designed by Niels Diffrient, FIDSA, is marketed by Design Seating, Inc. At first glance it looks like nothing more than an architectural modern, fully adjustable lounge chair. The associated accessories, however, when integrated with it, turn the chair into a very comfortable personal computer workstation. There is a mast with a height-adjustable platform so that the computer's screen can be set at a comfortable height for viewing combined with a tiltable platform below it to hold documents and the keyboard. A separate mast combines a fully adjustable lamp and a round tray table. Both these masts are carefully coordinated with the design of the chair. This chair is reminiscent of an

A chair with adjustable-height armrests. (Courtesy of Scan Contract.)

The Omnific chair, designed by Marta Tornero, converts from arms up to arms down—and vice versa—with a simple two-second adjustment. (Courtesy of Panel Concepts.)

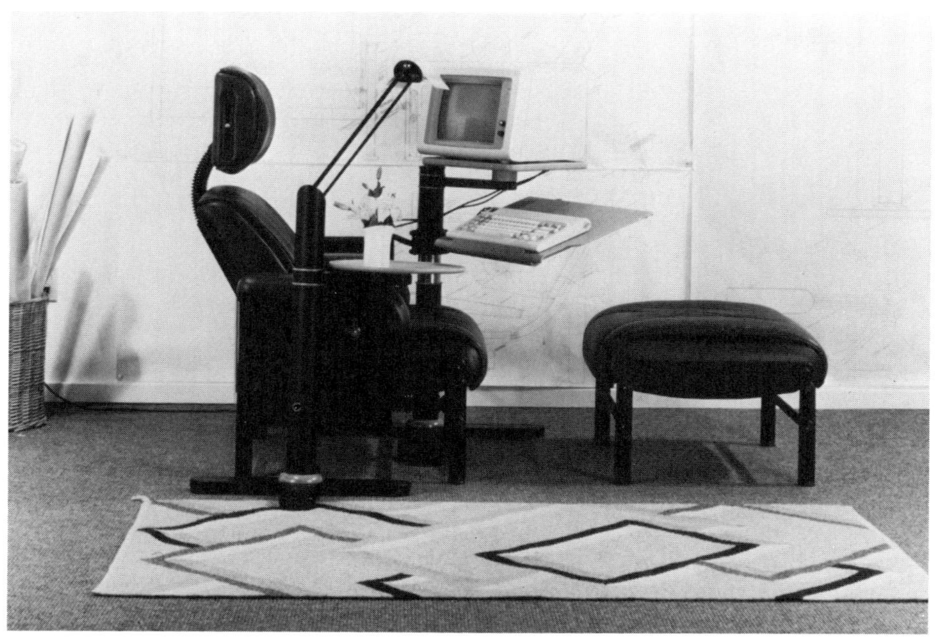

The integrated personal computer workstation for home or office. Diffrient's Jefferson chair reclines and most everything is adjustable. It is now being marketed by Design Seating, Inc. (Courtesy of Niels Diffrient, FIDSA. Photo by Bill Kontzias.)

Chairs without backs with forward-tilting seats. (Courtesy of Hag, Inc.)

experimental chair produced by Comforto several years ago combining a typewriter with an adjustable chair to form an integrated secretarial station.

By the year 2000 the computer technology now so evident in the office and on the factory floor will probably spawn the microprocessor-controlled chair (MPCC). As soon as a person sits down in the MPCC, the microprocessor in the chair's control center will automatically measure the sitter's popliteal height, weight, stature, arm reach, and eye height, sitting. After it digests these measurements, it is programmed to adjust the chair to the sitter automatically. However, it will probably have to be equipped with a manual override just in case the microprocessor is unable to handle the wide variations in the sizes of human bodies and body parts.

In connection with the MPCC, open-celled foam will probably be used as cushioning so that the microprocessor can also adjust the density of the cushioning to control the firmness of the seat and back cushions.

The microprocessor will also remember all of these adjustments and code them for each individual sitter who uses the chair. You plug in the code and the chair adjusts for your comfort.

An experimental combination chair and data-processing terminal. (Courtesy of Comforto, a Haworth Company.)

Another integrated workstation with a forward-sloped seat and a tiltable writing surface. (Courtesy of Hag, Inc.)

Note: Danish doctor A. C. Mandal first proposed the forward-sloping seat and has carried out extensive investigations of it in use.

Chapter 19

BIFMA and Other Standards

Standards are useful tools for evaluating furniture and panels for the office. There are specific standards that you can ask your office furniture and panel system suppliers to meet when they give you proposals or bids to supply these items.

Recently a landmark was reached by the Business and Institutional Furniture Manufacturers Association (BIFMA). The culmination of a 12-year program to formulate and publish safety and performance standards for office furnishings came with the publication of the ANSI/BIFMA Panel Systems Standard.

BIFMA has grown from a membership of 6 in 1973 to a membership of more than 250 manufacturers of nonresidential furniture and related products, including international associate members in Italy, France, Germany, Switzerland, Canada, Japan, Korea, Spain, the United Kingdom, The Netherlands, Taiwan, and England. U.S. BIFMA members account for more than 90 percent of the industry's volume in this country.

Within that same period BIFMA has published seven voluntary standards, six of which have been submitted to and approved by the American National Standards Institute (ANSI). It should be emphasized that these standards are *voluntary;* they are not government regulations but standards adopted by the industry itself. Here is BIFMA's description of them:

> The material presented in the BIFMA Standards was developed as a result of the efforts of the BIFMA Engineering Standards Committee, and particularly by its specific subcommittees. The Standards have been reviewed by a broad representation of governmental and commercial testing and procurement and interior design organizations. The Standards are intended to provide manufacturers, specifiers and users with a common basis of evaluating the safety, durability and structural adequacy of the specified office furniture . . . *independent* of construction materials, manufacturing processes or mechanical or aesthetic designs. The Standards define specific tests, the laboratory equipment that can be used, the conditions of tests and the recommended minimum acceptance levels to be used in evaluating these products. (italics added)

In effect the BIFMA standards allow manufacturers to make sure that the office furniture they make is strong, durable, and safe. The standards do not tell manufacturers how to design or restrict their ability to do so, as long as the furniture meets performance tests. Manufacturers can use materials, processes, or mechanical devices of choice and can style the pieces anyway they want to and still meet the standards. Design freedom is not hindered in any way.

As previously stated, these standards are voluntary; BIFMA was not required by law to produce them nor must they be obeyed. Bills have been introduced in at least 23 state legislatures, however, concerning working conditions for office workers using computer terminals. Some of these bills could mandate how furniture is designed and made. In Sweden and Germany such laws are in effect. For instance, an office chair with a four-pronged base can no longer be sold in Germany. The law says that five-pronged bases must be used so that the chair will not tip over easily, even though some engineers here say that the width of the span of the chair base is much more important to stability than the addition of another prong.

Discussion of this kind of design regulation has reached the federal level. Recently Stephen D. Channer, BIFMA's Executive Director, testified concerning the contract industry's record of voluntary standards formulation before the Subcommittee on Health and Safety, Committee on Education and Labor, U.S. House of Representatives.

Industry Acceptance

Make no mistake about it. These ANSI/BIFMA tests are for safety and performance and they are important. Why?

It has taken quite a while (since the chair standard was first issued in 1977, in fact) but now, some manufacturers of office and other heavy duty chairs and stools are for the first time including in their advertising and literature the fact that their seating passes the ANSI/BIFMA tests. Interior designers and specifiers are also just now beginning to insist that chairs offered to them for their clients pass these tests and meet the standard.

One reason the standards are being accepted is that after their origination by a BIFMA committee, the result is passed on to ANSI, our national standards-making body, for approval by ANSI's committees. On approval by ANSI, the standards are designated ANSI/BIFMA, numbered, printed by ANSI, and at that point made available through either organization at nominal prices. ANSI's approval makes sure that these furniture standards meet the general requirements applied to all standards by that body. ANSI standards result from a national consensus of manufacturers, consumers, and scientific, technical, and professional organizations plus government agencies.

Another reason for their acceptance is that committees of both organizations do not disband when a standard is finally approved. The committees constantly continue to work on updates, improvements, and revisions to keep the standards timely and relevant.

ANSI/BIFMA Standards

At this writing, the six Standards originating from BIFMA that have been accepted by ANSI and published are those for general office chairs, lateral files, vertical files, lounge seating, desks, and panel systems. BIFMA has also published a First Generation Voluntary Upholstered Furniture Flammability Standard for Business and Institutional Markets (1978, revised in 1980) as well as a glossary entitled Industry Product Definitions (1982, revised 1989).

Office Chairs

A look at ANSI/BIFMA Standard X5.1-1985 for general office chairs will give you the flavor of the tests that chairs must pass. This standard supersedes previous ANSI/BIFMA chair standards. Below are some of the tests.

First, there are a variety of back pull tests, ranging from 150 to 300 pounds. The purpose of these tests is to simulate the user "tilting back" or "exerting pressure on the chair back." Second, there is a base test, which involves the gradual application of a 2,500-pound static load to measure the base's strength. A third test drops 225- and 300-pound weights in free fall from a height of 6 inches to measure the strength of the seat and base together against impact. Swivel chairs receive a cycling test requiring that the swivel must complete 120,000 revolutions without binding or failing under a 225-pound load placed slightly off center. Office chairs that tilt must undergo 200,000 cycles of tilt operation with a 225-pound weight at the center of the seat.

In impact tests, chairs must withstand 100,000 drops of 100- and 125-pound weights from a height of 2 inches without failure. This measures the ability of the chair to withstand users dropping into the seat. The chair arms

A chair-testing facility. (Courtesy of Steelcase Inc.)

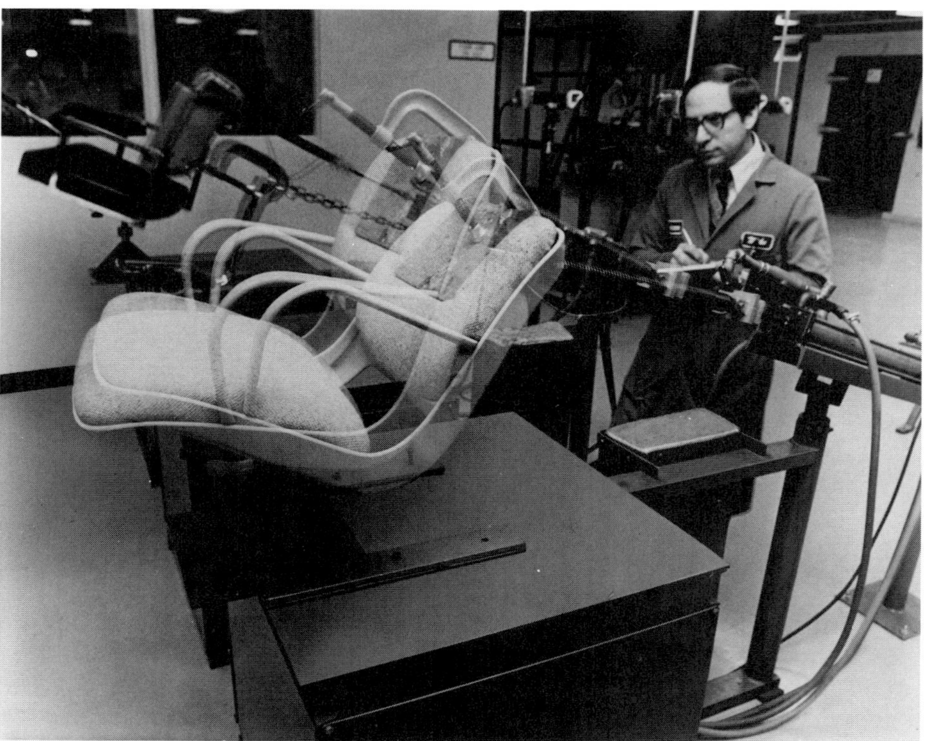

A swivel-tilt chair being tested for back durability. A 100-pound load is placed on the back for 120,000 cycles to simulate 12 years of ordinary use. (Courtesy of Steelcase Inc.)

must stand up under vertical loads of 200 and 300 pounds on each arm, as well as horizontal arm strength tests of 100 and 150 pounds. There is also a separate back durability test with a 100-pound force applied just below the top of the chair back; this must go on for 120,000 cycles before the chair passes.

This ANSI/BIFMA standard also includes two leg strength tests—front load applications of 75 and 125 pounds as well as side load applications of 75 and 115 pounds.

For chairs with casters, a 300-pound load is placed on the chair base and the chair is moved at least 30 inches in a rolling cycle; 100,000 cycles are required for hard casters, but only 36,000 cycles are asked of casters with soft treads. Tests are also conducted to determine front and rear stability. The above tests vary, depending on the type of chair being tested. Five types of chairs are recognized: (1) side chair, nonrotating, nontilt with a fixed back; (2) rotary desk chair; (3) rotary posture chair; (4) rotary clerical chair; and (5) rotary secretarial chair.

The National Furniture Center, Federal Supply Service (within the General Services Administration) incorporates this ANSI/BIFMA standard into its own specifications. For some of its government agency clients the service makes the tests tougher and demands specific dimensions of chair seat and back, a specific range of seat height adjustment (16 to 20 inches), a 3-inch range of back height adjustment, a 7-degree range of seat tilt adjustment, a 15-degree range of back tilt adjustment, a 5-prong base, specific padding grades and thicknesses, a minimum 21-ounce 100-percent nylon cover that meets an American Society for Testing Materials (ASTM) standard and an ASTM standard for chrome finishes, among other things. Perhaps, most important, it incorporates BIFMA's 1978 Upholstered Furniture Flammability Standard as part of the federal requirements. This standard contains tests for screening upholstery components, covers, and filler materials for flammability as well as tests of finished upholstered products for resistance to cigarette ignition. Similar tests are performed to meet requirements of the Upholstered Furniture Action Council for residential upholstered furniture.

Other Furniture and Equipment

Tests for Lateral Files (X5.2-1989) contain the following:

A retention test to make sure that the drawer suspensions do not disengage accidentally when a drawer is open and an upward force is exerted on the bottom. Drawers are tested to see that they do not rebound out of the cabinet when they are slammed shut and also to see that the stops keep the drawer from falling out of the case.

Further tests include evaluations of stability and racking (withstanding a set of forces that tend to twist the case), a test to determine how well the lock works, an outstop test, and an interlock test. The interlock mechanism

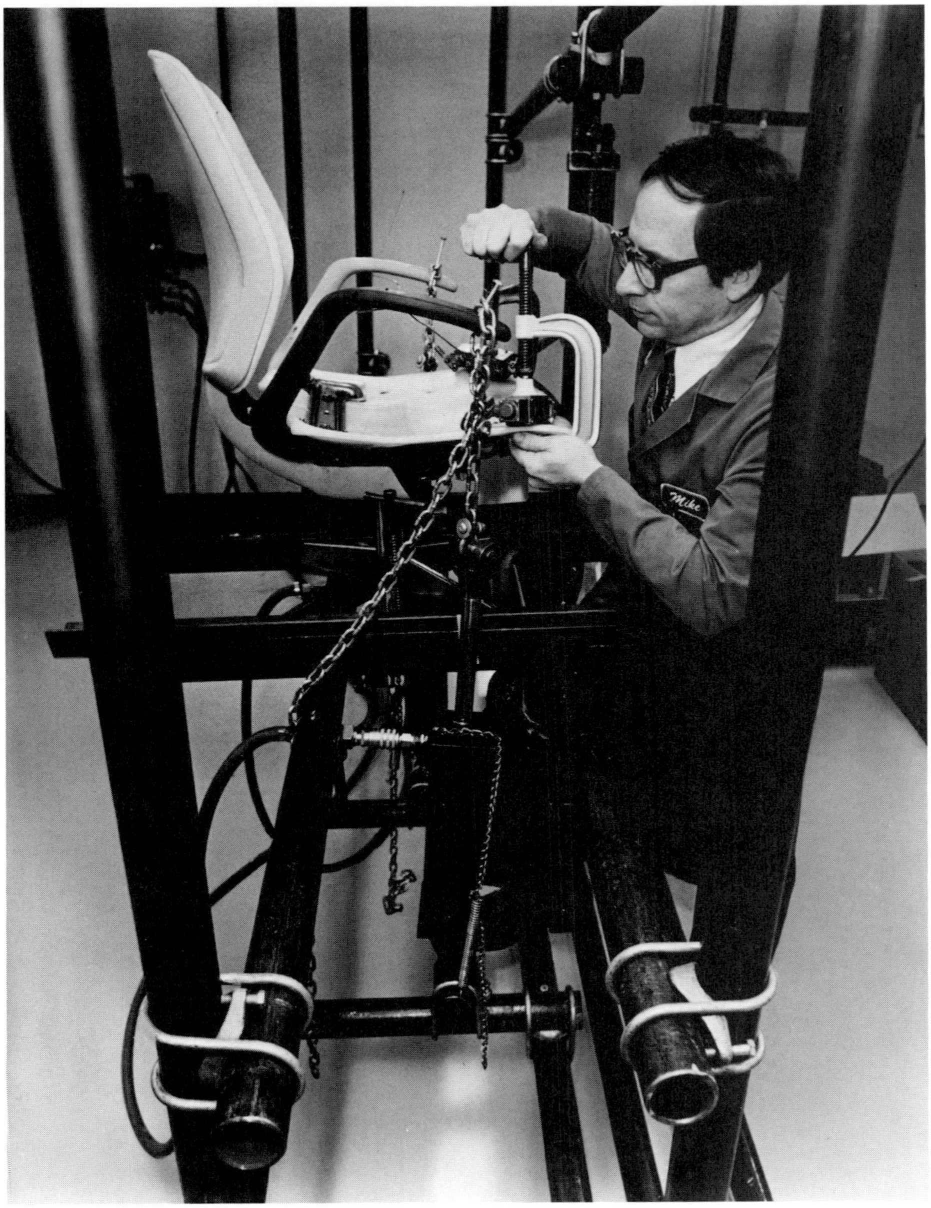

During this 100,000-cycle arm durability test, a chair is subjected to the equivalent of 10 to 12 years of use. An 80-pound load is applied to the end of both arms at the point where a person generally exerts pressure when getting out of a chair. (Courtesy of Steelcase Inc.).

In this file drawer service test, weight is loaded into a drawer that is mechanically opened and closed 100,000 times. (Courtesy of Steelcase Inc.)

A pneumatic system testing a desk lock. (Courtesy of Steelcase Inc.)

limits the number of drawers that can be pulled out at one time, so that the file does not tip over from the asymmetrical weight of the drawers.

Perhaps the most important tests in this standard are those for cycling and strength. Drawers with a center pull must undergo 75,000 open-close cycles, roll-out shelves are subjected to 55,000 cycles, and receding doors are run for 20,000 cycles. Receding doors also receive a drop test of 10,000 cycles.

Strength tests are of two types: static loads and proof loads. The top static load test, for instance, distributes a load of 3 pounds per linear inch over the top of the file and must not affect the operation of the top drawer or roll-out shelf. The proof load test increases the weight to 5 pounds per linear inch with the same requirement. The strength tests for fixed shelves, drawers, and roll-out shelves are similar.

Tests for Vertical Files (X5.3-1989) involve a battery of tests that, while they are not identical, are analogous to those used for lateral files, just as X5.4-1990 Office Furnishings—Lounge Seating demands tests similar to but not identical to the ones for General Office Chairs in X5.1-1985.

The tests in X5.5-1989 for Office Furnishings—Desk Products are almost like those in the file tests but add a drop test where one end of a fully loaded desk is raised and then dropped twice—once on each end.

The X5.6-1986 Panel Systems Standard requires tests for panel stability, panel mechanical strength, and panel mounted component dislodgement, as well as tests similar to those used for desks and files, such as static load tests for shelves, cabinets, and worksurfaces and similar cycling and weight tests for panel-mounted drawers similar to those used for drawers in desks and files.

ANSI/HFS 100-1988

BIFMA was and continues to be involved in ANSI/HFS 100-1988, the American National Standard for Human Factors Engineering of Visual Display Terminal Workstations, which was issued in 1988 and developed in cooperation with the Human Factors Society. Almost all of the portions of this standard that concern furniture design and interior design are covered in this book; the few not covered we do not feel are important to furniture and interior design.

ANSI A117.1-1986

To provide assured access to your offices for physically handicapped workers and visitors, as well as workspaces usable by the handicapped, you may want to consult ANSI A117.1-1986, the American National Standard for Buildings and Facilities—Providing Accessibility and Usability for Physically Handicapped People. The cost of making these provisions is usually quite low and well worth the effort.

Standards for Melamine Laminates

Formica®, Nevamar®, Wilsonart® and Micarta® are familiar brand names of melamine laminates that are major components in office furniture and systems. One can ask that these products meet certain standard tests, depending on the properties that you want in the product. For most grades, tests set up by the National Electrical Manufacturers Association (NEMA) are standard, but some manufacturers use various tests from the American Society for Testing Materials (ASTM) as well.

Why NEMA? Because melamine laminates were originally developed and used for electrical insulation. It wasn't until the 1920s that research breakthroughs led to their decorative use for furniture and countertops.

The standard tests measure resistance to wear, scuffing, impact, dimensional change, boiling water, high temperature, radiant and conductive heat, light, and stains. NEMA also has tests for cleanability and appearance (absence of defects).

There are several varieties of melamine laminates that are especially formulated to satisfy specific needs. Some laminates have higher than standard resistance to fire, X-rays, abrasion, laboratory chemicals, impact, and static electricity. Although ''antistat'' surfaces are mostly used in ''clean rooms'' to hold down dust, they may become important in offices because of the need to keep static electricity and dust away from computers.

In selecting laminates for offices, it is important to remember that matte-textured finishes are desirable to keep down glare. It is also important that office worksurfaces reflect from 30 to 50 percent of the light they receive to ease eye strain when using white paper. Medium oak, teak, and light walnut usually fall within this range as do typical office greys and beiges. Dark walnut and rosewood contrast too much with white paper and become distracting. White laminate is too light; its lack of contrast with white paper will make your eyes wander away from the work. The laminate manufacturer can furnish information on reflectance for specific patterns and colors.

Standards for Textiles

Because there are so many tests for textiles at present, the Association for Contract Textiles has been formed to work toward standard textile tests.

Chapter 20

Tips on Selecting Traditional Wood Office Furniture

Up to this point we have been talking about panel systems and chairs that are predominantly made of metal and plastic. Another category of furniture is made predominantly of wood and used heavily in the executive suite, as well as in executive workplaces at home: traditional wood office furniture. It take a different body of knowledge to buy it well.

The first step is to look at the styles that are available: The bulk of traditional office furniture being made is manufactured with eighteenth-century English style characteristics, although French Court and some nineteenth-century American rustic is available. This last is the style usually found in roll-top desks. Of course you can find almost any style around in antique stores, flea markets, and the like.

User Needs

Whatever style you like and shop for, there is one overriding principle that must be kept in mind: You must satisfy the needs of the person who's going to use the furniture. These are some of those needs:

Amount of Worksurface

Whatever furniture you end up with, enough worksurface area must be provided so that the worker does not feel cramped. If the worker likes to spread papers over a large area, then that large area is needed. If the worker likes to leave papers on the desk or worktable overnight, this will increase the amount of surface needed and might dictate the choice of a roll-top desk where the top can be closed and locked to cover the papers at night. Roll-tops usually have several small drawers and pigeonholes for the person who likes that sort of storage.

Office Appliances

Although the style of traditional furniture comes from the past by definition, some traditional furniture makers have adapted these beautiful designs so that the furniture fits the needs of today. One example is eighteenth-century tables that are now available to hold printers for computers. They have paper slots and paper shelves underneath, and some of them are on casters

There are lots of drawers, pigeonholes, and compartments in this roll-top desk and upper deck. (Courtesy of National Mt. Airy.)

A printer table in eighteenth-century styling. (Courtesy of COUNCILL Business Furniture.)

so that they can be moved about. As mentioned above, Alma makes an eighteenth-century-style panel system. It is perhaps ironic that traditional styles of the past in wood are being used with ultramodern computers, but wood itself is compatible with electronics. It carries no charges of static electricity and thus poses no problem for computers.

Another example is the desk for the secretary who uses a typewriter as well as a word processor; the secretarial return must be long and deep enough to hold both machines. The word processor can then be connected to the printer with its separate table.

Incidentally, a secretarial desk should have a purse hook and a shelf for personal belongings under one of its tops and a stationery organizer in the typing pedestal.

Be sure to provide enough worksurface for adding machines or calculators, needed reference materials, telephones, staplers, and binders. If a computer is to be used at a workplace, be sure to investigate the use of what is called an articulating keyboard shelf. This item is adjustable in height and can be easily hinged to the underside of the worksurface. Since it is hinged so that it disappears when not in use, it does not disturb the traditional styling of the piece.

Storage

Most eighteenth-century-style desks and credenzas can be ordered with a large variety of drawers, shelves, and cabinets; credenzas are especially flexible in this regard. In fact, you usually have to specify what units will make up the credenza and there is usually a choice of drawers for the desk pedestals. It is important to determine what kinds of materials will be stored. For example, if the worker maintains files, are letter, legal and/or computer printout files needed? How many inches of each type are needed? Are hanging files needed? If desk and credenza together cannot satisfy filing needs,

A specially designed eighteenth-century desk with the Corridor® system in place to accommodate wire management needs and a computer. (Courtesy of Sligh Furniture Co.)

separate filing cabinets in traditional styling are available. If a bookcase is needed, the dimensions of the books used in each office should be determined.

Patterns of Office Use

The author has designed several traditional offices where the worker used a table for conferences while desk paperwork was done on a kneehole credenza behind the table, so that when paperwork was being done, the user faced away from the conference table. The credenza worksurface must be deep enough so that it is comfortable for paperwork. This type of workplace demands a swivel chair. An arrangement of this kind is often preferred by people who work on confidential material because they do not want visitors to see their confidential papers. The style of working will affect what components go into the credenza and may affect the height of the credenza if this person likes to type and/or uses a word processor or a computer. You might have to approach the makeup of the credenza in the same way as you would approach the makeup of a secretarial station. In any case, the selection of furniture for any office should be made so that the worker who is going to use it will have the necessary worksurfaces and storage in proper places and sizes to suit his or her pattern of office use. There should also be enough wire holes with grommets and/or access plates to handle the wiring.

Space

How are you going to get the furniture into the space? If the sofa is too long to get onto the elevator or too bulky to get around a corner, will it be necessary to take a window out and use a crane to get it in? Or, will you have to take it upstairs on top of the elevator? Questions of this kind frequently arise.

One such instance involved the design of a secret military conference room. All that was provided to the designer was a partial blueprint of a floor of a building in an unknown location, with no entrances, stairways, or elevators shown on the print. The only defense the designer had was to state in writing that the designer was not responsible for making sure that the 14-foot conference table could actually be placed in the conference room. Happily, there were no problems with the set-up and delivery.

Secretarial workstation includes elements of the Devonshire eighteenth-century styled panel system. (Courtesy of the Alma Companies.)

Woods and Finishes

In shopping for traditional office furniture, you will find lots of mahogany. Look for Honduras mahogany, not some less expensive, weaker species such as sapele or Lauan. (Remember that it does come from the endangered tropical rainforests.) Cherry and some walnut, predominantly American black walnut, are also available. Some very expensive traditional furniture is made from French walnut. On genuine wood or wood-veneered pieces, hand-rubbed finishes are best and the finer ones may take as many as 30 operations for the finish alone. Some of these wood desks and conference tables can be had with tops of gold-tooled leather (several colors) or exotic veneers, such as Carpathian elm burl. Some wood-inlay and marble tops are also available.

It is important to think about how the piece of furniture is to be used.

This executive office includes desk, chairs, credenza and overhead cabinets, all from the Devonshire system. (Courtesy of the Alma Companies.)

If you want the elegant leather or unusual wood top (or even an ordinary wood top) and want to make it more durable, think about having an abrasion-resistant glass or polycarbonate slab cut to fit so that it can be placed over the desk or conference table top to protect it from wear and scratches. This kind of protection is also useful if any paper cutting is done on the top. An alternative would be to order a melamine laminate top that matches the finish on the balance of the desk or conference table. Their use does not compromise the styling of the furniture, and it certainly does extend the life of the top. Stay away from printed vinyl surfaces. The problem here is that if vinyl printed to resemble wood is scratched or torn, you need a resident artist to repair the finish.

When buying furniture, ask whoever sells it how to maintain it, and get the exact names of the preparations needed to clean it and keep it looking new. Remember that a traditional style with raised or carved ornamentation will require a lot of dusting.

A reproduction of a Chippendale architect's table from Circa 1765. Even in olden times, height and tilt worksurface adjustments as well as task lighting were needed. (Courtesy of Baker Furniture.)

The return of this L-shaped desk accommodates computer equipment. (Courtesy of COUNCILL Business Furniture.)

Most eighteenth-century traditional furniture is made with two kinds of bases: the plinth base, which is plain and flush-to-the-floor; and the scroll or ogee base, which has been sawn or scrolled in curved vertical patterns. With plinth bases, some desks and credenzas come with hidden adjusters. The plinth bases are easier to clean around than scrolled bases, which need to be cleaned under as well. In the best desks, bases are usually made from solid wood of the species you select.

Construction and Features

Some traditional desks have overhang (also called conference) tops for those who want to confer with up to five people at their desks. Desks without conference tops usually have two pull-out reference slides (also called dictation or armrest slides), one at the top of each pedestal, and some of them have a slide on the opposite (approach) side, so that a stenographer facing the executive can use it for taking notes.

If the top of the desk or table is veneered with the wood of your choice, the better ones will have edges made of that solid wood. Of course, some traditional furniture is made from solid woods entirely, but that is more expensive.

Most well-engineered traditional desks have a center drawer with a locking mechanism that also locks all of the drawers in both pedestals simultaneously. A good desk will usually have a hidden utility shelf hidden under the rear part of the center of the desk. Several drawer options are usually offered for each pedestal, depending upon how much and what kind of storage is needed by the user.

Drawer construction is another consideration. While there are some solid wood drawer fronts in the market, most traditional desks and credenzas made from fine woods have veneered drawer fronts; there should be five plies in each for strength and longevity.

There is no reason to worry about buying wood-veneered surfaces; with modern glues and veneering methods the surfaces do not come apart. The fronts should be attached to the drawer sides with dovetailed construction; the same construction should be used to connect the sides to the back of the drawer. Dovetailing is a method of furniture construction that has stood the test of time since it was invented by the Egyptians about 5,000 years ago. Drawers should also be fully boxed in, with the drawer bottom fitting into a precut groove in all four sides.

You may see some desks with molded plastic drawers that have attached wood fronts to make it easier to replace drawer fronts, which take a beating sometimes. The drawers also allow replacements in some lines that change the style of the desk when the fronts are changed.

The interior frame for drawer pedestals should be made from knot-free and defect-free hardwood, preferably birch, beech, or maple. All pedestals should have corner blocks on all four corners at the top and bottom for structural strength and longevity. Incidentally, drawer sides in some of the finer desks are made of solid mahogany, cherry, or walnut, but oak is frequently used and works just as well. Drawer interiors should be fully finished and waxed.

Drawer motion hardware is also important. Box drawers on the very finest traditional wood furniture are hand-fitted and waxed, so that they require no side or bottom hardware for smooth operation. Most better traditional furniture today, however, is fitted with steel drawer guides that slide on steel and nylon bearings. There are many variations on the market, but side guides rolling on steel or nylon bearings work out the best. Good box drawers will have adjustable interior partitions; usually one top box drawer is fitted with a pencil and paper clip tray.

Filing drawers require a different kind of steel and nylon guide, primarily because they must carry more weight and the user must have access to the full length of the filing drawer. The guide for this type of drawer is called a full progressive suspension; the good ones roll on steel ball bearings and usually slide in three stages. Full suspension means that the drawer body slides completely out from under the top so that you can see everything in the drawer. Before buying a traditional desk with file drawers, have a file drawer filled with paper demonstrated so that you can see whether or not the suspension works well. A good file drawer will have interior partition adjustments so that either legal or letter size paper can be stored in either ordinary or hanging file folders.

There are several auxiliary pieces of traditional furniture available in some lines, including trophy cases; telephone, coffee, lamp, wall, and small round tables; and both lateral and vertical filing cabinets where extra capacity is needed. Most makers include matching bookcases in their lines. Make sure that they have wood braces underneath each shelf end screwed into both the sides and the shelves (unless they have adjustable shelves). Bookcases may be open without doors; if they have doors, the doors can be solid or veneered, with plain or crown glass, or with wire gratings.

When picking out a traditional desk chair or conference chair, there is one primary rule: *Before buying it, sit in it.* If it is your own chair, make sure it has the features you want: swivel, tilt, seat and back height adjustment, lumbar support, casters, or whatever—but above all, make sure it's comfortable for you. Any traditional chair should be tried out by the person who will be using it—before it is bought. Also check to see that the arms do not hit the desk that will be used with the chair; the arms should fit under the top at the kneehole.

As for fabrics, a slightly nubby 100 percent nylon treated with a stain repeller is best, both because it is long-wearing and because the nubbiness allows a certain amount of air flow around the buttocks. This flow does not happen with vinyl; the result is pooling of perspiration, which is not only uncomfortable but also can lead to fungal infection. Wool fabrics are almost as good as nylon, and there are some very good wool-nylon blends on the market.

The sofa should have the same types of fabric. These fabrics are now woven in traditional patterns and colors for easy cleaning and long wear. The sofa should have a kiln-dried hardwood frame that is sealed and corner-blocked with eight-way hand-tied spring construction resting on the frame underneath the pillows. Sit on the sofa, too, before you buy it.

Make sure that conference and visitor seating is of roughly the same construction as the sofa; a similar upholstery cover should be used. Try out this auxiliary seating to see that it is comfortable. The seat height should be about 16 inches so that shorter people will also be comfortable.

One final word of caution: When you fall in love with an antique or a piece of used traditional furniture, make sure that it will fill your need before you buy it.

Chapter 21

FUNDI: A Revolutionary New Office Workstation from Public Works Canada

The next revolution in office furniture may have already started with the unveiling of the FUNDI III workstation by the Directorate of Architectural and Building Sciences (ABS) of Public Works Canada. The development of FUNDI was initiated by Peter A. D. Mill, former Director of ABS.

FUNDI III is an example of participatory design that embodies many of the design principles discussed in this book. It began like this: Environmental complaints by office workers increased during the 1970s as the pace of office automation intensified. In response, ABS developed a mobile diagnostic workstation as a monitoring tool to pinpoint the environmental causes of office workers' satisfaction and dissatisfaction. Calling it a *Func*tional *Di*agnostic *U*nit, they adopted the acronym FUNDI.

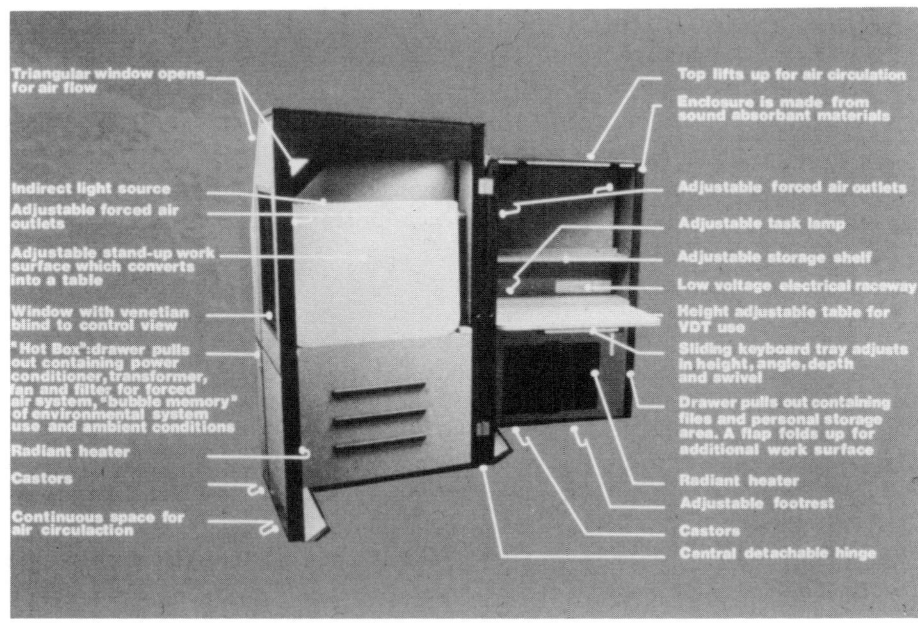

Features of FUNDI. (Courtesy Directorate of Architectural and Building Sciences, Public Works, Canada.)

As Audrey Kaplan, Project Manager, expressed it, ABS wanted to know

1. how individuals cope with environmental stresses in the office setting and
2. what the environmental and ergonomic requirements of traditional and new electronic offices are. (Kaplan 1985)

Since 1980, development of FUNDI has continued. The illustrations below show FUNDI III, the third generation model, which ABS calls "the mini-environmental modifier." It is the result of many years of "micro-environmental diagnostics" aimed at improving the environment of the office of the future. Mill says, "The FUNDI design is a collection of ideas, notions and hunches from different disciplines on the essential components for optimal office accommodation."

It resulted from a multi-disciplinary effort, including the use of staff and outside consultants in the fields of ergonomics, acoustics, administration, illumination, electrical engineering, data analysis, information management, architectural diagnostics, interior design, industrial design, computer installation, thermal comfort, office automation, finance, maintenance, cabinet making, mechanical engineering, editing, and VDT emissions.

Mill also stated,

> Through this work ABS has attempted to anticipate and mitigate the potentially adverse impacts of office automation on work environments. The Directorate's studies in recent years have consistently demonstrated that the "climate" of the work environment exerts a crucial influence on both employee productivity and the expenditures associated with the design and operations of public buildings. A logical conclusion is that building occupants must be allowed to influence their micro-environments and the design of new buildings.

Worker Complaints

ABS research has shown that lack of visual and aural privacy ranks first as the most important problem in Canadian government offices. The dimensions of this problem are affected by the aural, thermal, visual, functional, and air quality characteristics of the workspace.

The most important health issues that emerged from this research were eye strain and headaches; as many as 65 percent of those answering questionnaires said that the quality of the visual environment was inadequate.

According to Kaplan, the next most important health issue was

> air quality with respect to its distribution near the work station. In most instances approximately 10 cfm (cubic feet per minute) of outside air was being delivered to the overall floor, although this level was less at the work station. Public Works has now developed a test method using carbon dioxide as a tracer gas to insure that 20 cfm minimum outside air is delivered at each work station. (1985)

The next most important problem found was temperature-associated discomfort; people were either too warm or too cold.

FUNDI III addresses these problems and others, drawing on previous ABS research, which includes a field test of 16 earlier model FUNDIs in the Department of Communications from January of 1984 to March of 1985.

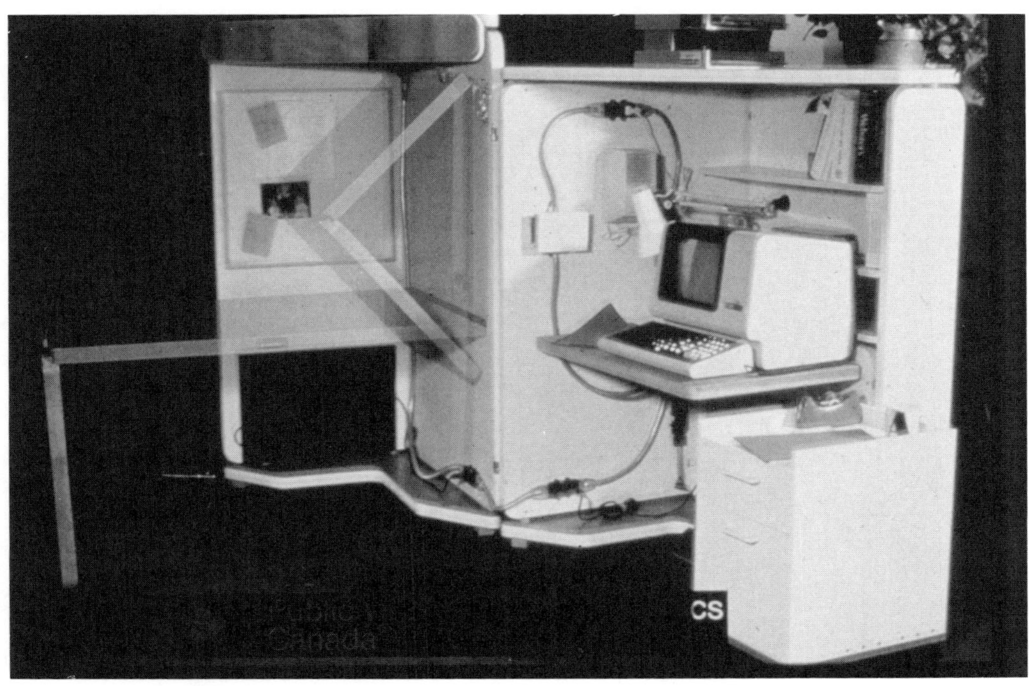

Some examples of various FUNDI configurations, open and closed.

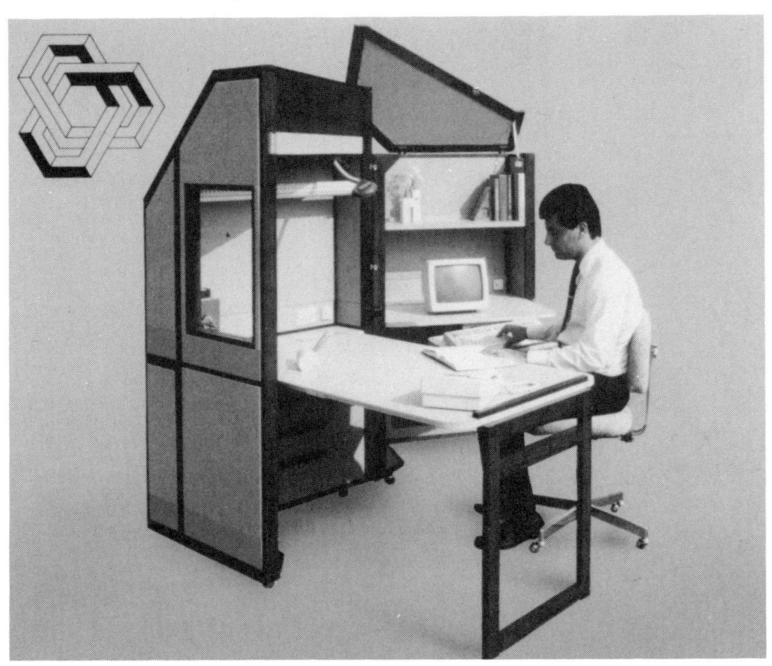

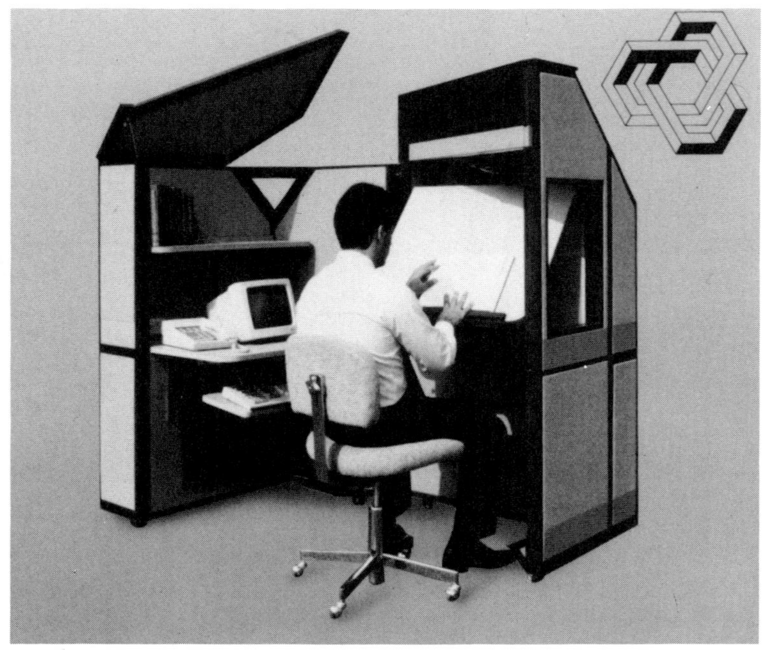

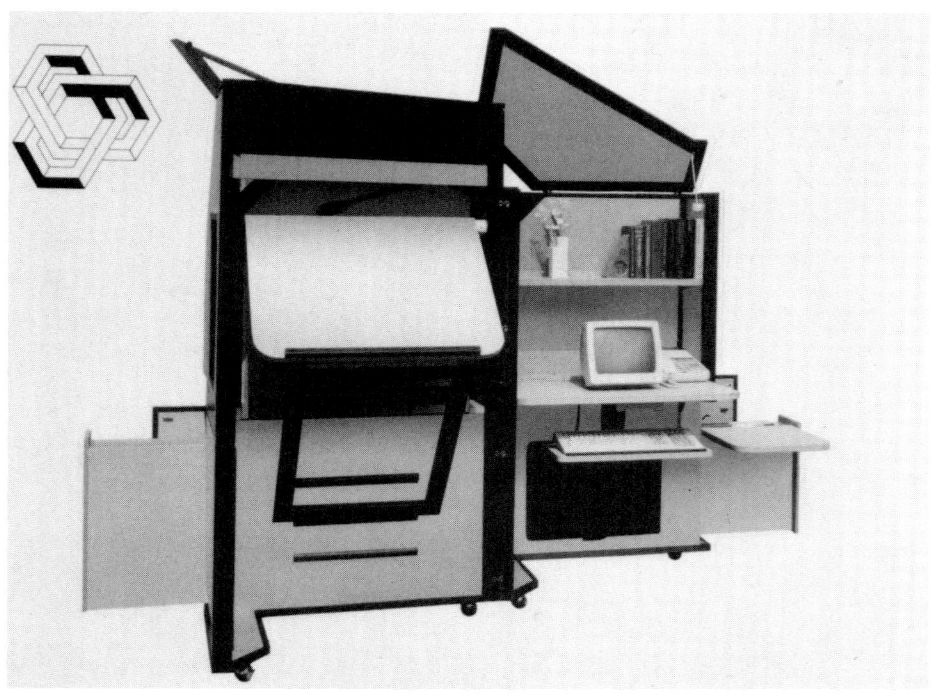

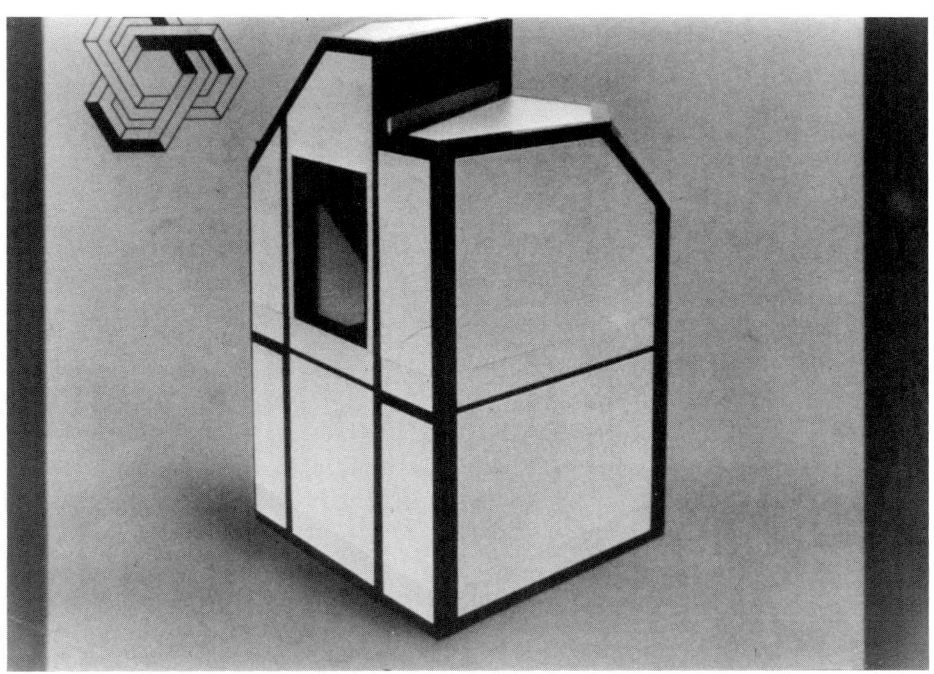

Design Characteristics of FUNDI III

Mobility

The unit has casters for easy moving and reconfiguration; the center of gravity is low and it is light in weight. One aim here has been to make it easy for even small people to move and reconfigure it. When not in use it can be moved out of the way or to storage.

The mobility of FUNDI allows instant changes to cope with the constant variations of job requirements and the continuing alteration of work flow patterns in the dynamic electronic office. It also permits the individual to select locations in regard to social preferences; friends can work next to friends, if work flow is not disturbed.

Security

FUNDI can be closed and locked as needed, whether for security requirements or when the worker is away from the office.

Flexibility for Adjustment and Reconfiguration

Essentially FUNDI is a kit of parts that enables its elements to be configured in a wide variety of ways for almost any type of office workstation from executive to clerical. The kit-of-parts approach allows the user to choose components needed for individual job requirements and also, within limits, the color, material, and finish of the components. Further, the parts are designed so that many of them can be adjusted to the personal size preferences of the user *by* the user; specially trained technicians are not needed.

Other Features

A triangular skylight on one section opens for air flow; on the other section, the skylight top lifts up to two positions to direct air circulation down to the occupant.

Another window on one section with a venetian blind controls visual privacy. Visual privacy can also be controlled by putting the unit in a half-open position. There are adjustable forced-air outlets on both sections equipped with filters as necessary. Each section has a radiant heater panel below the worksurfaces where the heat can be directed to the legs and feet, the body parts which usually get cold first in the office. The heaters (and the incandescent lights) have rheostat controls that permit settings from high/full to low/minimum. Since one of the principal reasons behind the development of FUNDI is to conserve energy, it also uses air movement to assist in cooling.

On one side there is a directionally adjustable indirect light source, an adjustable stand-up worksurface that can be converted into a worktable, and a "hot box" drawer containing a power conditioner, a transformer, and the fan and filter for the forced-air system. In addition it contains the bubble memory (more of this later) to record how workers use the system in varying ambient conditions, which are also recorded. The components in this drawer are modular for ease of servicing and replacement.

On the other side of the unit, there is an adjustable task lamp, an adjustable storage shelf, a horizontal low-voltage electrical raceway, and a drawer. This drawer is for files and personal storage, with a flap that folds up for additional worksurface area. The unit has provisions for computer use, including a height-adjustable table, a sliding, swiveling keyboard tray that adjusts in height, angle, and depth, and a footrest that is adjustable for angle and distance. An accordion-like channel permits the separation of the two sections by a limited distance for reconfiguration.

The FUNDI enclosure is made from sound absorbent materials. A mobile drawer pedestal is included in the kit of parts. When the FUNDI is closed, either this mobile pedestal or the chair may be placed within it.

FUNDIs will be equipped with an infrared sensor that automatically turns off heating, cooling, and light controls. When the worker leaves the station and the station is closed, the sensor automatically shuts down all power coming into it.

The design of FUNDI utilizes flat wire under carpet squares for power, telephone, and data transmission.

The tall section is just under 70 inches high; the shorter section is 12 inches lower. When closed, FUNDI measures less than 40 inches square and occupies less than 11 square feet; open and in use, it occupies less than 60 square feet. We feel that the use of FUNDIs in offices could significantly reduce the amount of square feet needed while greatly improving the quality of the interior environment.

Where FUNDI is used, less heat, light, and air are needed at the building level, since the FUNDI has its own supplemental heat and air movement capability. It can be placed in a building as required and is not limited by the location of a ceiling air supply because it is equipped with internal ducting and a fan that can circulate air freely to the occupant.

The comprehensive 16-FUNDI field trial mentioned above took place in about 2,500 square feet of offices of the Canadian Department of Communications in the Journal Tower North, a typical office building constructed in 1975.

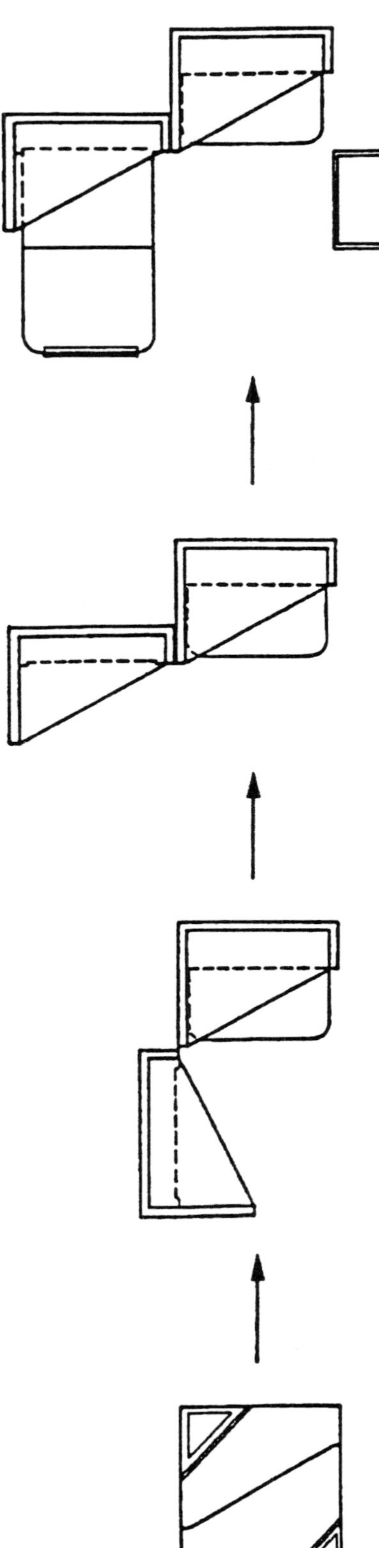

Diagrams show how the FUNDI opens from a locked box (bottom) to a fully open workstation. The positions are variable so that the occupant can place the two main sections for as much privacy and space as is preferred.

Field Test Results and Further Refinements

In evaluating user response to the FUNDIs, Kaplan stated:

> The general response to the FUNDIs was positive and occupants rated the units more positively than other types of open plan work stations. The users reported that they had improved visual privacy, similar degrees of noise disturbance and slightly improved voice privacy compared to their experience in other open plan offices. They felt that they had greater control over task lighting although they maintained that they did not have more control over temperature and ventilation. . . . The screening was rated the most positively. They also liked the compactness of the unit and the control features, particularly the lights, fan and footrest. (1985)

The process of experimentation with and refinement of FUNDI continued. In response to user demand during the trials, a 10-to-12-minute video cassette tape of an animated graphics training package was developed to tell users what features are available and how FUNDIs features can be used.

Use of the various features of FUNDI and user-selected settings will be monitored by a bubble memory microprocessor specifically designed for this purpose and developed from ABS research over a ten-year period. In this way, environmental thresholds can be determined for the variety of tasks in the office; the bubble memory will also keep track of when the FUNDI is used and by how many people.

These user settings will be compared with those made by an autonomous mobile robot called Roche I. The technology used for this robot is an outgrowth of ongoing robotic research and was conceived by ABS in conjunction with the Carnegie Mellon Robotics Research Center. The robot contains an ultrasonic sensor so that it can ''recognize'' furniture for accurate inventory controls and record the changing locations and configurations of furniture. Floor plans can then be developed from these records. The ultrasonic sensor will also prevent Roche I from bumping into furniture, walls, and people. In addition, the robot is expected to monitor the humidity, air particulate levels, and acoustic characteristics of the office environment and digitize this information for ongoing analyses.

Results from field tests performed on approximately 200 FUNDIs have been used to develop further the final characteristics of the design and control systems planned for FUNDI IV.

Other Experiments in the Field

In the early 1970s, the author was a member of a research team, ARC, which experimented with the use of self-contained individual environmental units to help with the recovery of patients in a mental hospital. These contained a bed, a partition, a desk, and walls with a window and a venetian blind. We feel that this gave the patients, our clients, a sense of control over an individual space. The author speculates that this sense of control given to the user is perhaps the most attractive feature of the FUNDI concept.

When these environments were in place and fully occupied in a ward, the large room looked like a neighborhood. The FUNDI report from ABS

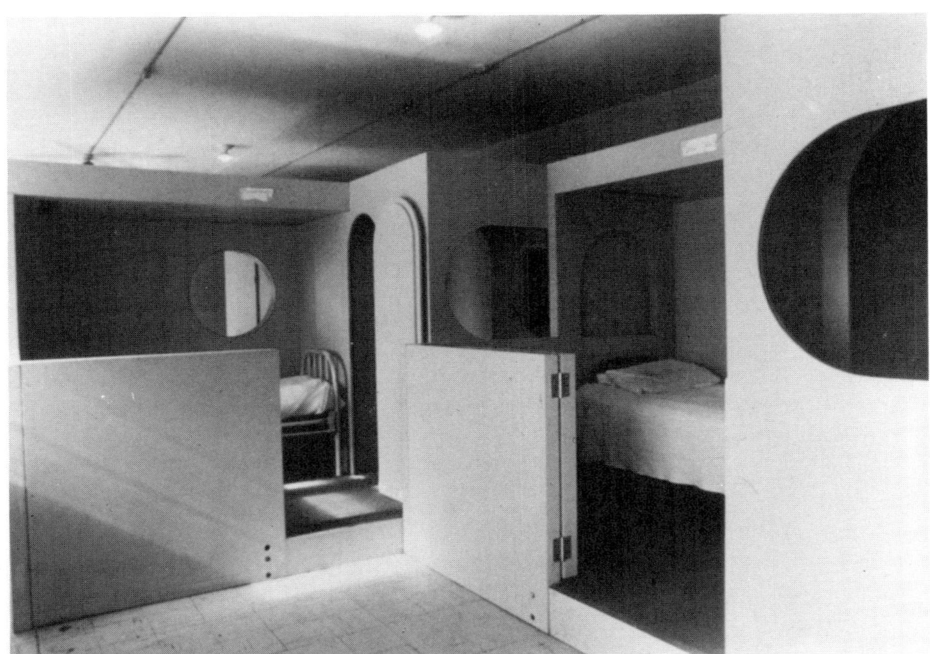

Individual environments in a mental hospital when first installed, before personalization. (Courtesy of the ARC Group, Incorporated.)

ends with this question: "What happens when the office becomes a 'neighborhood' and reflects such cultural values as privacy, identity, wayfinding, security and other phenomena?"

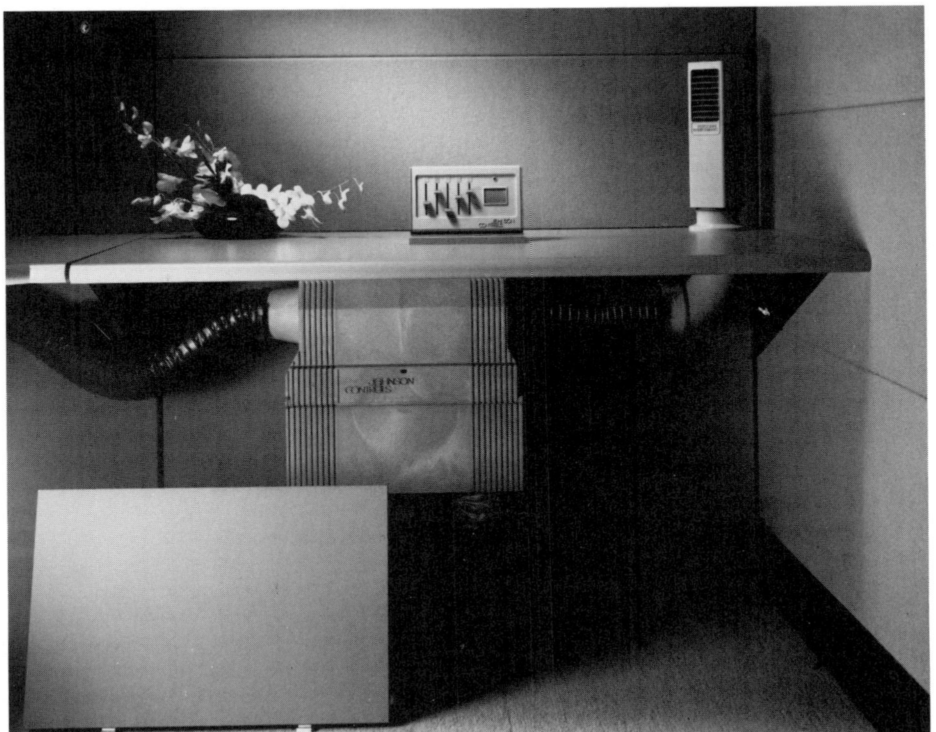

An installation of one of Johnson's Personal Environments. (Courtesy of Johnson Controls.)

Although ABS is not working on the FUNDI project at this writing, some of the FUNDI consultants have been involved with Johnson Controls in Milwaukee in designing a "Personal Environment."[1] Sponsors of the project include Apple Computer, Herman Miller, Milliken, Steelcase, Tate Access Floors, Teknion and Westinghouse Furniture.

Johnson's Personal Environment is a battery of controls that allows individual workers in open offices with panel systems to adjust air temperature, air velocity, supplemental heat from a radiant panel, sound masking, and lighting by moving five levers on a desktop control box. Most of these features were a part of FUNDI, as well.

In a departure from the usual ceiling plenum distribution of air (and sometimes wiring), cables and conditioned air are distributed to individual workstations through a raised floor and the furniture system panels. By eliminating the need for a ceiling plenum, 2 to 5 feet of vertical space can be saved on each floor. With this arrangement, more floors and therefore more rentable space can be built within a given building height than could be done using conventional air handling methods.

Indirect lighting is used for all areas except personal workstations, where individually controlled task lighting is furnished. Electronic filters remove dust and smoke particles, while a charcoal filter eliminates most of the gaseous contaminants. Sound control is accomplished by the workers' ability to generate white sound in each workstation.

When the worker leaves the workstation, a motion sensor detects the departure and sets the Personal Environment controls to the most energy-efficient levels; on the worker's return the air flow and temperature are returned to preselected levels. An Apple computer monitors settings in each office; when it determines the need for more warm or cooled air, it will call for it from central equipment.

[1]These included Pleasantine Drake, Peter Mill, Vivian Loftness, and Volker Hartkopf.

PART V

The Productivity Payoff

Chapter 22

A Case for Participatory Design

The late Douglas McGregor, in a book called *The Human Side of Enterprise,* published in 1960, defined a management philosophy, Theory Y, that forms a basis for the use of participatory design in offices today.

He characterized the typical American business enterprise run under what he called Theory X as a highly hierarchical organization, with all the marching orders originating from the chief executive officer, just as a general runs an army. Harsh disciplinary actions usually accompany this management style where Theory X reigns and independent thought and actions are discouraged.

Theory Y is the complete opposite of Theory X. Y assumes that workers will respond to challenges by taking on responsibility for decisions in the best interests of the enterprise. Theory Y organizations give their workers the freedom to act independently and participate in decision-making processes. Theory Y puts the emphasis on employee participation, rather than on the hierarchical strictures of Theory X (McGregor 1960).

Since 1960, however, the office world has changed in two important ways: the first is that office technology has made quantum advances and the second is that the office workers valued most in an organization are a different kind of people than they were then. For one thing, they are better educated. *Corporate Design* said, ''High school graduates had surged from 45% of the labor force in 1952 to 85% in 1982. An interesting precedent was also set in 1982 when college graduates outnumbered college dropouts for the first time'' (Ginzberg 1984).

Changes in office technology have also altered and will continue to alter job duties. The increased capacity and use of computers and their associated peripheral devices increases the ability of individual office workers to perform several different kinds of tasks without much instruction or supervision. In other words, workers become more autonomous, making many of their own decisions. They also become more specialized in many situations, knowing more about their jobs than anyone else and therefore knowing more about what they need in a workplace and its design.

Changes in job duties frequently come from the addition of new equipment, triggering a need for a change in workstation design. If the worker does not participate in the design of it, the workstation can become unsuitable, uncomfortable, and/or overcrowded; productivity and employee satisfaction can drop and the enterprise loses.

People Want to Participate

Two Steelcase studies, performed in 1978 and 1980 by Louis Harris & Associates, found that 91 percent of the more than 1,000 office workers surveyed ''feel that it is very or somewhat important for them to have a say in . . . decisions about getting whatever they need to feel comfortable in their jobs. . . . fewer office workers now have a voice in . . . office decisions than would like to'' (Steelcase 1978).

In 1980, Michael Brill, President of the Buffalo Organization for Social and Technological Innovation (BOSTI), said that in studies done by his organization up to that point, ''81% of the workers surveyed (more than 10,000) so far are not allowed to participate in design decisions, 79% want to participate in them and 72% are dissatisfied because they aren't allowed to participate in them'' (Brill 1980).

The situation was largely unchanged in late 1986, when a third Steelcase-sponsored study found that 61 percent of office workers say that a participatory style of management is very important at all levels of decision making, but only 29 percent say they have it, and only 25 percent of top executives consider it important to office workers (1987).

Similarly, the Steelcase survey produced the information that while 62 percent of office workers said that it is very important that executives initiate meetings with all levels of staff, only 30 percent said that such meetings take place in their jobs, and only 31 percent of top managers believed that this issue is important to office workers. A real gap was apparent.

Dissatisfaction with the Open Plan

The desire to participate clearly exists. Dr. Francis Duffy, co-author of this book and principal author of the influential British ORBIT 1 Study, has said,

> The study team predicts that highly skilled and valued staff will become more demanding in their expectations and requirements. User preferences with regard to other aspects of office design will also become more important. For example, there are now a number of studies which show considerable staff resistance to working in open plan offices. The consensus seems to be an increasing dislike of open plan because of disturbance, loss of privacy and stress. (1983)

The following are examples of studies showing worker dissatisfaction with open-plan offices.

As early as 1972, Malcolm J. Brookes reported on a study of 120 office employees who moved from a conventional mixture of open-plan, semiprivate, and private offices to a landscaped open-plan office. While the workers liked the aesthetics of their new offices, they felt they were less efficient and less utilitarian than their former quarters. They complained about the increase in the noise level, the number of visual distractions, and the loss of privacy.

J. Nemecek and E. Grandjean in 1973 did a survey of large-space, open-plan offices and came to similar conclusions, confirming Brookes' results (Nemecek and Grandjean 1973).

In April, 1983, *Design* magazine said, "A comparative study of conventional and open plan offices at a West Midland local authority provides further evidence that open plan layouts may be significantly less healthy and less productive work settings" (1983).

Fifty-nine employees working in separate, enclosed offices in a traditional Town Hall and 359 employees working in open-plan offices in a new, adjacent building answered questionnaires about their working conditions. Here are some of the results:

1. While 54 percent of those in separate offices registered general satisfaction with them, only 28 percent of those in the open plan agreed.
2. Of those in the open plan, 73 percent felt that there was a lack of privacy; 47 percent of those in conventional offices felt the same way.
3. In the open plan 69 percent objected to distractions and disturbances; only 50 percent of those in enclosed offices did.
4. Of those in the open plan, 70 percent felt that their personal productivity was reduced; only 49 percent of the workers in conventional offices agreed.
5. Only 16 percent of those in enclosed offices reported headaches, while 39 percent of those in the open plan had them.
6. Of the workers in the open plan, 46 percent said that they had infectious illnesses; the figure was 24 percent for workers in conventional offices.

Dr. Duffy points out that in Sweden and West Germany, where the open plan was once so popular, many new office buildings are being constructed with private offices and group offices, rather than in a continuous open plan (Duffy 1987).

In Sweden this trend is helped along by laws requiring that before a new building is built or an old one remodeled, the people who are going to work there must be consulted about the design of the architecture and interiors.

More Individual Control

Dr. Duffy cites another trend, seen particularly in Germany and Holland, toward more individual control of the workstation environment. Control is expressed, for example, in the right to open windows, to adjust task lighting, to personalize the individual workplace, and to control local air-conditioning, and in the right to a window view. The Steelcase studies cited show that a majority of office workers say that they do not have the right temperature and 58 percent of those studied have used fans, heaters, or other appliances to make their workstations more comfortable.

The Influence of Individual Work Styles

Another factor influencing the desire for more individual personal control of the workplace is the existence of differing work styles among office workers. Ronald Goodrich (1986), in a study of office workers for U.S. senators, found these differences:

- Those who rely principally on the visual processing of information ''need to read and see things, so they have more paper to store.''
- ''Others rely more on auditory means and seem more comfortable with conversation and discussion.''
- There are those who organize their work material horizontally and laterally spread piles of papers on available surfaces, sometimes in a relaxed, disorderly, and cluttered manner.
- In contrast, those who organize their work vertically use shelves, files, bins, and tacking surfaces and do not scatter papers about. They are usually more organized.

Goodrich also points out that there are great differences in storage needs between ''pack rats,'' who must save everything and ''neat rats,'' who save only bare essentials. He also mentions that there are differences in the amounts of personalization of the workplace that individual office workers want.

Participation in office design is necessary to accommodate these differences in work styles.

The Real Expert

Thus we see that there is substantial dissatisfaction with the office environment and the workers' desire to participate in the design of it is also substantial. Dr. Arthur I. Rubin, of the National Bureau of Standards, says,

> A good fit between the user and the office systems requires detailed analysis of the job. The real expert on many tasks is frequently the job occupant. Potential benefits of involvement are: greater degree of commitment and cooperation as a result of participating in the change process and improvement in the quality of the design decisions because of the expertise of the users supplementing those of the other design team members. (1983)

Perhaps it is time to allow the ''real expert'' to be involved with the design of the workplace.

Dr. Peter Ellis has said,

> Is it possible that if we created the most perfect office facility in the world, we would still not satisfy the people who used it if they themselves had not been involved? . . . It is not the objective qualities only which matter, but the relations between these and the people who use them. Maybe what people are telling us when they express dissatisfaction with the environment is that they want to be *involved.* And the evidence is mounting that this is not just a luxury which is going to make people feel better, but that it makes for greater efficiency and effectiveness. (1986b)

Studies of Participatory Design

There are several studies in the United States, Canada, England, and France that show the success of participatory design.

Under the leadership of architect Sam Sloan, the author was one of four consultants who pioneered (on a fairly large scale) the participatory design process in the United States in 1972 for the Northwest Regional Offices of the Federal Aviation Administration (FAA) in Seattle. More than 350 office workers had told us what they wanted and needed, and though most of them did not believe it would happen, they got what they asked for.

Here's a quote from George T. Harris, former editor of *Psychology Today:*

> When a radical design group consulted Seattle white-collar workers about office furniture and layout for a new FAA building, morale and satisfaction soared. Compared with FAA workers in a fancier building in Los Angeles, Dr. Robert Sommer (another member of the radical design group) reports, the Seattle workers were significantly happier, more pleased with everything—from their jobs to the air conditioning system. (Harris 1977)

Every FAA office worker in the the Seattle building was offered a chance to participate in the design of his own space (and every worker accepted); each filled out a 15-page questionnaire and each was interviewed by a member of the design team. In contrast, at the new Los Angeles FAA Southwest Regional Offices, only 2 percent of the workforce said that they had participated actively in the design process there.

In Seattle, with 13 desks, 15 chairs, 100 fabric swatches, 6 credenzas, 10 telephone colors, and even 6 different in-and-out baskets to choose from, the power of selection was real and was exercised. These choices were not just the means of satisfying personal whims; by choosing the worker participated in the design of the individual workplace.

The participatory office design process was not repeated on a large scale in the United States until 1982, when 2,358 office employees of Union Carbide got the same privileges that the Seattle workers had had, as Dr. Duffy reported in the first chapter. There he also described the pioneering participatory design work of Herman Hertzberger at Centraal Beheer in Holland.

France From France comes a report of perhaps the most comprehensive known participatory office design project, the headquarters building for the Banque Populaire at Cahors.

To understand why this bank would choose to involve not only its staff but its customers, it should be pointed out that the bank is a cooperative owned by its customers, who are the only shareholders.

After the site and the architects were chosen, a first step in the process was to administer questionnaires to the staff. Questions covered not only working conditions (light, noise, temperature, ventilation, adequacy of furnishings, and so on) but also the organization and the way it worked by departments and as a whole. The results of the analysis of the questionnaires yielded the initial criteria for layout and furnishing.

The next step was to bring all interested people into the design process. Four study groups of between 15 and 20 people each were formed, one for employees, one for customer shareholders, one for local dignitaries, and one for management. The groups served under the direction of the architects, who were assisted in the process by communications consultants experienced in group dynamics.

Canada Donald V. Nightingale has published his findings from a thorough survey of 1,000 employees in 20 matched industrial organizations in Canada. Ten of the organizations were formally participative in decision making, and the other half made decisions in a conventional hierarchical way. Nightingale reported,

> Significant worker control over decision-making does lead to positive outcomes and this relationship is found when the nature of the work is controlled. In other words, attitudes can be improved even in organizations in which major task design is impossible. Apparently, uninspiring work can be tolerated if employees have the right to exercise influence over other areas of their work lives. (Nightingale 1981)

England Colin Cave, a partner in Duffy Eley Giffone Worthington (DEGW), has written about a study by the British Institute of Management of 300 of its subscriber companies with more than 1,000 employees, which concluded that consultation and employee participation had vastly increased in recent years. In all, 82 percent of the respondents had employee councils or committees; 77 percent said they used these groups for consultation (Cave 1981).

In England, Francis Duffy and Peter Ellis concluded a successful participatory design project for a warehouse for Unipart, the parts division of BL (formerly known as British Leyland), the British automaker. The entire workforce was brought into the design process, from top management down to shop floor workers. Frequently the designers were mediators when different opinions existed among the workers.

Satisfaction and Length of Participation

A 41-month study by Gere Picasso (1985), formerly Environmental Research Manager for AT&T Communications, shows that the longer employees participate in the office design process, the more satisfied they are.

One hundred thirty-five employees of an AT&T unit were moved from conventional offices to newly designed open-plan offices. The employees were given questionnaires on seven environmental issues: lighting, visual and acoustical privacy, perception of privacy, office layout, communications, and workplace satisfaction. Questionnaires were administered before the move, one month after, 14 months after, and 41 months after. The three questionnaires administered after the move constituted a very thorough post-occupancy evaluation (POE). One month before move-in, a 40-minute presentation was given to all employees moving to the new offices, telling them what to expect from their new office space and how they could control and adjust it.

Due to promotions and changes in employment during the 41-month period, a decreasing percentage of the employees participated in all of the questionnaires and the presentation.

The group that had participated in all of the questionnaires and the presentation showed higher satisfaction on six out of seven of the environmental issues than the others who had participated less.

Ms. Picasso puts it this way:

> Overwhelmingly, the personnel liked their environment, were proud of it and felt their status and work was supported by it. It is significant, however, how this changed from initial exposure to this type of environment.
>
> After being carefully educated and after having spent some time in the new environment, there was a marked increase, 15 per cent, in overall satisfaction. It should be noted, however, that this satisfaction level was achieved at a substantial budget reduction from previous company moves. Further, energy consumption was reduced through lower lighting levels and space utilization (density) was increased. So, in summary, more people were put in less space at lower first cost and lower long-term cost, with an *increase* in environmental satisfaction. (1985)

(In the next chapter, productivity increases for this project are reported.)

The Importance of Dialogue

The 1978 Steelcase study advocating office worker participation sums up the problem:

> There is, in effect, a collision course indicated here—too little consultation with office workers affected by change, too much avoidance of the privacy issue by office decision-makers, too little understanding by office workers of the reasons office decision-makers feel the open plan has important advantages over a conventional plan office, and too little dialog between office workers and office decision-makers about potential drawbacks.
>
> Increased employee participation in the office planning process would clearly go a long way toward alleviating the intensity of the collision. Unfortunately, unless employees come to feel truly involved in the decisions that most affect their office environment, this aspect of democracy in the workplace might become another "hot issue" over the next ten years, rather than a tool for solving a communications problem, with the stake being productivity in the workplace. (1978)

The communications problem was still there in late 1986 when the Steelcase survey (published in 1987) showed that only 50 percent of the executives feel it very important that management should encourage a free exchange of information among employees and departments, while 74 percent of office workers feel this way. Only 33 percent of office workers said that a free exchange was a reality in their jobs (Steelcase 1987).

The 1989 Office Environment Index (OEI) (Steelcase 1989) showed a marked drop in the percentage, from 69 to 55 percent, of office workers who say their organizations have standards programs that entitle them to "a certain type of workspace, furniture and accessories."

The OEI 1989 authors (Louis Harris Associates) comment that,

> The apparent decline of office standards—or at least the perception of them—may be related to attempts on the part of management to foster a "participatory" workplace by leveling some of the symbols of hierarchy. If this is the

> case, the "gaps" that persist between office workers' aspirations and the reality they face in participating fully in the organization suggest that a change in symbolism may not be enough. (Steelcase 1989)

As a "gap" example, only 51 percent of office workers say that they have "some choice of details of their workspace, furniture or accessories," while higher percentages of top executives (61 percent) and facilities managers (59 percent) say that they do (Steelcase 1989).

It was also found in OEI 1989 that nearly 7 in 10, 69 percent, of office workers surveyed felt it "very important" to have "the right kind of physical environment" in order "to do as much work as they reasonably can" (Steelcase 1989). This seems to be especially true for office workers in technical jobs (77 percent), unions (76 percent), and government jobs (73 percent).

OEI 1989 also reveals that top management and facilities managers tend to underestimate the value workers place on the office environment. A lesser 60 percent of top executives and 58 percent of facilities managers thought that workers would say this, with gaps of 9 and 11 percentage points, respectively.

CAOSSPP

Following its sponsorship of the studies by the American Productivity Center (Steelcase 1983), Steelcase established a Computer-Assisted Office Survey and Space Planning Program (CAOSSPP) that can be used by its dealers. The dealer gets a series of seven questionnaires for each project, four on the whole project attacking (1) the problems of project identification (and definition), (2) group needs, (3) relative closeness, and (4) the general analysis of Personal Workstations, plus three questionnaires totalling 43 pages for each workstation occupant. After the questionnaires are filled out, the dealer sends them to Steelcase for computer analysis. The printout is then sent back to the dealer so that it can be used for the design of individual workplaces (the printout even gives the exact number of square inches needed for each worksurface) and for the design of the office as a whole. The Steelcase design process for its dealers' use was derived from Steelcase's own procedures in planning its new corporate development center, which opened in 1989.

It is true that Herman Miller, a furniture and systems manufacturing competitor, and several large space-planning firms have had similar questionnaires and programs for years. When the largest office furniture manufacturer in the world goes into the questionnaire business, however, it is clear that participatory office design has arrived.

One of the three CAOSSPP questionnaires, *personal work areas* is reproduced in full in the Appendix, along with part of a prototype printout of information from the questionnaire.

The Computer Assisted Office Survey and Space Planning Program is one part of Steelcase's Environmental Support Services (E.S.S.) Program. The program provides a similar service for lighting visualization. The dealer fills out a "Lighting Visualization Analysis Request" form and provides a scaled floor plan as well as the graphic format he wants, with contour plots, transparencies, or prints. This material is processed on Steelcase's computer and the result is sent back to the dealer, who can then revise it if necessary and return it to find out the effects of the revisions.

The most important component of Environmental Support Services is the E.S.S. Design Program, a complete package of hardware and software for computer-aided interior design (see Chapter 7, Computer-Aided Office Design for a description). Steelcase has added a low-cost Workplace Audit to its battery of Environmental Support Services for evaluating the overall effectiveness of an office environment. Questionnaires are administered to employees and the answers are analyzed on a computer; specific recommendations can then be made.

We believe that the use of participatory design in offices has been held back because it cost so much to individually program each project that management frequently felt that the process was too expensive (and also too slow). Now, however, with the programs available such as those described above, the cost has come down and the process now can be accomplished much faster.

Quality Circles as an Office Design Tool

We have been talking about the process of initial planning or redesigning of offices. Maintaining participation in the handling of ongoing change is another vital aspect of the design process. For making necessary adjustments and changes on a continuing basis, a Quality Circle can be an excellent participatory design tool.

Essentially, a Quality Circle, as defined by the Quality Circle Institute (QCI), is

> a group of employees, performing similar work, who meet regularly to learn about basic Quality Circle techniques. They apply these techniques to identify problems within their jurisdiction, analyze these difficulties, and recommend solutions to management. When possible, they will initiate the necessary action to implement the solution. Normally, Circles will consist of three to twelve employees from the same work area. (Tate 1984)

Although they were first reported in Japan in 1961 as "Quality Control Circles," there is evidence that similar groups were in existence in the United States before then. An example is Phillips Petroleum's "66 Buzz Sessions." The ideas behind them draw heavily on the work of American psychologists Maslow, Herzberg, and Gordon as well as American management theorist Douglas McGregor.

It has been estimated that by 1983 there were 14 million workers in Japan involved in such groups and that there were 8,000 business and government locations in the United States where Quality Circles were in use by that time.

QCI's clients, which number more than 3,000, include some exceptionally well-known companies, such as Hewlett Packard; IBM; Campbell Soup; Motorola; USX; Control Data; Digital Equipment; NCR; Northern Telecom; Texas Instruments; Federal Express; AT&T; Martin Marietta; Eastman Kodak; the U.S. Air Force, Army, and Navy; Aetna Life & Casualty; General Electric; Westinghouse; and several airlines—including United, Pan Am, Eastern, American, Singapore, and Finnair.

Quality Circles are in use in firms of all sizes, even those with 20 or fewer employees. A recent survey of 1,618 U.S. companies by the American Management Association found that 36 percent of them are using Quality Circles to solve work problems.

An important reason for the success of Quality Circles is that they save money. Here are two examples:

1. Nashville Electric Service in Tennessee saved more than $250,000 when one of its employee groups recommended a simple recycling project for cable equipment and insulators.
2. A company in Alabama saved over $2,500,000 through a simple change in the assembly line—another result of a Circle recommendation. (Tate 1984)

While neither of these examples comes from an office Quality Circle, they nonetheless show how savings can occur.

How Do Quality Circles Come About?

Here's a quote from QCI:

> To implement Quality Circles there has to be a determined support by management, a belief in people, and a willingness to provide the training that has proven so essential. Every organization is made up of different people, with different problems. Think of Quality Circles, not as a ''cure-all,'' but as a unique tool with which to generate an atmosphere in which people solve their own problems. (Tate 1984)

Great emphasis is placed on participation. Groups should be small enough to give all the members a chance to participate fully. Seven or eight members is the ideal size. Membership must be voluntary; no one should be coerced or pressured into being a member, and anyone who wants to participate should be able to join.

A well-trained facilitator must be present in order to make sure that the group is productive. One of the authors has participated in several different kinds of brainstorming groups. A trained facilitator was absolutely necessary for them to function productively. Brainstorming is an essential part of the Quality Circle process.

Leaders and members also get training. A Quality Circle cannot be started on the spur of the moment but requires careful preparation and training to operate successfully.

Purposes of Quality Circles

According to QCI, Quality Circles

Reduce errors and enhance quality

Inspire more effective teamwork

Promote job involvement

Increase employee motivation

Create a problem-solving capability

Build an attitude of ''problem prevention''

Improve company communications

Develop harmonious manager/worker relationships

Promote personal and leadership development

Develop a greater safety awareness (Tate 1984)

Incidentally, we should dispel the notion that Quality Circles are only used for manufacturing operations; successful circles are operating in offices as well, notably at Westinghouse Electric in Pittsburgh. Their construction group has a successful office Quality Circle in that group's information and communication center. That circle, composed of secretaries, attacked the problem of how to train their bosses to dictate more efficiently (they recommended that their bosses organize better and speak more clearly). Martin Marietta also operates several successful office Quality Circles.

Banks are joining the Quality Circle parade as well. Citibank has at least 15 in New York and Republic Bank in Houston has at least 18. Other banks with Quality Circles include the Central Bank of Denver, Connecticut Savings Bank, Continental Bank of Chicago, First National Bank of Chicago, First Tennessee Bank, and Seattle First National Bank.

Quality Circles are turning up among city and state government workers. In Hayward, California police detectives set one up and a private area for interviews was the result. Utility workers in the same city also formed a circle that was able to produce better maintenance yard layouts. A Michigan state civil service circle simplified the process for reviewing job applicants, reducing a one-year backlog and clearing it within three months.

A quote from a circle member is noteworthy: ''The thing that I like most about Quality Circles is that the employee is considered the expert, and the owners are willing to listen to us explain the problem and the solution'' (Tate 1984).

The following chapter will examine increases in office productivity resulting from workers' participation in the design of their offices.

Chapter 23

Increased Productivity from Design

Productivity Increases through Participatory Design

Among interior design strategies that have yielded significant results in increasing productivity in the office, participatory design is probably the most important over all. Several examples of the successful use of this strategy are described below.

AT&T Communications

Ms. Gere Picasso, formerly Environmental Designer for AT&T Communications, designed new offices for sales representatives at AT&T's National Telemarketing Center in Kansas City, Missouri, using the participatory design process and involving every office employee. AT&T workers at the telemarketing center market products and services over the phone. A single sale of more than $100,000 is not uncommon for this operation.

The first step in the design process was a general survey of employees' physical needs in terms of space allocations, storage space, furniture, and other equipment. The second step was another survey, this time about job satisfaction, the accuracy of job descriptions, management support, and employee assessment of their own errors.

According to Picasso, "In addition to providing us with the input we would need to design a user-responsive environment," the two surveys were "virtually the first signal the employees received that someone did care that they were out there and that management was, in fact, concerned about their needs" (Picasso 1986).

The design of the new offices included moving them from a basement to the third floor of a new office building, increasing each workplace from 25 to 65 square feet, replacing single panels with three-sided and four-sided panel enclosures, and replacing furniture with adjustable chairs and VDT tables. Both task and ambient lighting were installed.

During the period covered by the surveys, salaries remained unchanged, but financial incentive awards were put in place. The results were remarkable:

1. The sale-closing rate went from one out of ten calls to seven out of ten calls.
2. A post-occupancy evaluation showed that the sales representatives had a much more positive outlook on their jobs, their environment, and themselves after they had worked in their new offices for seven and a half months.
3. Sales produced from this group went from $3.5 million per month before the move to more than double that amount, $7.1 million per month (an increase of 102.8 percent), after the move to the offices newly designed with employee input.

Because of the success of this program, it has been used in other AT&T locations, and Ms. Picasso has done similar design jobs for Wang, Holiday Inns, and The Bank of America.

TRW

According to Don Stuckle (1985) of TRW, a significant increase in productivity occurred when 39 software designers housed in a common bullpen office participated in the design of new private offices at TRW's Space Park facility in Redondo Beach, California. After 12 months, the designers reported that their productivity had increased 39 percent on the average; the range was 10 to 200 percent. They attributed the increase to the gain in privacy, better acoustics, more comfortable chairs, and advanced hardware, which they helped choose.

Merck

Carl Ruff (1985) has described another large participatory design project carried out for Merck & Company in Rahway, New Jersey. Merck hired Duffy, Incorporated of New York City, to guide the redesign of its present offices and develop guidelines for the design of future office spaces to handle the continuing advances in technology.

Duffy interviewed 27 senior Merck executives to identify important managerial issues; material gathered in these interviews formed the basis of a questionnaire that was sent to 2,000 workers, asking them, among other things, "to rate 29 specific workstation features on satisfaction and importance to them personally as well as to their job effectiveness" (Ruff 1985). The survey was conducted and the completed questionnaires were analyzed by a Rutgers University Graduate School MBA team. Of those sent questionnaires 72 percent responded.

According to Ruff, 98 percent of the respondents

> considered their personal workstation to have a significant influence on their overall attitude toward their work. In rank order, specific workstation features of most importance to the respondents were: lighting of the worksurface, ability to concentrate, suitability for work done, overall appearance, adequate HVAC, and the ability to adjust. (1985)

From the results of the survey, design guidelines were developed. Ruff reported,

> To date they have been used in three major renovation projects and for two major moves to leased buildings, involving more than 700 Merck office workers. The calculated return on investment for the projects undertaken thus far

> has been 25 percent or greater. The most extensive renovation undertaken included a complete conversion to a full range of advanced office functions for a group of 74 international office workers. For this project, the return on investment, which included the purchase of the advanced technology, was calculated to be over 50 percent. (1985)

Ruff stated that another result of this project was a reduction in average turnaround time from four days to six hours for more than 100,000 telexes handled by this group annually (1985).

Aetna

Participatory design has been a fact of office life for more than ten years at Aetna; cooperation between researchers and employees has been extensive and Carol Sullivan calls their offices a ''real-life research laboratory'' (Sullivan 1990).

Methods used have included work-in mockups (17,000 square feet of them) complete with furniture, carpet, lighting, power distribution, HVAC and window treatment options. Questionnaires and interviews (with both numerically scaled and open-ended questions) have yielded information about work, comfort, satisfaction with environmental elements, and the effect of these on productivity. Group discussions with employees have been held, and post-occupancy evaluations have also been conducted.

After employees were moved from bullpen spaces to panel system workstations with ergonomic chairs and task lights, productivity increased 66.9 percent. A reorganization also coincided with the move. Later, the increase in productivity leveled off at 53 percent. There were also significant increases in employee satisfaction with the environment (Sullivan 1990).

American Productivity Center Studies

The following are examples and quotations selected from studies done by the American Productivity Center and sponsored by Steelcase.

1. London Life, a company that insures more than 2 million Canadians, has its headquarters in London, Ontario. At a time when ''most of its offices within its 600,000 square feet of office space were arranged in typing pool fashion, with makeshift tables for terminals, homemade storage cabinets and inadequate distraction and noise control'' (Steelcase 1983a), London Life began a research project that lasted almost a year.

First, the company polled its employees to identify problems. ''The polls indicated that inadequate facilities and equipment were the most serious obstacles to productivity improvement.''

London Life then hired a designer to ask more questions, principally these two: (1) What do you need to do your job? (2) Whom do you need to be close to?

As a result of the questioning, the designer recommended that London Life purchase systems furniture, after a lengthy evaluation of furniture systems on the Canadian market.

The polls were continued throughout the process with these results:

> Productivity improvements have been accomplished through participative planning. As a result, little apprehension is expressed by employees, an accomplishment for a company that has undergone a major organizational change and staff reduction (2,100 to 1,500 through attrition) during the same period. Top management recently announced a corporate productivity increase of 10.6% last year. (Steelcase 1983a)

London Life before systems furniture. (Courtesy of Steelcase Inc.)

2. The following statement from Polaroid describes the value of employee participation in planning and design:

> The corporate culture at Polaroid has been a decisive factor in the shaping of office automation efforts and policy. Autonomous initiatives of individual and business units are highly valued. Top down directives tend to be incompatible with the corporate culture at Polaroid and when workers participate in planning they are more likely to accept the program. (Steelcase 1983a)

One example of hard dollars savings occurred in Polaroid's materials laboratory. The employees there suggested the purchasing of word-processing equipment; the company purchased the equipment. Before this was done, the laboratory had two professional people each earning $30,000 per year and six typists each earning an average of $16,667 per year for total salary costs of $160,000. After the new machines were installed, three professional people with annual salaries totalling $90,000 ($30,000 each) could now handle the workload that formerly required eight employees at a total annual salary of $160,000. Annual cost savings: $70,000.

3. Honeywell invited employee participation in the selection and configuration of office furniture systems to meet the challenge of increased computerization and reached the conclusion that "design of the system must be based on data from the user." A further comment is interesting:

> Introduction of technology into an office may be furthered by exposing the appropriate personalities. Management observed that their electronic systems were more readily accepted in offices where extroverted, "social" personnel used the systems first. Apparently such persons were more likely to discuss the technology over lunch, seek out new uses for the system, and encourage their colleagues to overcome basic fears. Where more reserved, introverted persons were the initial users, interest and development of applications were slow to evolve.

> Finally the branch managers experienced a favorable employee response to the open landscape concept. While some employees were potentially confronted with less privacy and more distraction, the majority responded favorably due to more professional appearing surroundings and greater personal space than was possible with conventional designs. (Steelcase 1983a)

While Honeywell has not measured exact productivity gains from these designs, spokesmen for the company believe that significant gains have been achieved.

4. The Southern Company is the second largest utility company in the United States and the largest investor-owned utility. In 1979 its Southern Company Services subsidiary started a program to increase productivity in its Engineering Division.

"To provide visibility, the Engineering, Productivity and Information Center (EPIC) was created. EPIC, a conference room with walls covered by graphic representations of engineering productivity measures, was built

London Life after systems furniture. (Courtesy of Steelcase Inc.)

specifically for this purpose. At one time 97 charts representing the progress of 193 productivity indicators were in use. Employees strive to improve their measures and many units within engineering post charts in their own office areas. A competitive spirit has developed as the EPIC concept is utilized, in microcosm, throughout the organization'' (Steelcase 1983a).

One example of the results is that ''labor savings of 3 to 1 have been realized over manual drafting with automated drafting equipment. Engineering has five complete automated drafting systems operating on three shifts producing 30 to 35% of their drawings'' (Steelcase 1983a).

The main theme running through all of these Steelcase-American Productivity Center case histories is: *Get full cooperation and participation from all employees. Find out what they need. Involve them in the productivity process.*

Productivity Increase from the Use of Headsets

Modern Office Technology (1984) has reported a research study performed by H. B. Maynard & Co., of El Segundo, California for Plantronics of Santa Cruz, California, a major supplier of telephone headsets.

In Maynard's observation of more than 2,000 telephone transactions, it was found that a worker using a telephone handset struck 113.4 keys per minute on a computer keyboard with only one free hand to work with. Using a headset, the rate increased to 200 strokes per minute using both hands, a gain of 43 percent in productivity.

The same research showed that replacing conventional handsets with headsets can:

Speed response to incoming telephone calls by 72%

Speed local call placement time by 48%

Speed long distance call placement by 40%

Speed order hand-up time by 59%

Improve overall efficiency by as much as 11% in typical office environments, given the individual improvements cited above. (*Modern Office Technology* 1984)

Productivity Increases from Panel System Installations

Westinghouse has released the results of a study performed by Human Factors/Industrial Design, at the offices of Blue Cross/Blue Shield in Detroit.

The workers studied were a group of 122 white collar workers involved mostly in repetitive paper tasks: claims processing, correspondence, and general clerical work. They were involved in changing from a bullpen office with no divider panels or partitions to a different office furnished with divider panels and other components of the Westinghouse Open Office System.

Another insurance company office before systems furniture. (Courtesy of Steelcase Inc.)

According to Westinghouse, "The goal of the study was to document any measurable changes in productivity that could be attributed to a change to Westinghouse Open Office System furnishings" (Brookes and Mitchell 1982).

Blue Cross/Blue Shield had developed sophisticated productivity rating procedures over the years for each type of job and for each employee.

The same insurance company after systems furniture showing the privacy of compact workstations. (Courtesy of Steelcase Inc.)

Still another insurance company office before. (Courtesy of Steelcase Inc.)

For the purposes of this study the results of these procedures for a period of eight months before the move were compared with results eight months after the move. The control group was a second cluster of workers performing similar tasks who did not move from their bullpen offices.

The group of workers who moved into offices furnished with Westinghouse's panel system furnishings showed an increase in productivity of 5.5 percent at a time when the national average increase in white collar productivity was estimated to be at 0.4 percent; comparatively there was no significant change in the productivity of the control group, who did not move during this period.

The value of the increase in productivity was calculated to be $979 per year per worker, based on an employee cost of $17,798 for salary, benefits, and payroll taxes paid per year. Dividing the workstation cost, $1,877, by the value of the improvement in productivity shows that the pay-back period for the cost of the new workstations was 23 months.

Steelcase has reported the results of a joint study by a major insurance company and The Alfred P. Sloan School of Management of MIT. This study was conducted when the insurance company replaced open bullpen arrangements of conventional desks and chairs in three departments with a panel system.

Ninety-four people worked in the space before the change; afterward it housed 124 people; the space per person shrank from 97.5 to 86.5 square feet. In spite of the shrinkage in square feet allocated to each workstation, a year after the panel system was installed the three departments had accomplished productivity increases of 5.8 percent, 12.6 percent, and 17.1 percent, an average of 11.83 percent.

Although the conditions of the Westinghouse- and Steelcase-sponsored studies were different, and although the panel systems involved were not the same, the number of workers involved in each study was almost identical, 122 and 124, samples large enough to enhance the validity of both studies.

Another study demonstrating productivity increases was conducted by the U.S. Army Corps of Engineers' Construction Engineering Research Laboratory at the Defense Logistic Agency's Defense Construction Supply Center in Columbus, Ohio. The study showed that the introduction of panel systems furniture was responsible for a 20.6 percent increase in a group of office workers' productivity when compared to two other groups, one using conventional steel furniture and the other working with improved conventional steel furniture. The increased productivity paid the costs back in 10.8 months (Francis and Dressel 1990).

Dr. T. J. Springer has written about a study done at Wells Fargo Bank in San Francisco. He said,

> A change from conventional furniture to open plan systems furniture resulted in a overall productivity increase of 15.4 percent two months after the installation of the new furniture. An additional 13 percent improvement, for a total of 28.4 percent, was reported in the subsequent month. (Springer, 1986)

This other insurance company after; managers are provided with 75-inch high panels. (Courtesy of Steelcase Inc.)

One reason for improved productivity from the use of panel systems may be improved acoustics, since Dr. Springer has reported several older studies showing good results from reducing noise levels.

On the basis of the studies reported above, it seems fair to say in this situation that we can look for productivity increases ranging from 5.5 percent to 28.4 percent when this change occurs. When the introduction of panel systems is combined with participatory design procedures, the increase in productivity can reach 66.9 percent.

Productivity Increases through Improved Lighting

Studies from the National Lighting Bureau show that improved lighting can also result in increased productivity in the office.

Stimulated by conditions of inadequate illumination and reflected glare on VDT screens and keyboards, the lighting system at Control Data Corporation's Sunnyvale, California Operations Group was redesigned. The result was a 6 percent increase in productivity and a 65 percent reduction in energy consumption. Over all, there was a simple payback period of 23 days.

The presence of reflected glare in a drafting room at Pennsylvania Power & Lighting Company in Allentown, Pennsylvania prompted the improvement of the lighting system. The changes brought an increase in productivity of 7.5 percent; operating and maintenance costs were reduced 76 percent. The costs of the project were paid back in 73 days.

When the lighting in the drafting area at Superior Die Set Corporation in Oak Creek, Wisconsin was revamped, increased productivity of more than 11 percent and reduced operating and maintenance costs together caused a simple payback period of project costs in less than 24 days (National Lighting Bureau 1988).

Productivity Increases from Adjustable Furniture

Solid evidence that computer terminal operators like adjustable furniture at the workstation came from studies done in Switzerland by Etienne Grandjean, M.D. and his colleagues at the Swiss Federal Ergonomic Laboratories. They first found a reduction in physical complaints when they offered adjustable worksurfaces and an increase in complaints when only fixed worksurfaces were used.

Physical complaints included headaches (perhaps from visual overload and fatigue); muscle, joint, and tendon pain (especially in the neck, back, and wrist); irritability; depression; anxiety; eye strain; and glare discomfort (Grandjean et al. 1982).

In a subsequent research project they found that, among other things

> 97% of the operators surveyed felt that a height-adjustable keyboard table was useful, 97% felt that a height-adjustable screen surface was useful, 97% felt that the screen distance should be adjustable and 92% felt that the inclination of the screen should be adjustable. (Grandjean et al. 1983)

In Bloomington, Illinois, Dr. T. J. Springer conducted a study in the offices of a major insurance company. He looked at workers using adjustable computer furniture and compared their output with workers using conventional, nonadjustable office furniture while both groups were doing the same tasks.

He found that

> Improvements in performance were observed for each of the alternative (adjustable) workstation designs when compared to the present company standard. The NKR and IBM workstations resulted in a 15% improvement in data entry performance and 10% improvement in interactive dialog transactions.
>
> Employees showed a strong preference for the NKR, IBM and Gutmann workstations on the basis of comfort, ease of adjustment, space and adequacy with which job needs were met. (Springer 1982)

The two most important benefits the employees liked were the increased comfort and the ability to adjust the furniture themselves. The specific features they appreciated were the height adjustability of the screen, keyboard, and writing surfaces. (These workstations were equipped with the auxiliary writing surfaces we mentioned earlier.) The features of the seating that they liked were the seat height, back height, and back tilt adjustments as well as the ability to turn while seated.

Increased productivity as a result of Dr. Springer's work paid back the increased cost of the adjustable furniture in 22 weeks for data entry tasks and in 36 weeks for dialog tasks.

In Cincinnati, Ohio, Dr. Marvin J. Dainoff, formerly of the National Institute for Occupational Safety and Health (NIOSH), and his associates conducted a similar study:

> An experimental simulation of a VDT entry task was conducted during five 3-hour sessions in which subjects worked under ergonomic conditions alternating between good and poor features as defined by adjustments of working and seating surfaces, lighting and glare. Performance measures were taken during each session and a battery of psychophysical/physiological measures and subjective complaints were taken before and after each work session. Preliminary results indicate a 24.5% improvement in performance as well as a decrease in musculoskeletal complaints attributed to good ergonomic design characteristics. (Dainoff et al. 1982)

IBM and Wrightline workstations were used together with ergonomically designed lighting and glare reduction equipment to produce the total result. Dr. Dainoff and his colleagues performed a second study almost identical to the one above; this second study showed a productivity increase of 17.5 percent.

IBM, NKR (Swedish), Gutmann, and Wrightline split-top, adjustable terminal tables as well as Comforto and Gutmann chairs were used in these studies and were specifically commended by the subjects. There are now at least two dozen companies that manufacture similar adjustable, split-top terminal tables with varying capabilities. About two dozen manufacturers make reasonably adjustable chairs. Use the criteria in Chapter 18 to check chairs out and use Chapter 8 for worksurfaces; then look at the prices in terms of the features you want for each.

Another productivity study was performed by C. N. Ong (1984) of the Department of Social Medicine and Public Health at the University of Singapore. The study shows that a 37.15 percent increase in productivity and a 92.8 percent reduction in errors occurred among 36 female data-entry op-

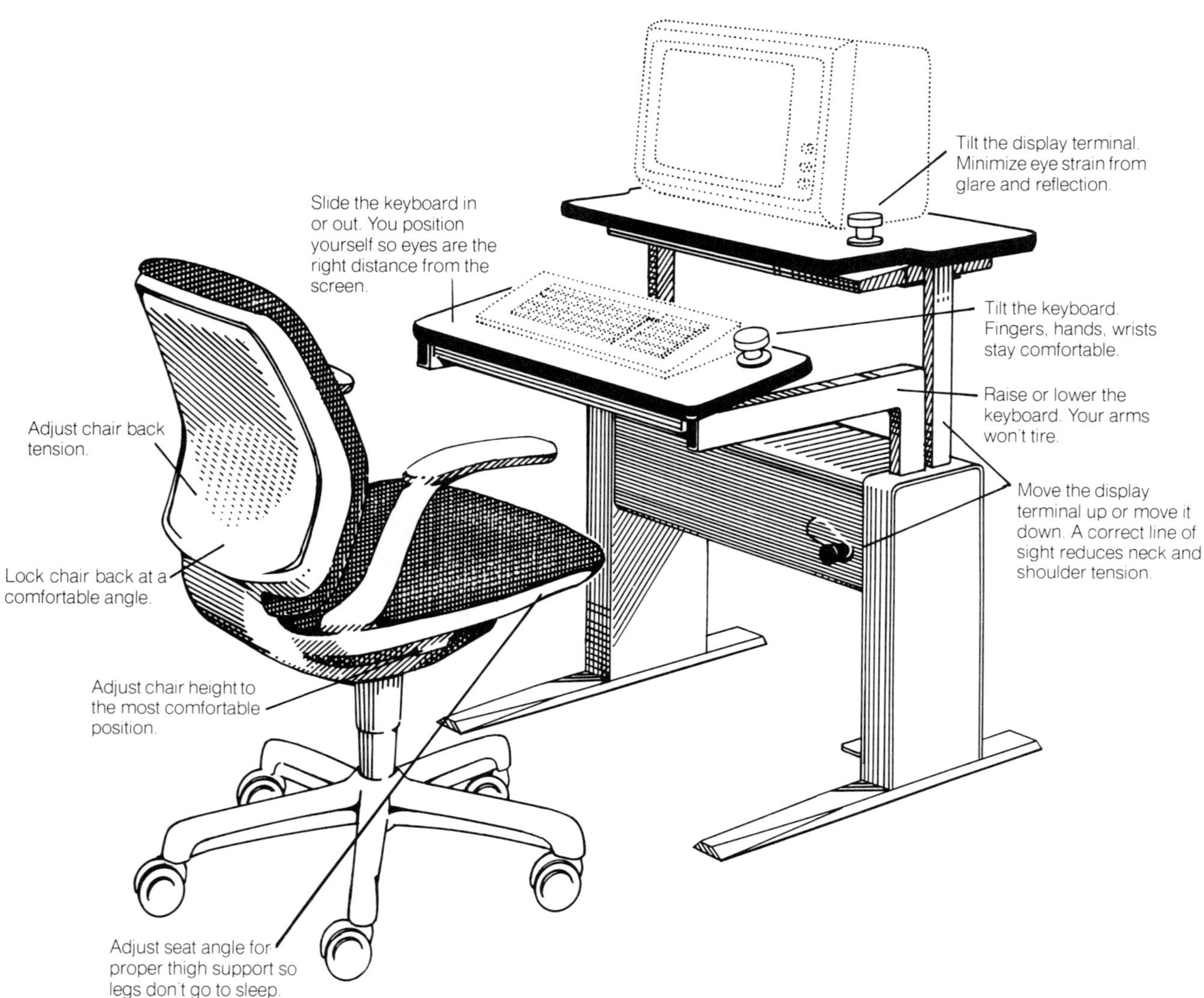

This fully adjustable chair and fully adjustable split-top computer terminal table are the type of furniture used in the Dainoff and Springer productivity studies. (Courtesy of Steelcase Inc.)

erators over a period of 12 months after their Singapore Airlines computer center work area had been redesigned and their "work-rest regime revised." The report of the study says that "A better environment led to significantly less visual and muscular complaints (Ong 1984). Dr. Ong reports that adjustable chairs were used.

Since the workers were given a comprehensive questionnaire to answer before the redesign, participatory design was a factor here. The questionnaire answers identified possible causes for the "high prevalence of subjective symptoms" such as the "illumination level, improper working posture, badly designed tables and chairs and insufficient rest pauses" (Ong 1984).

Dr. Ong points out that since the operators in Singapore are smaller in size than Western workers, furniture designed for the larger Western people did not fit and was a major cause of physical complaints in Singapore, according to the information obtained from the questionnaires (Ong 1984).

Determining the Pay-Back Period

From the American studies above comparing the performance of operators using adjustable furniture with the performance of operators using conventional nonadjustable furniture, we find a range of increases in productivity from 10 to 24.5 percent, with an average increase of 16.75 percent.

Fully adjustable auxiliary surfaces and an adjustable document holder attached to the computer terminal table. (Courtesy of Watson Furniture Systems.)

The cost of a good adjustable chair should be about $250, and a good split-top adjustable table should cost about $475, for a total of $725. These prices could be reduced if large quantities are bought. We assume good lighting.

Using the 24.5 percent increase in productivity, the value of the productivity increase for a terminal operator who receives $12,000 per year in earnings and benefits is $2,940. The workstation pays for itself in a little over three months.

At the $15,000 level the value of the increase is $3,675 and the payoff period is 2⅓ months. At $18,000 the value is $4,410 and the time goes down to less than 2 months. (A survey by the Administrative Management Society (AMS) showed in 1989 that lower level data-processing employees averaged $19,167 per year.)

At the $21,000 level the figures change to $5,145 and less than 1⅔ months. When employees reach the $24,000 level the value is $5,880 and the time required to pay for the workstation furniture is less than 1.5 months. (The 1989 AMS survey mentioned above pegged lead computer operators' salaries at an average of $23,900 per year.)

At $30,000 the dollar figure becomes $7,350 and the time goes down to less than 5 weeks. When the salary and benefits reach $36,000 the increased productivity is worth $8,820 and the workstation furniture is paid for in less than one month.

At the 16.75 percent level of productivity increase, the figures look like this:

Salary Level	Value of Increase	Time to Pay for Furniture
$12,000	$2,010	A little more than 4 months
$15,000	$2,512.50	3.5 months
$18,000	$3,015	Less than 3 months
$21,000	$3,517.50	2.5 months
$24,000	$4,020	A little more than 2 months
$30,000	$5,025	1⅔ months
$36,000	$6,030	Less than 1.5 months

Even if the productivity increase is as little as 10 percent, the figures still look attractive:

Salary Level	Value of Increase	Time to Pay for Furniture
$12,000	$1,200	A little more than 7 months
$15,000	$1,500	A little less than 6 months
$18,000	$1,800	A little less than 5 months
$21,000	$2,100	A little more than 4 months
$24,000	$2,400	A little less than 4 months
$30,000	$3,000	A little less than 3 months
$36,000	$3,600	Less than 2.5 months

To sum up, adjustable workstation furniture not only means more comfort and less physical complaints but also, after paying for itself quickly, continues to show a profit as the increased productivity continues. Obviously, these effects are heightened as the salary of the individual concerned rises.

Synergistic Productivity Gains

The stakes in raising productivity levels are huge. According to AT&T Communications, for the United States, wages and related costs for the office stood at $600 billion in 1981 and by 1989 were estimated to have risen to $1.5 trillion. Each one percent gain would save about $6 billion at the 1981 level and that same one percent value rises to $15 billion at the estimated 1989 level.

Adding up the productivity gains from the studies above, we now have:

From participatory design—from 10.6 to 102.8 percent

From adjustable furniture—10 to 37.15 percent

From the introduction of panel systems—5.5 to 17.1 percent

From the improvement of lighting systems—6 to 11 percent

From the introduction of headsets substituting for handsets—11 percent

It would be misleading simply to add the higher numbers up and say that office productivity can be increased up to X percent. For one thing, all offices don't have telephone situations where it would be necessary to substitute headsets for handsets. Also, and more important, the studies above were conducted in different situations by different investigators. For another thing, we do not know how these changes work together or how synergy (several factors acting at the same time in the same place) works in the office situation. For instance, if we add the London Life increases previously mentioned to the other three strategies above, our total is increased, but we cannot know how much of that series of increases is due to employee participation or how much of it could be attributed to the new furniture they bought.

The studies mentioned above with their definite percentages of gains are the only ones that we have found that we believe were rigorously conducted. In addition to these studies, however, there is a body of conventional wisdom indicating that the synergistic effect of several strategies working together produces far greater productivity gains.

Here is a group of statements that we found interesting:

1. An unnamed Citibank spokesman has said that the company's 1981 office automation program has resulted in "better customer relations, 50% better productivity and a 40% reduction in staff."

2. Three cases described in this chapter, London Life, Honeywell, and Polaroid, indicate that participatory design can produce largely unmeasured productivity gains. It is also significant that like Citibank, each organization reduced staff while increasing productivity.

3. Computer companies' salespeople are claiming that the use of their computers alone can increase productivity from 50 to 500 percent. A result in this range occurred at Travelers' Insurance's Constitution State Management Company subsidiary when just the addition and use of personal computers increased the amount of premiums analyzed from $7 million to $34 million per year without adding any people to the payroll.

4. There are two statements from the British CALUS study (1983) that speak to the points above:

A quote from an unnamed U.S. bank: "We didn't let anybody go.

Automation has enabled us to do more, to increase productivity, to offer more and better services to customers.'' From an insurance firm: ''Sixteen years ago the combined staff of the group was 13,000; now with double the business it is 8,000'' (College of Estate Management 1983).

The authors believe that increases in productivity are just beginning and that there is much more to increasing productivity than the examples in this book. While the studies mostly identify effective individual strategies, we await further detailed studies using more than one of them in the same place at the same time, as in the examples from AT&T Communications and Aetna.

First Steelcase Questionnaire for the Personal Work Area

About You and Your Job

Before you continue with this section, please make sure your Department/Employee Identification Number is entered on the following answer sheet.

Please fill in the oval on the answer sheet that has the letter that corresponds with your choice. Use the No. 2 lead pencil provided to fill in the ovals. Do not mark outside the ovals.

1 Do you have any special physical needs *(such as disabilities; special size or weight; allergies to smoke or fabrics)* which might influence the design of your personal work area?

A Yes **B** No

If yes, please explain this need in Question No. 53 at the end of this questionnaire.

2 Do you have to talk or communicate frequently with people that sit near you?

A Yes **B** No

3 Do you have business discussions in your personal work area that should not be overheard by other people *(confidential phone calls, personal interviews, etc.)*?

A Yes **B** No

Please describe these types of discussions in Question No. 54 at the end of this questionnaire.

4 If yes, please indicate the number of hours spent per week in these confidential business discussions:

Hours per week: **A** 1-4 **B** 5-10 **C** 11-20 **D** More

About You and Your Job (continued)

5 If you work on confidential items which should not be seen by other people, please indicate the items and the hours per week that you work on them:

	Item	Hours per week 1-4	5-10	11-20	More
.1	None	0			
.2	CRT/VDT Screen	A	B	C	D
.3	Paper Materials (such as budgets, salary data, or personnel records)	A	B	C	D
.4	Flip Charts or Marker Boards	A	B	C	D
.5	Other*	A	B	C	D

**(Please describe in Question No. 55 at the end of this questionnaire.)*

6 Is your personal work area used by people on other work shifts?

A Yes **B** No

7 How many years have you been with the company?

A Less than 1 yr. **B** 1-2 yrs. **C** 3-5 yrs. **D** 6-10 yrs. **E** More

8 How many years have you been at your present job?

A Less than 1 yr. **B** 1-2 yrs. **C** 3-5 yrs. **D** 6-10 yrs. **E** More

Activities

The activities you perform as part of your job are a key factor in the design of your workplace.

Listed on the right are general classifications of activities you may perform in your personal work area. Please read through the definitions carefully.

- *Select the three key activities that are most important in your job.*
- *Turn to the pages indicated to answer the questions pertaining to those activities.*
- *Identify the equipment you use during those activities in the Equipment section on page 27.*

Written Entry/Completing Forms (page 11)
An activity that requires you to write or fill in printed forms, such as phone messages, bills, receipts, and invoices. These items may be numbered, stamped, or processed in a way that requires little time with each piece of paper.

Writing Text (page 13)
This includes writing memos or other communications such as reports and letters.

Drawing/Drafting (page 15)
This includes creating engineering drawings, sketches, charts, artwork, or similar activities.

Using the Telephone (page 17)
Here the reference is to telephoning as a major task, requiring you to spend a *large* amount of time on the phone for business purposes. Examples: transferring calls, taking orders, placing orders, conversations.

Machine Operation (page 19)
This means operating one or more machines as a major activity. This would include: typing, CRT/VDT operation, calculating. (Do not include times when you use a machine outside your personal work area.)

Reading Written Materials (page 21)
This means reading or scanning written materials to gain information, determine action or to handle incoming mail or work. Examples: books, magazines, mail, manuals.

Meetings and Group Activities (page 23)
This means any activity with another person, or persons, *within your personal work area.* Includes: discussions, presentations, interviews, performance reviews.

Sorting, Filing, Handling Materials (page 25)
Includes putting files away, arranging items into proper order or piles, removing staples and separating materials, but excludes writing, e.g.: batching, sorting, filing, stamping.

Illustrations for Question 10

(A) Stacked **(B)** Side-by-Side **(C)** Overlapped

Written Entry/Completing Forms

9 An activity that requires you to write or fill in printed forms, such as phone messages, bills, receipts, and invoices. These items may be numbered, stamped, or processed in a way that requires little time with each piece of paper.

Hours per week: **A** 1-4 **B** 5-10 **C** 11-20 **D** More

10 Picture the materials you need on your desk during this activity. Please indicate the quantities used at one time and whether the items are used in stacks, side-by-side or overlapped (see illustrations at left). *If an item is not used, leave blank.*

	Items	Quantity Needed and How Used
.1	None	**0**
.2	Forms, Memos, Mail, Note Paper	**1 2 3 4** or more **A** Stacked **B** Side-by-Side **C** Overlapped
.3	Computer Printouts/Plots	**1 2 3 4** or more **A** Stacked **B** Side-by-Side **C** Overlapped
.4	Cards, Checks, Envelopes	**1 2 3 4** or more **A** Stacked **B** Side-by-Side **C** Overlapped
.5	File Folders, Books, Binders, Magazines	**1 2 3 4** or more **A** Stacked **B** Side-by-Side **C** Overlapped
.6	Drawings, Blueprints, Artwork	**1 2 3 4** or more **A** Stacked **B** Side-by-Side **C** Overlapped
.7	Other	**1 2 3 4** or more **A** Stacked **B** Side-by-Side **C** Overlapped

Illustrations for Question 12

(A) Stacked **(B)** Side-by-Side **(C)** Overlapped

Writing Text

11 This includes writing memos or other communications such as reports, letters.
Hours per week: **A** 1-4 **B** 5-10 **C** 11-20 **D** More

12 Picture the materials you need on your desk during this activity. Please indicate the quantities used at one time and whether the items are used in stacks, side-by-side or overlapped (see illustrations at left). *If an item is not used, leave blank.*

	Items	Quantity Needed and How Used
.1	None	**0**
.2	Forms, Memos, Mail, Note Paper	**1 2 3 4** or more **A** Stacked **B** Side-by-Side **C** Overlapped
.3	Computer Printouts/Plots	**1 2 3 4** or more **A** Stacked **B** Side-by-Side **C** Overlapped
.4	Cards, Checks, Envelopes	**1 2 3 4** or more **A** Stacked **B** Side-by-Side **C** Overlapped
.5	File Folders, Books, Binders, Magazines	**1 2 3 4** or more **A** Stacked **B** Side-by-Side **C** Overlapped
.6	Drawings, Blueprints, Artwork	**1 2 3 4** or more **A** Stacked **B** Side-by-Side **C** Overlapped
.7	Other	**1 2 3 4** or more **A** Stacked **B** Side-by-Side **C** Overlapped

Drawing/Drafting

13 This includes creating engineering drawings, sketches, charts, artwork, or similar activities.

Hours per week: **A** 1-4 **B** 5-10 **C** 11-20 **D** More

14 Picture the materials you need on your desk, not your drafting board, during this activity. Please indicate the quantities used at one time and whether the items are used in stacks, side-by-side or overlapped (see illustrations at left). *If an item is not used, leave blank.*

Illustrations for Question 14

(A) Stacked **(B)** Side-by-Side **(C)** Overlapped

	Items	Quantity Needed and How Used
.1	None	**0**
.2	Forms, Memos, Mail, Note Paper	**1 2 3 4** or more **A** Stacked **B** Side-by-Side **C** Overlapped
.3	Computer Printouts/Plots	**1 2 3 4** or more **A** Stacked **B** Side-by-Side **C** Overlapped
.4	Cards, Checks, Envelopes	**1 2 3 4** or more **A** Stacked **B** Side-by-Side **C** Overlapped
.5	File Folders, Books, Binders, Magazines	**1 2 3 4** or more **A** Stacked **B** Side-by-Side **C** Overlapped
.6	Drawings, Blueprints, Artwork	**1 2 3 4** or more **A** Stacked **B** Side-by-Side **C** Overlapped
.7	Other	**1 2 3 4** or more **A** Stacked **B** Side-by-Side **C** Overlapped

Before you continue with this section, please make sure your Department/Employee Identification Number is entered on the following answer sheet.

Illustrations for Question 16

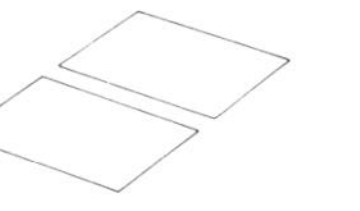

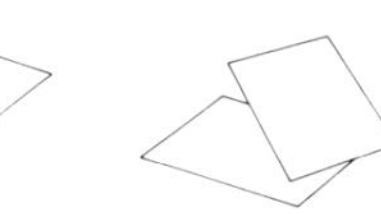

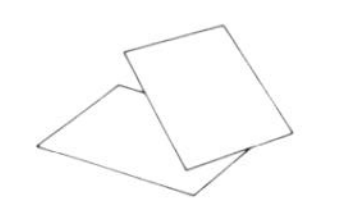

(A) Stacked **(B)** Side-by-Side **(C)** Overlapped

Using the Telephone

15 Here the reference is to telephoning as a major task, requiring you to spend a *large* amount of time on the phone for business purposes. Examples: transferring calls, taking orders, placing orders, conversations.
Hours per week: **A** 1-4 **B** 5-10 **C** 11-20 **D** More

16 Picture the materials you need on your desk during this activity. Please indicate the quantities used at one time and whether the items are used in stacks, side-by-side or overlapped (see illustrations at left). *If an item is not used, leave blank.*

	Items	Quantity Needed and How Used
.1	None	**0**
.2	Forms, Memos, Mail, Note Paper	**1 2 3 4** or more **A** Stacked **B** Side-by-Side **C** Overlapped
.3	Computer Printouts/Plots	**1 2 3 4** or more **A** Stacked **B** Side-by-Side **C** Overlapped
.4	Cards, Checks, Envelopes	**1 2 3 4** or more **A** Stacked **B** Side-by-Side **C** Overlapped
.5	File Folders, Books, Binders, Magazines	**1 2 3 4** or more **A** Stacked **B** Side-by-Side **C** Overlapped
.6	Drawings, Blueprints, Artwork	**1 2 3 4** or more **A** Stacked **B** Side-by-Side **C** Overlapped
.7	Other	**1 2 3 4** or more **A** Stacked **B** Side-by-Side **C** Overlapped

Illustrations for Question 18

(A) Stacked

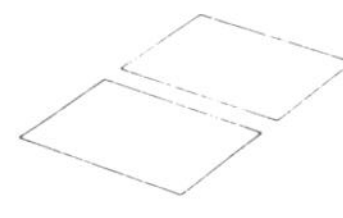

(B) Side-by-Side

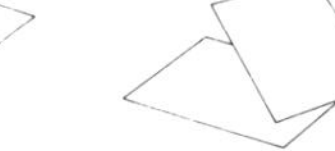

(C) Overlapped

Machine Operation

17 This means operating one or more machines as a major activity. This would include typing, CRT/VDT operation, calculating. Do not include times when you use a machine outside of your personal work area.

Hours per week: **A** 1-4 **B** 5-10 **C** 11-20 **D** More

18 Picture the materials you need on your desk during this activity. Please indicate the quantities used at one time and whether the items are used in stacks, side-by-side or overlapped (see illustrations at left). *If an item is not used, leave blank.*

	Items	Quantity Needed and How Used
.1	None	**0**
.2	Forms, Memos, Mail, Note Paper	**1 2 3 4** or more **A** Stacked **B** Side-by-Side **C** Overlapped
.3	Computer Printouts/Plots	**1 2 3 4** or more **A** Stacked **B** Side-by-Side **C** Overlapped
.4	Cards, Checks, Envelopes	**1 2 3 4** or more **A** Stacked **B** Side-by-Side **C** Overlapped
.5	File Folders, Books, Binders, Magazines	**1 2 3 4** or more **A** Stacked **B** Side-by-Side **C** Overlapped
.6	Drawings, Blueprints, Artwork	**1 2 3 4** or more **A** Stacked **B** Side-by-Side **C** Overlapped
.7	Other	**1 2 3 4** or more **A** Stacked **B** Side-by-Side **C** Overlapped

Illustrations for Question 20

(A) Stacked **(B)** Side-by-Side **(C)** Overlapped

Reading Written Materials

19 This means reading or scanning written materials to gain information, determine action, or to handle incoming mail or work. Examples: books, magazines, mail, manuals.
Hours per week: **A** 1-4 **B** 5-10 **C** 11-20 **D** More

20 Picture the materials you need on your desk during this activity. Please indicate the quantities used at one time and whether the items are used in stacks, side-by-side or overlapped (see illustrations at left). *If an item is not used, leave blank.*

	Items	Quantity Needed and How Used
.1	None	**0**
.2	Forms, Memos, Mail, Note Paper	**1 2 3 4** or more **A** Stacked **B** Side-by-Side **C** Overlapped
.3	Computer Printouts/Plots	**1 2 3 4** or more **A** Stacked **B** Side-by-Side **C** Overlapped
.4	Cards, Checks, Envelopes	**1 2 3 4** or more **A** Stacked **B** Side-by-Side **C** Overlapped
.5	File Folders, Books, Binders, Magazines	**1 2 3 4** or more **A** Stacked **B** Side-by-Side **C** Overlapped
.6	Drawings, Blueprints, Artwork	**1 2 3 4** or more **A** Stacked **B** Side-by-Side **C** Overlapped
.7	Other	**1 2 3 4** or more **A** Stacked **B** Side-by-Side **C** Overlapped

Illustrations for Question 22

(A) Stacked **(B)** Side-by-Side **(C)** Overlapped

Meetings and Group Activities

21 This means any activity with another person or persons, *within your personal work area.* Includes discussions, presentations, performance reviews, interviews.
Hours per week: **A** 1-4 **B** 5-10 **C** 11-20 **D** More

22 Picture the materials you need on your desk during this activity. Please indicate the quantities used at one time and whether the items are used in stacks, side-by-side or overlapped (see illustrations at left.) *If an item is not used, leave blank.*

	Items	Quantity Needed and How Used
.1	None	**0**
.2	Forms, Memos, Mail, Note Paper	**1 2 3 4** or more **A** Stacked **B** Side-by-Side **C** Overlapped
.3	Computer Printouts/Plots	**1 2 3 4** or more **A** Stacked **B** Side-by-Side **C** Overlapped
.4	Cards, Checks, Envelopes	**1 2 3 4** or more **A** Stacked **B** Side-by-Side **C** Overlapped
.5	File Folders, Books, Binders, Magazines	**1 2 3 4** or more **A** Stacked **B** Side-by-Side **C** Overlapped
.6	Drawings, Blueprints, Artwork	**1 2 3 4** or more **A** Stacked **B** Side-by-Side **C** Overlapped
.7	Other	**1 2 3 4** or more **A** Stacked **B** Side-by-Side **C** Overlapped

Illustrations for Question 24

(A) Stacked

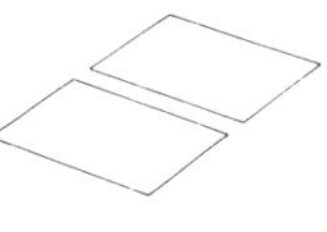

(B) Side-by-Side

(C) Overlapped

Sorting, Filing, Handling Materials

23 Includes putting files away, arranging items into proper order or piles, removing staples and separating materials, but excluding writing. Examples: batching, sorting, filing, stamping.

Hours per week: **A** 1-4 **B** 5-10 **C** 11-20 **D** More

24 Picture the materials you need on your desk during this activity. Please indicate the quantities used at one time and whether the items are used in stacks, side-by-side or overlapped (see illustrations at left). *If an item is not used, leave blank.*

	Items	Quantity Needed and How Used
.1	None	**0**
.2	Forms, Memos, Mail, Note Paper	**1-2** **3-4** **5-6** **7** or more **A** Stacked **B** Side-by-Side **C** Overlapped
.3	Computer Printouts/Plots	**1-2** **3-4** **5-6** **7** or more **A** Stacked **B** Side-by-Side **C** Overlapped
.4	Cards, Checks, Envelopes	**1-2** **3-4** **5-6** **7** or more **A** Stacked **B** Side-by-Side **C** Overlapped
.5	File Folders, Books, Binders, Magazines	**1-2** **3-4** **5-6** **7** or more **A** Stacked **B** Side-by-Side **C** Overlapped
.6	Drawings, Blueprints, Artwork	**1-2** **3-4** **5-6** **7** or more **A** Stacked **B** Side-by-Side **C** Overlapped
.7	Other	**1-2** **3-4** **5-6** **7** or more **A** Stacked **B** Side-by-Side **C** Overlapped

Equipment

Before you continue with this section, please make sure your Department/Employee Identification Number is entered on the following answer sheet.

25 For the machines/equipment you require in your personal work area, please indicate the following information about its use:

- The number of hours per week you use the machines/equipment.
- Whether the machines/equipment you use are shared with *one* other person. Indicate with whom you share your equipment in Question No. 56 in the back of the questionnaire. (Do not include departmental equipment shared by 3 or more people.)

If a piece of equipment is not used, leave blank.

	Items	Hours per Week Used				Mark if Item is Shared
		1-4	5-10	11-20	More	
.1	None	0				
.2	Manual Typewriter	A	B	C	D	E
.3	Electric Typewriter	A	B	C	D	E
.4	Personal Computer	A	B	C	D	E
.5	VDT/CRT	A	B	C	D	E
	Detached Keyboard	A Yes		B No		
.6	Processing or Memory Device	A	B	C	D	E
.7	Printer/Plotter	A	B	C	D	E
.8	Dictator/Transcriber	A	B	C	D	E
.9	Calculator	A	B	C	D	E
.10	Microfilm/Fiche Viewer	A	B	C	D	E
.11	Telephone	A	B	C	D	E
.12	Drawing/Drafting Board	A	B	C	D	E
.13	Electric Stapler	A	B	C	D	E
.14	Automatic Time/Date Stamp	A	B	C	D	E
.15	Other*	A	B	C	D	E

(Please describe in Question No. 57 at the end of this questionnaire.)

On and Around Your Desk

Before you continue with this section, please make sure your Department/Employee Identification Number is entered on the following answer sheet.

26 Please indicate which of the following *accessory* items you keep on your work surface:

A In/Out Trays **B** Stapler **C** Calendar or Appointment Book
D Tape Dispenser **E** Rolodex **F** Other

27 Do you require a space to put some or most of these items away at night?

A Yes **B** No

28 Please indicate the number of hours per week that you spend with visitors who come into your personal work area for five minutes or more:

	No. of Visitors at One Time	Hours per Week				
		0-1	2-3	4-10	11-20	More
.1	One	**A**	**B**	**C**	**D**	**E**
.2	Two	**A**	**B**	**C**	**D**	**E**
.3	Three	**A**	**B**	**C**	**D**	**E**

Storage/Filing

The facts you give here describe the amount of storage space you need. Please indicate the total number of inches of materials which you should store in your personal work area. Indicate only those materials you presently need to store.

- *Do not make entries for items you do not store.*
- *Do not include materials that are shared by others.*
- *Do not include what you may expect to store in the future.*

Carefully measure the contents as shown using the measuring tape.

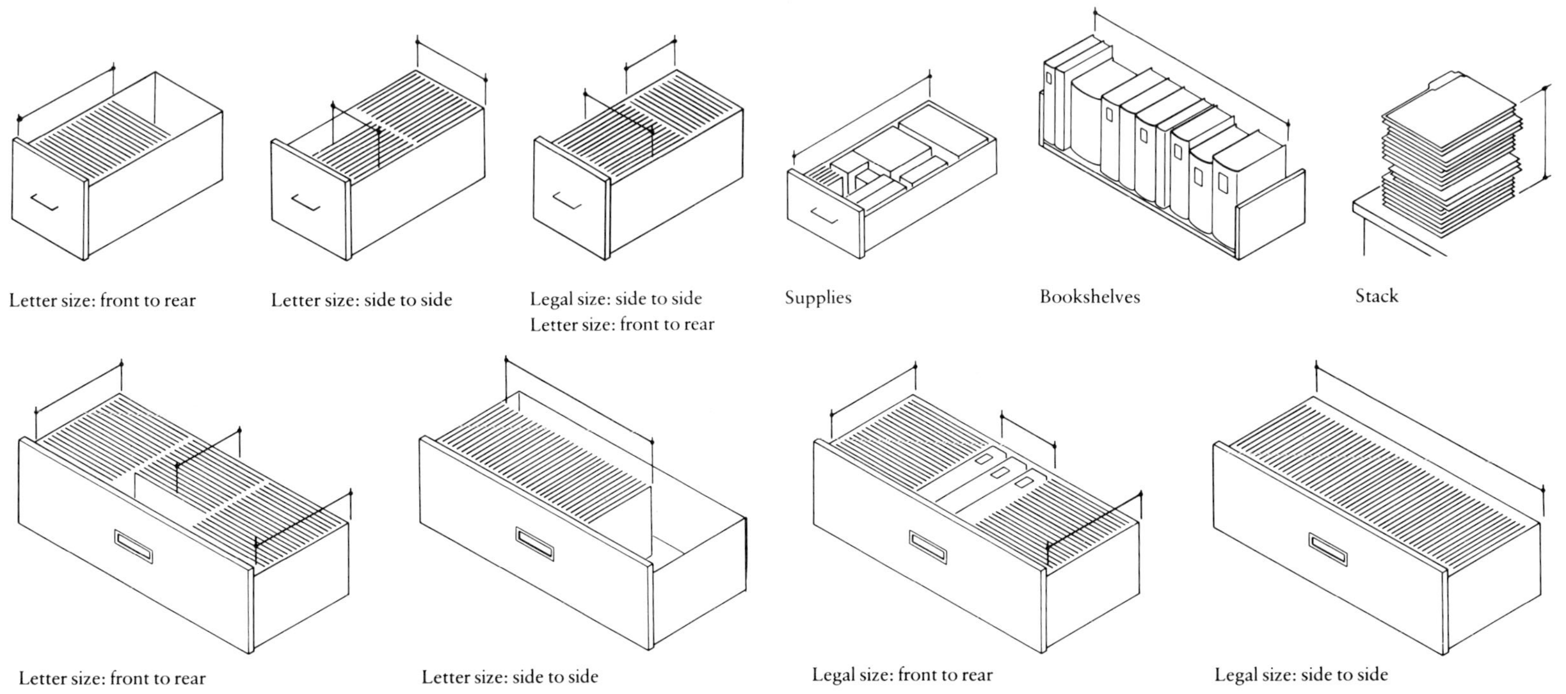

Storage/Filing (continued)

Do not include materials that are shared by others.

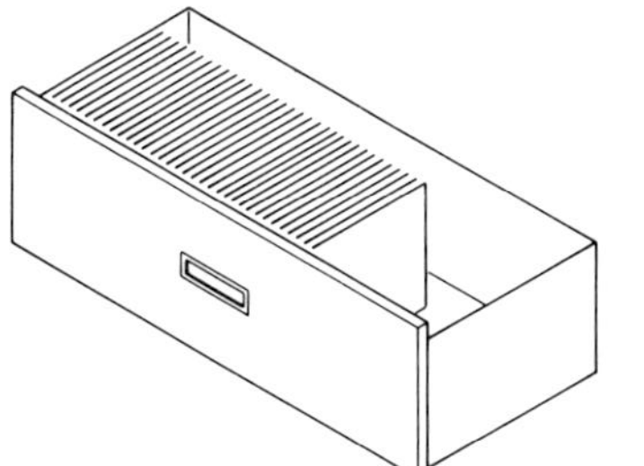

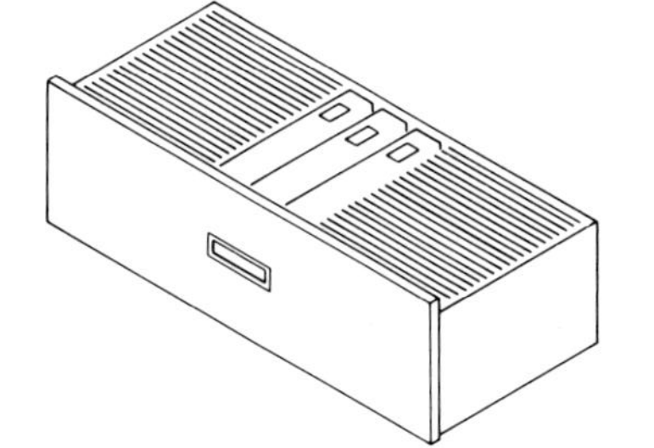

Files and Printouts

29 Letter size files (8½″ x 11″)

A 1″-15″ **B** 16″-30″ **C** 31″-45″ **D** 46″-60″ **E** 61″-75″
F 76″-90″ **G** 91″-105″ **H** 106″-120″ **I** More

30 Legal size files (8½″ x 14″)

A 1″-15″ **B** 16″-30″ **C** 31″-45″ **D** 46″-60″ **E** 61″-75″
F 76″-90″ **G** 91″-105″ **H** 106″-120″ **I** More

31 Computer printouts (14⅞″ x 8½″ paper size)

A 1″-15″ **B** 16″-30″ **C** 31″-45″ **D** 46″-60″ **E** 61″-75″
F 76″-90″ **G** 91″-105″ **H** 106″-120″ **I** More

32 Computer printouts (14⅞″ x 11″ paper size)

A 1″-15″ **B** 16″-30″ **C** 31″-45″ **D** 46″-60″ **E** 61″-75″
F 76″-90″ **G** 91″-105″ **H** 106″-120″ **I** More

33 Computer printouts (9½″ x 11″ paper size)

A 1″-15″ **B** 16″-30″ **C** 31″-45″ **D** 46″-60″ **E** 61″-75″
F 76″-90″ **G** 91″-105″ **H** 106″-120″ **I** More

Storage/Filing (continued)

Do not include materials that are shared by others.

Bulk Storage

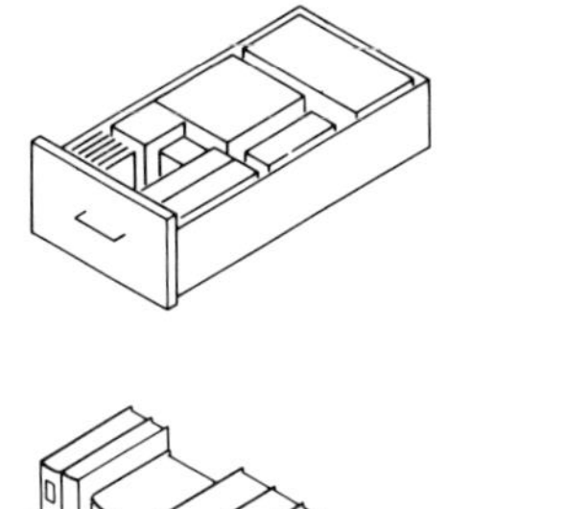

34 Pads, stationery, envelopes

A 1″-15″ **B** 16″-30″ **C** 31″-45″ **D** 46″-60″ **E** 61″-75″
F 76″-90″ **G** 91″-105″ **H** 106″-120″ **I** More

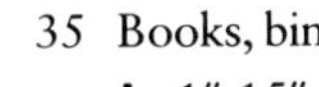

35 Books, binders, magazines

A 1″-15″ **B** 16″-30″ **C** 31″-45″ **D** 46″-60″ **E** 61″-75″
F 76″-90″ **G** 91″-105″ **H** 106″-120″ **I** More

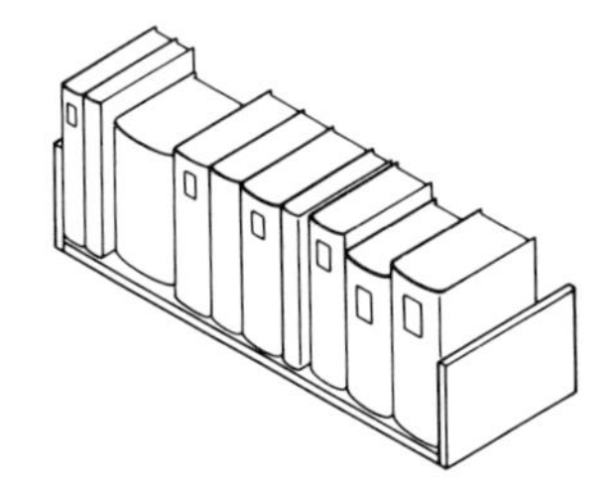

36 Large books (12″ or higher)

A 1″-15″ **B** 16″-30″ **C** 31″-45″ **D** 46″-60″ **E** 61″-75″
F 76″-90″ **G** 91″-105″ **H** 106″-120″ **I** More

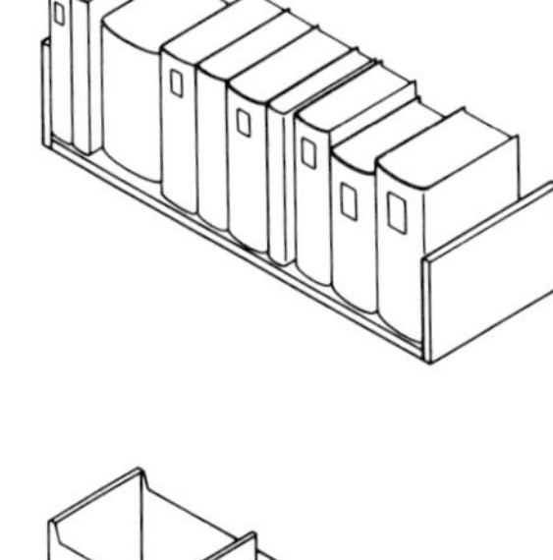

37 Index cards (3″ x 5″)

A 1″-15″ **B** 16″-30″ **C** 31″-45″ **D** 46″-60″ **E** 61″-75″
F 76″-90″ **G** 91″-105″ **H** 106″-120″ **I** More

38 Index cards (4″ x 6″)

A 1″-15″ **B** 16″-30″ **C** 31″-45″ **D** 46″-60″ **E** 61″-75″
F 76″-90″ **G** 91″-105″ **H** 106″-120″ **I** More

39 Index cards (5″ x 8″)

A 1″-15″ **B** 16″-30″ **C** 31″-45″ **D** 46″-60″ **E** 61″-75″
F 76″-90″ **G** 91″-105″ **H** 106″-120″ **I** More

Storage/Filing (continued)

Do not include materials that are shared by others.

Computer Support Materials and Microfilm

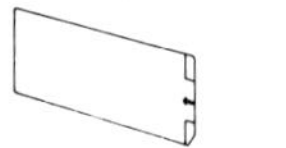

40 Computer cards, aperture cards, magnetic cards (3¼″ x 7⅜″)

A 1″-15″ **B** 16″-30″ **C** 31″-45″ **D** 46″-60″ **E** 61″-75″
F 76″-90″ **G** 91″-105″ **H** 106″-120″ **I** More

41 Tape cartridges and cassettes

A 1″-15″ **B** 16″-30″ **C** 31″-45″ **D** 46″-60″ **E** 61″-75″
F 76″-90″ **G** 91″-105″ **H** 106″-120″ **I** More

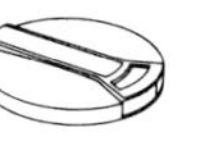

42 Hard disk cartridges

A 1″-15″ **B** 16″-30″ **C** 31″-45″ **D** 46″-60″ **E** 61″-75″
F 76″-90″ **G** 91″-105″ **H** 106″-120″ **I** More

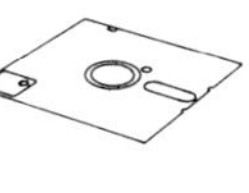

43 Floppy disks

A 1″-15″ **B** 16″-30″ **C** 31″-45″ **D** 46″-60″ **E** 61″-75″
F 76″-90″ **G** 91″-105″ **H** 106″-120″ **I** More

44 Magnetic tape (reels)

A 1″-15″ **B** 16″-30″ **C** 31″-45″ **D** 46″-60″ **E** 61″-75″
F 76″-90″ **G** 91″-105″ **H** 106″-120″ **I** More

45 Microfiche (4″ x 6″)

A 1″-15″ **B** 16″-30″ **C** 31″-45″ **D** 46″-60″ **E** 61″-75″
F 76″-90″ **G** 91″-105″ **H** 106″-120″ **I** More

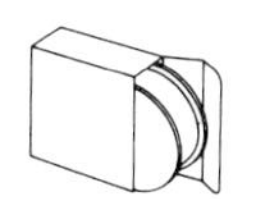

46 Microfilm rolls (4″ x 4″ x 1″)

A 1″-15″ **B** 16″-30″ **C** 31″-45″ **D** 46″-60″ **E** 61″-75″
F 76″-90″ **G** 91″-105″ **H** 106″-120″ **I** More

Additional Storage Requirements

47 If you store blueprints/drawings in your personal work area, please indicate how they are stored. *(Indicate all that apply).*

A Rolled
B Flat
C Hanging
D Folded in Files

48 What do you expect your storage requirements to be in the future?

A No change – I'll have to store the same quantities of materials.
B Increased – I'll have to store more materials.
C Decreased – I'll have to store less materials.

49 For any additional storage requirements, indicate all that apply to you:

A I store other materials in my work area which have not been listed in this section. *(List under Question No. 58 at the end of this questionnaire.)*
B I store materials in other places that should be in my personal work area. *(List under Question No. 59 at the end of this questionnaire.)*
C I have no other storage requirements.

In Your Own Words

Some questions just can't be computerized. Your own words are needed. Please use the spaces following to provide the information needed.

____
Department/Employee Identification Number

____
Name

50 Briefly and candidly describe what you do in your job!

51 What do you like best about your current personal work area?

52 What do you feel needs the most improvement in your personal work area?

53 If your response to Question 1 (page 5) was Yes, please list the special physical needs or requirements that you have.

54 If your response to Question 3 (page 5) was Yes, please list the types of confidential conversations you have in your personal work area.

In Your Own Words (continued)

55 If you responsed to Question 5.5 (page 7), please describe the items that should not be seen by others.

56 If you share equipment with one other person (Question 25, page 27), state what and with whom.

57 If you responded to Question 25.15 (page 27), please describe the other machines/equipment you require in your personal work area including the dimensions.

58 If your response to Question 49A (page 39) was Yes, please describe the additional materials you store in your work area.

59 If your response to Question 49B (page 39) was Yes, please describe what materials are stored in other places and where they are located.

Partial Printout of Information from Steelcase Questionnaire

Requestor Name/Address
SOUTHERN CALIFORNIA MFG CO
1001 WARNER AVENUE
TUSTIN, CALIFORNIA 92680

Analysis I.D.
001076

Project Number
9001

Project Description
SOUTHERN CALIFORNIA MFG. CO.
TUSTIN HEADQUARTERS

Report Title
PLACEMENT CHART

Report I.D.
OA-AA-50-1 **INCON. RESOLUTION = AVERAGE**

Page **1**

Date **04/08/83**

Time **17:21:11**

	1	2	3	4	5	6	7	8	9	10	11	12	13	14	15	16	17	18	19	20	21	22	23	24	25	26	27	28	29	30	
1																															1
2																															2
3																															3
4																															4
5																															5
6																															6
7							18			31			27			23															7
8																															8
9																															9
10							14			16			22			20			21												10
11																															11
12																															12
13							10			15			32			08			12			24									13
14																															14
15																															15
16							09			17			07			11			06			04									16

17							17
18							18
19	30	25	29	13	03	26	19
20							20
21							21
22			02	05	19	01	22
23							23
24							24
25				28			25
26							26
27							27
28							28
29							29
30							30

REF	GROUP	GROUP DESCRIPTION	LOCTN	SQFT
1	1000	V.P. GENERAL MANAGER	22,22	
2	2000	DIVISION SALES MANAGE	22,13	
3	3000	MARKETING SERVICES MA	19,19	
4	4000	MAJOR ORDER	16,22	
5	5000	GUEST SERVICES	22,16	
6	6000	ORDER ENTRY	16,19	
7	7000	DEALER SERVICES	16,13	
8	8000	PIC MANAGEMENT	13,16	
9	9000	DATA CENTER DATA ENTR	16, 7	
10	10000	SYSTEMS	13, 7	
11	11000	INVENTORY CONTROL	16,16	
12	12000	DATA BASE	13,19	
13	13000	PURCHASING	19,16	
14	14000	CONTROLLER	10, 7	
15	15000	GENERAL ACCOUNTING	13,10	
16	16000	ADMINISTRATIVE SERVIC	10,10	
17	17000	PAYROLL COST ACCOUNTI	16,10	
18	18000	BUDGET AND INTERNAL A	7, 7	
19	19000	SECRETARIAL STAFF	22,19	
20	20000	ENGINEERING MANAGEMEN	10,16	
21	21000	STANDARDS ENGINEERING	10,19	
22	22000	MANUFACTURING ENGINEE	10,13	
23	23000	PROJECT ENGINEERING	7,16	

REF	GROUP	GROUP DESCRIPTION	LOCTN	SQFT
24	24000	PRODUCT ENGINEERING	13,22	
25	25000	PERSONNEL	19,10	
26	26000	MAIN ENTRANCE LOBBY	19,22	
27	27000	PLANT ENTRANCE 3	7,13	
28	28000	PRESENTATION ROOM	25,16	
29	29000	2ND ENTRANCE FROM OUTS	19,13	
30	30000	COMPUTER ROOM	19, 7	
31	31000	MAIL ROOM	7,10	
32	32000	COPYING MACHINE	13,13	

REF	GROUP	GROUP DESCRIPTION	LOCTN	SQFT

Requestor Name/Address
SOUTHERN CALIFORNIA MFG CO
1001 WARNER AVENUE
TUSTIN, CALIFORNIA 92680

Analysis I.D.
001076

Project Number
9001

Project Description
SOUTHERN CALIFORNIA MFG. CO.
TUSTIN HEADQUARTERS

Report Title
ADJACENCY INCONSISTENCIES

Report I.D.
OA-AA-30-2

INCON. RESOLUTION = AVERAGE

Page
1

Date
04/08/83

Time
17:21:11

FROM REFERENCE NUMBER	FROM GROUP ID	TO REFERENCE NUMBER	TO GROUP ID	FROM / TO VALUE	TO / FROM VALUE	ASSUMED VALUE	INCONSISTENCY LEVEL
3	3000	4	4000	C	B	B	
		6	6000	C	B	B	
		8	8000	B	C	B	
		16	16000	C	D	C	
4	4000	5	5000	C	B	B	
		6	6000	B	C	B	
		7	7000	B	C	B	
		8	8000	C	D	C	
		9	9000	C	D	C	
		10	10000	B	D	C	**
		11	11000	B	C	B	
		12	12000	C	D	C	
		16	16000	B	D	C	**
		19	19000	D	E	E	
		22	22000	D	C	C	
		24	24000	B	C	B	
5	5000	16	16000	C	D	C	
		17	17000	E	D	E	
		19	19000	B	A	A	
6	6000	7	7000	A	C	B	**
		11	11000	B	A	A	
		12	12000	C	B	B	
		15	15000	D	B	C	**
		19	19000	D	C	C	
		24	24000	D	C	C	

Requestor Name/Address
SOUTHERN CALIFORNIA MFG CO
2001 WARNER AVENUE
TUSTIN, CALIFORNIA 92680

Project Number
9001

Project Description
SOUTHERN CALIFORNIA MFG. CO.
TUSTIN HEADQUARTERS

Report Title
GROUP LIST

Analysis I.D.
001076

Report I.D.
OA-AA-10-1

INCON. RESOLUTION = AVERAGE

Page
1

Date
04/08/83

Time
17:21:11

REF NO	GROUP ID NO	GROUP DESCRIPTION	SQ FT	REF NO	GROUP ID NO	GROUP DESCRIPTION	SQ FT
1	1000	V.P. GENERAL MANAGER		31	31000	MAIL ROOM	
2	2000	DIVISION SALES MANAGER		32	32000	COPYING MACHINE	
3	3000	MARKETING SERVICES MANAGER					
4	4000	MAJOR ORDER					
5	5000	GUEST SERVICES					
6	6000	ORDER ENTRY					
7	7000	DEALER SERVICES					
8	8000	PIC MANAGEMENT					
9	9000	DATA CENTER DATA ENTRY					
10	10000	SYSTEMS					
11	11000	INVENTORY CONTROL					
12	12000	DATA BASE					
13	13000	PURCHASING					
14	14000	CONTROLLER					
15	15000	GENERAL ACCOUNTING					
16	16000	ADMINISTRATIVE SERVICES					
17	17000	PAYROLL COST ACCOUNTING					
18	18000	BUDGET AND INTERNAL AUDIT					
19	19000	SECRETARIAL STAFF					
20	20000	ENGINEERING MANAGEMENT					
21	21000	STANDARDS ENGINEERING					
22	22000	MANUFACTURING ENGINEERING					
23	23000	PROJECT ENGINEERING					
24	24000	PRODUCT ENGINEERING					
25	25000	PERSONNEL					
26	26000	MAIN ENTRANCE LOBBY					
27	27000	PLANT ENTRANCE 3					
28	28000	PRESENTATION ROOM					
29	29000	2ND ENTRANCE FROM OUTSIDE					
30	30000	COMPUTER ROOM					

Computer Assisted Office Survey and Space Planning — Relative Closeness

Requestor Name/Address
SOUTHERN CALIFORNIA MFG CO
1001 WARNER AVENUE
TUSTIN, CALIFORNIA 92680

Project Number
9001

Project Description
SOUTHERN CALIFORNIA MFG. CO
TUSTIN HEADQUARTERS

Page
1

Report Title
FINAL MATRIX

Date
04/08/83

Analysis I.D.
001100

Report I.D.
OA-AA-30-3

INCON. RESOLUTION = AVERAGE

Time
17:21:11

GROUP DESCRIPTION	GROUP ID NO	REF NO	TO ----> 1	2	3	4	5	6	7	8	9	10	1	2	3	4	15	6	7	8	9	20	1	2	3	4	25	6	7	8	9	30	1	2
V.P. GENERAL MANAGER	1000	1																																
DIVISION SALES MANAG	2000	2	-																															
MARKETING SERVICES M	3000	3	B	-																														
MAJOR ORDER	4000	4	-	-	B																													
GUEST SERVICES	5000	5	C	B	B	B																												
ORDER ENTRY	6000	6	C	-	B	B	-																											
DEALER SERVICES	7000	7	-	-	B	B	C	B																										
PIC MANAGEMENT	8000	8	C	-	B	C	-	-	C																									
DATA CENTER DATA ENT	9000	9	-	-	-	C	-	C	C	B																								
SYSTEMS	10000	10	-	-	-	C	-	B	C	B	A																							
INVENTORY CONTROL	11000	11	-	-	C	B	-	A	A	A	B	B																						
DATA BASE	12000	12	-	-	-	C	-	B	-	A	B	B	B																					
PURCHASING	13000	13	-	-	-	-	-	-	C	C	-	-	A	-																				
CONTROLLER	14000	14	B	C	C	-	-	-	C	C	-	-	-	-	C																			
GENERAL ACCOUNTING	15000	15	C	-	-	-	-	C	C	-	C	C	-	-	B	B																		
ADMINISTRATIVE SERVI	16000	16	-	-	C	C	C	B	B	C	-	-	C	-	C	B	B																	
PAYROLL COST ACCOUNT	17000	17	-	-	-	-	E	C	-	B	B	B	C	B	C	B	A	C																
BUDGET AND INTERNAL	18000	18	C	-	-	-	-	-	-	-	C	-	-	-	-	B	B	C	B															
SECRETARIAL STAFF	19000	19	A	B	A	E	A	C	C	C	-	-	C	-	-	B	C	C	C	C														
ENGINEERING MANAGEME	20000	20	B	-	-	-	-	-	-	C	-	-	C	C	B	C	-	C	C	-	C													
STANDARDS ENGINEERIN	21000	21	-	-	-	-	-	-	-	-	C	C	C	A	-	-	-	C	B	-	C	A												
MANUFACTURING ENGINE	22000	22	-	-	-	C	-	-	-	C	C	-	C	B	C	-	-	C	-	-	C	A	A											
PROJECT ENGINEERING	23000	23	C	-	-	-	-	-	-	-	C	-	-	-	B	-	C	C	C	C	C	A	C	B										
PRODUCT ENGINEERING	24000	24	-	-	-	B	-	C	C	-	-	-	C	B	C	-	-	B	-	-	-	A	C	C	C									
PERSONNEL	25000	25	-	-	-	-	-	-	-	C	C	-	C	-	-	C	-	-	A	-	B	C	C	-	-	-								
MAIN ENTRANCE LOBBY	26000	26	-	-	C	B	B	-	-	C	-	-	-	-	-	-	-	-	E	-	B	B	-	C	B	-	C							
PLANT ENTRANCE 3	27000	27	-	-	-	-	C	-	C	C	C	B	B	-	B	-	-	B	-	-	-	B	B	A	B	C	A	-						
PRESENTATION ROOM	28000	28	-	-	-	-	C	-	C	-	-	-	-	-	-	-	-	-	-	-	-	-	-	-	-	-	-	-	-					
2ND ENTRANCE FROM OU	29000	29	-	-	-	-	-	-	-	-	-	-	-	-	A	-	-	-	-	-	-	-	-	-	-	-	A	-	-	-				
COMPUTER ROOM	30000	30	-	-	-	-	-	-	-	-	B	B	B	-	-	-	-	-	B	-	-	-	-	-	-	-	B	-	-	-	-			
MAIL ROOM	31000	31	-	-	-	-	-	C	-	-	-	-	C	-	C	-	-	B	-	-	C	-	-	-	-	-	B	-	-	-	-	-		
COPYING MACHINE	32000	32	-	-	C	C	-	A	A	C	-	C	E	C	C	-	C	C	C	C	B	B	B	B	B	C	C	-	-	-	-	-	-	

'-' = 'D'

Requestor Name/Address
SOUTHERN CALIFORNIA MFG CO
1001 WARNER AVENUE
TUSTIN, CALIFORNIA 92680

Project Number
9001

Project Description
SOUTHERN CALIFORNIA MFG. CO
TUSTIN HEADQUARTERS

Report Title
INTERVIEW REPORT

Page
13

Date
04/08/83

Analysis I.D.
001100

Report I.D.
OA-AA-20-1

INCON. RESOLUTION = AVERAGE

Time
17:21:11

REF NO	GROUP ID NO	GROUP DESCRIPTION	TO REF NO	TO GROUP ID NO	TO GROUP DESCRIPTION	VALUE	REASONS	
7	7000	DEALER SERVICES						
			1	1000	V.P. GENERAL MANAGER	D		
			2	2000	DIVISION SALES MANAGER	D		
			3	3000	MARKETING SERVICES MANAGER	B	1 DIRECT CONTACT	
		VALUE INCONSISTENCY ***** 4 HAS C VALUE RUN ASSUMES B VALUE	4	4000	MAJOR ORDER	B	1 DIRECT CONTACT	
			5	5000	GUEST SERVICES	C	1 DIRECT CONTACT	2
		VALUE INCONSISTENCY ***** 6 HAS C VALUE RUN ASSUMES B VALUE	6	6000	ORDER ENTRY	A	1 DIRECT CONTACT	2
		VALUE INCONSISTENCY ***** 8 HAS D VALUE RUN ASSUMES C VALUE	8	8000	PIC MANAGEMENT	C	9 ORD FACE-FACE	
		VALUE INCONSISTENCY ***** 9 HAS D VALUE RUN ASSUMES C VALUE	9	9000	DATA CENTER DATA ENTRY	C	2 JOINT TASKS	9
		VALUE INCONSISTENCY ***** 10 HAS B VALUE RUN ASSUMES C VALUE	10	10000	SYSTEMS	D		
		VALUE INCONSISTENCY ***** 11 HAS B VALUE RUN ASSUMES A VALUE	11	11000	INVENTORY CONTROL	A	1 DIRECT CONTACT	
			12	12000	DATA BASE	D		
			13	13000	PURCHASING	C	1 DIRECT CONTACT	5
		VALUE INCONSISTENCY ***** 14 HAS C VALUE RUN ASSUMES C VALUE	14	14000	CONTROLLER	D		
		VALUE INCONSISTENCY ***** 15 HAS D VALUE RUN ASSUMES C VALUE	15	15000	GENERAL ACCOUNTING	B	5 PAPER FLOW	
			16	16000	ADMINISTRATIVE SERVICES	B	5 PAPER FLOW	
			17	17000	PAYROLL COST ACCOUNTING	D		
			18	18000	BUDGET AND INTERNAL AUDIT	D		
		VALUE INCONSISTENCY ***** 19 HAS C VALUE RUN ASSUMES C VALUE	19	19000	SECRETARIAL STAFF	D		

Computer Assisted Office Survey and Space Planning — Personal Work Area

Requestor Name/Address
SOUTHERN CALIF. MFG. CO.
1001 WARNER AVENUE
TUSTIN, CA

Project Number
9001

Project Description
SOUTHERN CALIFORNIA MFG. CO.
TUSTIN HEADQUARTERS

Report Title
DEPARTMENT LIST

Page
1

Date
03/17/83

Analysis I.D.
000860

Report I.D.
OA-WA-20-1

Questionnaire I.D.
1

Time
12:15:52

DEPARTMENT CODE	DEPARTMENT DESCRIPTION	DEPARTMENT MANAGER
03000	MARKETING SERVICES MANAGEMENT	B. GILBERT
04000	MAJOR ORDER	J. VOAKE
05000	GUEST SERVICES	D. WILKIN
06000	ORDER ENTRY	T. EASTON
07000	DEALER SERVICES	R. SCHERFF
08000	PIC AND SYSTEMS MANAGEMENT	B. DEVRIES
09000	DATA CENTER	R. KASALO
10000	SYSTEMS	M. RILEY
11000	INVENTORY CONTROL	S. HOPKINS
12000	DATA BASE	G. VRONE
13000	PURCHASING	B. DENHAM
14000	ACCOUNTING	T. TROLLAN
15000	GENERAL ACCOUNTING	T. TROLLAN
16000	ADMINISTRATIVE SERVICES	J. MCKAY PAYNE
17000	PAYROLL COST ACCOUNTING	R. FITZPATRICK
18000	BUDGET INTERNAL AUDIT	S. LONG
19000	SECRETARIAL	D. PLECHOT
20000	ENGINEERING MANAGEMENT	M. REED
21000	STANDARDS ENGINEERING	S. ROBART
22000	MANUFACTURING ENGINEERING	C. COOPER
23000	PROJECT ENGINEERING	K. SARRACH
24000	PRODUCT ENGINEERING Q.C.	K. JENKINS
25000	PERSONNEL	B. TAYLOR

Computer Assisted Office Survey and Space Planning — Personal Work Area

Requestor Name/Address
SOUTHERN CALIF. MFG. CO.
1001 WARNER AVENUE
TUSTIN, CA

Project Number
9001

Project Description
SOUTHERN CALIFORNIA MFG. CO.
TUSTIN HEADQUARTERS

Report Title
PROJECT FUNCTIONAL NEEDS SUMMARY
SURFACE AREA (ASCENDING)

Report I.D.
OA-WA-60-1

Analysis I.D.
000860

Questionnaire I.D.
1

Page 2

Date
05/18/83

Time
18:08:37

JOB TITLE	DEPT	COUNT	SURFACE LEN DEPTH	FILE STG LIN IN	BULK STG LIN IN	EQUIPMENT	DISPLAY WIDTH HGT	PRIVACY	CONFERENCE
MANAGER PERSONNEL DEPT 2006	25000	1	66 12 AREA 792	136	135	TYPEWRITER CALCULATOR TELEPHONE OTHER EQPT	15 22 AREA 330	ACOUSTIC- MED VISUAL- LOW MAX RECOVR 5 MIN RECOVR 0	CHAIRS 2
MANAGER ENGINEERING 2005	20000	1	56 16 AREA 896	181	285	CALCULATOR TELEPHONE	48 22 AREA 1056	ACOUSTIC- LOW VISUAL- LOW MAX RECOVR 8 MIN RECOVR 8	ROOMS 0.14
MANAGER MARKETING SERV 2001	03000	1	130 22 AREA 2860	151	90	CALCULATOR TELEPHONE	33 22 AREA 726	ACOUSTIC- LOW VISUAL- LOW MAX RECOVR 4 MIN RECOVR 0	ROOMS 0.07
MANAGER PURCHASING 2002	13000	1	132 24 AREA 3168	180	30	CALCULATOR TELEPHONE	195 24 AREA 4680	ACOUSTIC- HIGH VISUAL- LOW MAX RECOVR 21 MIN RECOVR 11	CHAIRS 1
MGR. PAYROLL COST ACC 2004	017000	1	157 30 AREA 4710	120	210	CRT/VDT CALCULATOR TELEPHONE	0 0 AREA 0	ACOUSTIC- HIGH VISUAL- HIGH MAX RECOVR 30 MIN RECOVR 30	

Requestor Name/Address
SOUTHERN CALIF. MFG. CO.
1001 WARNER AVENUE
TUSTIN, CA

Project Number
9001

Project Description
SOUTHERN CALIFORNIA MFG. CO.
TUSTIN HEADQUARTERS

Report Title
EMPLOYEE LIST
07000 DEALER SERVICES

Page
7

Date
03/17/83

Analysis I.D.
000860

Report I.D.
OA-WA-10-3

Questionnaire I.D.
1

Time
12:15:52

EMPLOYEE ID NO	EMPLOYEE NAME		JOB TITLE	SUPERVISOR		COMPANY SERVICE		JOB SERVICE
07001	SCHERFF	R.E.	MANAGER DEALER SERVI	GILBERT	B.	6- 10	YRS.	1- 2
1	JOB TITLE EMPL COUNT							
07002	LAURIE	B. .	SUPERVISOR DEALER SE	SCHERFF	R.	3- 5	YRS	< 1
1	JOB TITLE EMPL COUNT							
07010	ALVES	J.A.	DEALER SERVICE REPRE	SCHERFF	R.S.	6- 10	YRS	6- 10
07003	GRATZ	C.K.	DEALER SERVICE REPRE	SCHERFF	R.	NO SERVICE		NO SERVICE
07004	HAMILTON	A.F.	DEALER SERVICE REPRE	SCHERFF	R.	1- 2	YRS	1- 2
07005	ODEN	G.G.	DEALER SERVICE REPRE	SCHERFF	R.R.	6- 10	YRS	3- 5
07006	STEWART	K. .	DEALER SERVICE REPRE	SCHERFF	R.	3- 5	YRS	3- 5
07007	WIEBEBAILEY	N.W.	DEALER SERVICE REPRE	SCHERFF	R.S.	1- 2	YRS	1- 2
07008	WIGLE	M.W.	DEALER SERVICE REPRE	SCHERFF	R.S.	< 1	YR	< 1
07009	WILSON	B. .	DEALER SERVICE REPRE	SCHERFF	R. .	1- 2	YRS	1- 2
8	JOB TITLE EMPL COUNT							
07011	COFFEY	M.O.	TELEPHONE REP. ASSIS	LAURIE	B.	3- 5	YRS	1- 2
07012	GATES	S. .	TELEPHONE REP. ASSIS	LAURIE	R.	3- 5	YRS	1- 2
07013	PETERS	N.A.	TELEPHONE REP. ASSIS	LAURIE	B.	1- 2	YRS	1- 2
3	JOB TITLE EMPL COUNT							
07014	FRANKS	P.T.	CHANGE ORDER CLERK	LAURIE	B.A.	3- 5	YRS	1- 2
07015	VESELY	B.K.	CHANGE ORDER CLERK	LAURIE	B.	1- 2	YRS	1- 2
2	JOB TITLE EMPL COUNT							
15	DEPT EMPL COUNT							

Computer Assisted Office Survey and Space Planning — Personal Work Area

Requestor Name/Address
SOUTHERN CALIF. MFG. CO.
1001 WARNER AVENUE
TUSTIN, CA

Project Number
9001

Project Description
SOUTHERN CALIFORNIA MFG. CO.
TUSTIN HEADQUARTERS

Report Title
FUNCTIONAL NEEDS SUMMARY
07000 DEALER SERVICES

Analysis I.D.
000860

Report I.D.
OA-WA-50-1

Questionnaire I.D.
1

Page
10

Date
03/17/83

Time
12:15:52

EMPLOYEE NAME/ JOB TITLE		ID NO/ COUNT	SURFACE LEN	 DEPTH	FILE STG LIN IN	BULK STG LIN IN	EQUIPMENT	DISPLAY WIDTH	 HGT	PRIVACY		CONFERENCE		HUMAN FACTORS
SCHERFF	RE	07001	118 AREA	12 1416	136	135	TELEPHONE OTHER EQPT	45 AREA	11 495	ACOUSTIC- MED VISUAL- LOW MAX RECOVR MIN RECOVR	 6 0	CHAIRS ROOMS	1 0.02	RIGHT HANDED HGT > 6-2
MANAGER DEALER SERVI 2102		1	118 AREA	12 1416	136	135	TELEPHONE OTHER EQPT	45 AREA	11 495	ACOUSTIC- MED VISUAL- LOW MAX RECOVR MIN RECOVR	 6 0	CHAIRS ROOMS	1 0.02	
LAURIE	B	07002	81 AREA	22 1782	75	150		39 AREA	22 858	ACOUSTIC- LOW VISUAL- LOW MAX RECOVR MIN RECOVR	 0 0			RIGHT HANDED HGT > 6-2
SUPERVISOR DEALER SE 3003		1	81 AREA	22 1782	75	150		39 AREA	22 858	ACOUSTIC- LOW VISUAL- LOW MAX RECOVR MIN RECOVR	 0 0			
ALVES	JA	07010	170 AREA	30 5100	45	135	MICROFILM V TELEPHONE CRT/VDT TYPEWRITER	45 AREA	11 495	ACOUSTIC- LOW VISUAL- LOW MAX RECOVR MIN RECOVR	 39 6	CHAIRS ROOMS	1 0.00	RIGHT HANDED
GRATZ	CK	07003	131 AREA	30 3930	90	90	TELEPHONE CRT/VDT OTHER EQPT	57 AREA	22 1254	ACOUSTIC- LOW VISUAL- LOW MAX RECOVR MIN RECOVR	 6 0			LEFT HANDED

Computer Assisted Office Survey and Space Planning — Personal Work Area

Requestor Name/Address
SOUTHERN CALIF. MFG. CO.
1001 WARNER AVENUE
TUSTIN, CA

Analysis I.D.
000860

Project Number
9001

Project Description
SOUTHERN CALIFORNIA MFG. CO.
TUSTIN HEADQUARTERS

Report Title
FUNCTIONAL NEEDS SUMMARY
07000 DEALER SERVICES

Report I.D.
OA-WA-50-1

Questionnaire I.D.
1

Page
11

Date
03/17/83

Time
12:15:52

EMPLOYEE NAME/ JOB TITLE		ID NO/ COUNT	SURFACE LEN	SURFACE DEPTH	FILE STG LIN IN	BULK STG LIN IN	EQUIPMENT	DISPLAY WIDTH	DISPLAY HGT	PRIVACY	CONFERENCE	HUMAN FACTORS
HAMILTON	AF	07004	129 AREA	30 3870	60	90	CRT/VDT TELEPHONE	105 AREA	22 2310	ACOUSTIC- LOW VISUAL- LOW MAX RECOVR 3 MIN RECOVR 0		RIGHT HANDED
ODEN	GG	07005	141 AREA	30 4230	15	0	CRT/VDT TELEPHONE OTHER EQPT	0 AREA	0 0	ACOUSTIC- LOW VISUAL- LOW MAX RECOVR 28 MIN RECOVR 0		RIGHT HANDED
STEWART	K	07006	150 AREA	30 4500	45	105	CRT/VDT MICROFILM V TELEPHONE CALCULATOR	93 AREA	22 2046	ACOUSTIC- LOW VISUAL- LOW MAX RECOVR 1 MIN RECOVR 0		SPC PHYSICAL RIGHT HANDED
WIEBEBAILEY	NW	07007	81 AREA	30 2430	121	60	TELEPHONE OTHER EQPT CRT/VDT	54 AREA	22 1188	ACOUSTIC- LOW VISUAL- LOW MAX RECOVR 0 MIN RECOVR 0		RIGHT HANDED
WIGLE	MW	07008	142 AREA	30 4260	30	45	CRT/VDT TELEPHONE MICROFILM V CALCULATOR	120 AREA	24 2880	ACOUSTIC- LOW VISUAL- LOW MAX RECOVR 0 MIN RECOVR 0		RIGHT HANDED
WILSON	B	07009	144 AREA	30 4320	105	90	TELEPHONE CRT/VDT OTHER EQPT	69 AREA	22 1518	ACOUSTIC- LOW VISUAL- LOW MAX RECOVR 15 MIN RECOVR 5		RIGHT HANDED
DEALER SERVICE REPRE 4002		8	144 AREA	30 4320	90	90	CRT/VDT TELEPHONE OTHER EQPT	93 AREA	22 2046	ACOUSTIC- LOW VISUAL- LOW MAX RECOVR 15 MIN RECOVR 0		

Requestor Name/Address
SOUTHERN CALIF. MFG. CO.
1001 WARNER AVENUE
TUSTIN, CA

Project Number
9001

Project Description
SOUTHERN CALIFORNIA MFG. CO.
TUSTIN HEADQUARTERS

Report Title
FUNCTIONAL NEEDS SUMMARY
07000 DEALER SERVICES

Analysis I.D.
000860

Report I.D.
OA-WA-50-1

Questionnaire I.D.
1

Page
12

Date
03/17/83

Time
12:15:52

EMPLOYEE NAME/ JOB TITLE		ID NO/ COUNT	SURFACE LEN	SURFACE DEPTH	FILE STG LIN IN	BULK STG LIN IN	EQUIPMENT	DISPLAY WIDTH	DISPLAY HGT	PRIVACY	CONFERENCE	HUMAN FACTORS
COFFEY	MO	07011	198 AREA	30 5940	60	135	CRT/VDT TELEPHONE TYPEWRITER	45 AREA	11 495	ACOUSTIC- LOW VISUAL- LOW MAX RECOVR 2 MIN RECOVR 0		RIGHT HANDED
GATES	S	07012	301 AREA	30 9030	30	45	CRT/VDT TELEPHONE TYPEWRITER	60 AREA	22 1320	ACOUSTIC- LOW VISUAL- LOW MAX RECOVR 2 MIN RECOVR 2		RIGHT HANDED
PETERS	NA	07013	248 AREA	30 7440	120	211	OTHER EQPT CRT/VDT TELEPHONE TYPEWRITER	57 AREA	22 1254	ACOUSTIC- LOW VISUAL- LOW MAX RECOVR 2 MIN RECOVR 0		RIGHT HANDED
TELEPHONE REP. ASSIS 5007		3	301 AREA	30 9030	120	211	TYPEWRITER CRT/VDT TELEPHONE	60 AREA	22 1320	ACOUSTIC- LOW VISUAL- LOW MAX RECOVR 2 MIN RECOVR 0		
FRANKS	PT	07014	175 AREA	30 5250	45	30	CRT/VDT TELEPHONE OTHER EQPT DATE/TIME S	42 AREA	22 924	ACOUSTIC- LOW VISUAL- LOW MAX RECOVR 6 MIN RECOVR 6		RIGHT HANDED
VESELY	BK	07015	175 AREA	30 5250	45	30	CRT/VDT TELEPHONE OTHER EQPT DATE/TIME S	42 AREA	22 924	ACOUSTIC- LOW VISUAL- LOW MAX RECOVR 17 MIN RECOVR 0		RIGHT HANDED
CHANGE ORDER CLERK 5110		2	175 AREA	30 5250	45	30	CRT/VDT TELEPHONE DATE/TIME S OTHER EQPT	42 AREA	22 924	ACOUSTIC- LOW VISUAL- LOW MAX RECOVR 17 MIN RECOVR 0		

Computer Assisted Office Survey and Space Planning — Personal Work Area

Requestor Name/Address
SOUTHERN CALIF. MFG. CO.
1001 WARNER AVENUE
TUSTIN, CA

Analysis I.D.
000860

Project Number
9001

Project Description
SOUTHERN CALIFORNIA MFG. CO.
TUSTIN HEADQUARTERS

Report Title
INDIVIDUAL ANALYSIS

Report I.D.
OA-WA-30-1

Employee Name
GRATZ CK
07003

Title
DEALER SERVICE REPRE

Department
DEALER SERVICES
07000

Supervisor
SCHERFF R

Page
32

Date
03/21/83

Time
16:34:16

Worksurface

```
1. ACTV: TELEPHONE USAGE TIME          >20 HR
2. MATL: 2 BOOKS,BINDERS,MAGAZINE    24X12 IN
         1 FILE FOLDER               20X12 IN
         2 LETTER SIZE PAPER          9X11 IN
3. EQPT: CRT/VDT                     21X30 IN

1. ACTV: READING DOCUMENTS TIME       5-10 HR
2. MATL: 1 COMPUTER PRINTOUT         15X22 IN
         1 BOOKS,BINDERS,MAGAZINE    24X12 IN
         1 FILE FOLDER               20X12 IN
3. EQPT:

   SURFACE REQUIRED LENGTH:      131 IN
                    DEPTH:        30 IN
                    AREA:       3930 SQ IN
```

File Storage

```
   DESCRIPTION                              LIN IN
1. LETTER SIZE FILES STORAGE                76- 90

1. DAILY USAGE LETTER/LEGAL FILES           61- 75
1. WEEKLY USAGE PRINTOUTS                    1- 15

1. DEPARTMENT STRG LETTER/LEGAL              1- 15
2. INACTIVE STRG LETTER/LEGAL                1- 15
3. PURGED STRG LETTER/LEGAL                 16- 30

   FILE STORAGE REQUIRED:   90 IN
```

Bulk and Other Storage

```
   DESCRIPTION                              LIN IN
1. PADS,STATIONERY,ETC STORAGE              31- 45
2. BOOKS,BINDER,MAGAZINES STORAGE           16- 30
3. LARGE BOOKS (> 12 IN) STORAGE             1- 15

1. BLUEPRINT/DRWG STG:

   BULK STORAGE REQUIRED:   90 IN
```

Equipment

```
   DESCRIPTION        PLUG HRS LOC SHR   SIZE
1. TELEPHONE            P   21  F         9X10
2. CRT/VDT              P   10  R  YES   21X30
3. OTHER EQPT                4     YES    0X 0
```

Display

```
   DESCRIPTION                             QTY  SIZE
1. QTY MEMOS,LETTERS DISPLAYED              3   9X11
2. QTY PRINTOUTS,CHARTS DISPLAYED           2  15X22
3. OTHER MATERIALS DISPLAYED                3   0X 0

   DISPLAY SURFACE:      57 WIDE     22 HIGH

   ACCESSIBLE TO OTHERS:
1. MAIL/IN-OUT MATERIAL

   AIDS:                                  HRS/WK
1. TACKABLE SURFACE AID USAGE               >20
```

Privacy

```
1. SEEING FROM WORKAREA REQUIRED
   ANSWER: YES (COMMUNICATION)
2. TYPE OF PRIVACY MOST CRITICAL
   ANSWER: DEPARTMENTAL PRIVACY

1. VISUAL PRIVACY REQUIREMENT:            LOW
2. ACOUSTIC PRIVACY REQUIREMENT:          LOW
3. DISTRACTION RECOVERY TIME:
                    DAILY MAXIMUM:          6 MIN
                    DAILY MINIMUM:          0 MIN
```

Notes

Human Factors

```
                                          YEARS
1. LEFT HANDED
2. UNDER 40          YEARS

                                         HRS/WK
1. TIME SPENT IN WORKAREA                  > 20
2. TIME STANDING IN WORKAREA              NONE
```

Meetings and Conferences

```
   WORKAREA REQUIREMENTS:                 HRS/WK
1. OUTSIDE VISITORS IN WORKAREA           1- 4
2. ONE PERSON MEETINGS                    0.0
3. TWO PEOPLE MEETINGS                    0.0
4. THREE PEOPLE MEETINGS                  0.0
   AIDS:                                  PERCENT
   REQUIRES 0 CHAIRS

   GROUP REQUIREMENTS:                    HRS/MO
1. 4 PEOPLE MEETINGS                      0
2. 5-8 PEOPLE MEETINGS                    0
3. 9-12 PEOPLE MEETINGS                   0
4. > 12 PEOPLE MEETINGS                   0
   AIDS:
1. CHALK BOARD CONF      2. OTHER EQPT CONF
   REQUIRES  0.00 CONFERENCE ROOMS
```

References

Abelson, Philip H. 1982. ''The Revolution in Computers and Electronics.'' *Science* no. 4534; 752.

——. 1985. ''The Bell Laboratories Revisited.'' *Science* 227, no. 4686; 467.

Administrative Management. 1986. ''Off-Site Vaults.'' June, 64.

——. ''For Your Eyes Only. . . . Or Maybe Your Computer's.'' May, 74.

Administrative Management Society. 1988. ''1988 Office Salaries Survey.'' News Release, 12 August.

——. 1989. ''1989 Office Salaries Survey.'' News Release, August.

Allyn, Maureen F. 1988. ''Rising Factory Productivity Is Giving the Expansion Room to Run.'' *Fortune,* 1 August, 25–26.

Anderson, Howard. 1982. *Yankee Ingenuity* 6:5.

Andersson, B. J. G., and R. Ortengren. 1974. ''Lumbar Disc Pressure and Myoelectric Back Muscle Activity.'' *Scandinavian Journal of Rehabilitative Medicine* 3:115–121.

Anthony, Angelo. 1987. ''American Business Addresses Its Future.'' *Frequent Flyer,* May, 102–14.

——. 1988a. ''Tools for the Traveler.'' *Frequent Flyer,* February, 79–95.

——. 1988b. ''Tools for the Traveler.'' *Frequent Flyer,* September, 66 ff.

Apcar, Leonard M. 1985. ''Telecommuters Could Top 7.2 Million This Year.'' *The Wall Street Journal,* 5 February, 1.

The Architects' Journal (UK). 1985a. ''Energy Savings in Non-Domestic Buildings.'' 181, no. 14 (3 April); 53–58.

——. 1985b. ''Intelligent Building Blocks.'' 181, no. 5 (January 30): 47–54.

——. 1987. ''Life after Handover.'' 9 September, 5.

Architecture. 1988. ''Emergency Path Marking System.'' August, 136, 139.

AT&T Communications. 1986. Company brochure.

Attwood, Dennis. 1986. ''Ergonomics Implementation in Industry: A Case Study.'' In *19th Annual Meeting Proceedings,* 37–40. Human Factors Association of Canada.

Baldwin, M. W. 1983. ''Facilities Management by Computer.'' Presentation at an International Facilities Management Conference, Denver.

Barayon, Ramon Sender. 1988. ''John Ott, Light Pioneer.'' *Whole Earth Review,* 102–5.

Barden, John. 1988. ''Sitting Positions.'' *Designers' Journal* (UK) no. 41, (October): 74–78, 80.

BASF. 1986. "The Need for Conductive Carpet in the Contemporary Workplace." Williamsburg, Va.

Battle, Tim. 1987. "The Rise of Air Conditioning." *The Architects' Journal* (UK) 186: 33 and 34, 58–63.

Becker, Franklin. 1988. "How to Take the Crisis out of Office Relocations." *IFMA Journal*, Fall, 38–44.

Benz, Claus, Robert Grob, and Peter Haubner. 1983. *Designing VDU Workplaces*. Koln, West Germany: Verlag TUV Rheinland.

Best, Alistair. 1988. "Shelf Life." *Designers' Journal* (UK) no. 41 (October): 83–86.

Best, C. F. 1988. "An Evaluation of the Ergoscale." *The Ergonomist* (UK) 212 (January): 2–4.

Birell, James A., and Patrick N. White, 1982. "Using Technical Intervention to Behavioural Advantage." *Behaviour and Information Technology* (UK) 1:305–20.

Bogue, David T. 1990. "Order from Chaos: Evaluating Emerging Technologies in Information and Image Management." *Modern Office Technology* 35, no. 1 (January): 144, 146.

Bologna, Jack. 1985. "Internal Security: Issues and Answers." *Office Administration and Automation* 46, no. 7 (July): 33–37, 81.

Branscomb, Lewis M. 1982. "Electronics amd Computers: An Overview." *Science* 215:755–60.

Brill, Michael. 1980. "Productivity: How to Define It and Achieve It in the Office." Presentation at National Exposition of Contract Furnishings (NEOCON), June, Chicago, The Merchandise Mart.

Brookes, Malcolm J. 1972. "Changes in Employee Attitudes and Work Practices in an Office Landscape." In William J. Mitchell, ed., *Environmental Design: Research and Practice*, Proceedings of the EDRA 3/AR 8 Conference, 14-1-1–14-1-9.

Brookes, Malcolm J., and Peter P. Mitchell. 1982. "A Study of White Collar Productivity and Open Office System Furnishings." Brochure Published by Westinghouse Open Office Systems.

Bulkeley, William. 1982. "Pocket Terminal Said to Speed Access to Large Data Banks Is Unveiled." *The Wall Street Journal*, 26 March, 29.

Bureau of National Affairs. 1984. "VDT's in the Workplace: A Study of the Effects on Employment." Special Report 45-LDSR 30, Washington, D.C.

Cakir, A., D. J. Hart, and T. F. M. Stewart. 1980. *Visual Display Terminals: A Manual Covering Ergonomics, Workplace Design, Task Organization, Health and Safety*. New York: John Wiley & Sons.

Calver, Peter. 1989. "Wire Management in Furniture: The New British Standard." *Facilities* 7, no. 4 (April): 15–17.

Canestaro, N. K. 1987. "Open Office Programming: Assessment of The Workstation Game As a Planning Tool." *Dissertion Abstracts International*. University Microfilms no. 8720220.

Canestaro, Nancy K., and Ross G. MacLean. 1988. "Australian and U.S. Work Places: A Trade-Off Study." *Journal of Interior Design Education and Research* 14, no. 2 (Fall): 37–44.

Carlson, Jennifer A. 1986. "Defense Productivity Rockets 20 Percent with Open Plan Booster." *Facilities Design and Management*, July/August, 72–75.

Carolin, Peter. 1983. "Building Services Integration and Intelligence." *The Architects' Journal* (UK) 23 November, 114–32.

Carpet Cushion Council, 1986. "Selecting the Correct Contract Carpet Cushion for Every Traffic Area." Southfield, Mich.

Carrington, Tim. 1981. "Computer Linkups Let Traders Start Up Securities Firms at Home." *The Wall Street Journal*, 9 December, 25.

Carroll, Paul B. 1988. "Devices Expected to Hasten Age of Optical Storage." *The Wall Street Journal* 9 May, 25.

Caruso, Corrado, and Luigi Giffone, eds. for DEGW. 1987. "Space Planning & Facilities Management." *Habitat Ufficio* (Italy) 30 (February): 83–96.

Cave, Colin. 1981. "Changing Roles." *The Architects' Journal* (UK), 174, 45.

Centre for Advanced Land Use Studies (CALUS). 1983. *Property and Information Technology: The Future for the Office Market*. CALUS Research Report. Whiteknights, Reading, UK: British College of Real Estate Management.

Chace, Susan. 1983. "Tomorrow's Computer May Replace Itself, Some Visionaries Think." *The Wall Street Journal,* 6 January, 1.

Channer, Stephen D. 1983. "The Case for Furniture Befitting the Human Condition." *Modern Office Procedures* 28, no. 6 (June): 53–60.

Charles, Jeff, and John Miller. 1988. "Risks and Remedies, Noise: The Risks." *The Architects' Journal* (UK), 3 February, 47–56.

Cohen, Bernard. 1988. "Flooring of the Future." *Habitat Ufficio* (Italy), June, 32, 110–11.

Colombini, Daniela, ed. 1986. "L'Ergonomia Della Seduta." *Habitat Ufficio* (Italy), June, 20.

The Construction Specifier. 1989. "ASHRAE Adopts New Standards, Guidelines." 13, 15, December.

Contract. 1986. "Naugastat Helps Eliminate Static in Electronic Work Settings." April, 68.

——. 1987. "Thomas & Betts." July, 97.

——. 1988. "County Legislators Pass First Ergonomics Bill." July, 18.

——. 1989. "Court Alters Part of Suffolk VDT Law." January, 13.

Cook, Billy G. 1988. "Designing for Security from the Inside Out." *Architecture,* August, 125–26.

Cooper, Jerry, 1986. "Controlling Restaurant Noise." *Interior Design,* June, 232–34, 268–69.

Cooper, Rodney, 1988. "Post Bang New Deals." *Designers' Journal* (UK), February, 38–42.

Cooper, Rodney, and Alan Hart. 1984. "Sweeping Cables under the Carpet." *Designers' Journal* (UK), 2 February, 42–45.

Cooper, Walter A., and Kristine J. Ottervik. 1987. "Universal Cabling and Wire Management." *Interior Design,* May, 284, 285, 572, 573.

Corlin, Len, and Anne Falluchi. 1976. "The Open Plan—Love It or Adjust!—Users Evaluate Their Experiences." *Contract* 18, no. 7:51–53.

Cornell, Paul. 1988. "The Biomechanics of Sitting." Grand Rapids, Mich.: Steelcase, Inc., form no. S-065.

——. 1988. "High Backrest Support in Seating." Grand Rapids, Mich.: Steelcase, Inc., form no. S-066.

Craig, Marianne. 1983. *Office Workers Survival Handbook—A Guide to Fighting Health Hazards in the Office."* London: BSSRS Publications.

Cross Information Company. 1985. *Intelligent Buildings/Information Systems—IBIS.* Boulder, Col.

Crossen, Cynthia. 1985. "Fair Chairs." *The Wall Street Journal,* 2 August, 15.

Dainoff, Marvin J. 1984. "Ergonomics of Office Automation—A Conceptual Overview." In *Proceedings of the 1984 International Conference on Occupational Ergonomics,* vol. 2: Reviews, 72–80. Rexdale, Ontario: Human Factors Conference, Inc. (Human Factors Association of Canada/Association canadienne d'ergonomie).

Dainoff, Marvin J., Laurie Fraser, and B. J. Taylor. 1982. "Visual, Musculoskeletal and Performance Differences Between Good and Poor VDT Workstations: Preliminary Findings." *Proceedings of the Human Factors Society 26th Annual Meeting,* 144. Santa Monica: Human Factors Society.

Damon, A., H. W. Stoudt, and R. A. McFarland. 1966. *The Human Body in Equipment Design.* Cambridge, Mass.: Harvard University Press.

Daniels, Gilbert S. 1952. *The "Average Man"?* Technical Note WCRD-53-7, December. Aero Medical Laboratory, Wright Air Development Center, Wright Patterson Air Force Base, Ohio.

DeGroot, J. P, and R. Vellinga. 1984. "Practical Usage of Adjustable Features in Terminal Furniture." In *Proceedings of the 1984 International Conference on Occupational Ergonomics* 1: 308–12. Rexdale, Ontario: Human Factors Conference, Inc.

Derven, Ronald. 1985. "New Occupancy Sensors Are Automatic Watt Misers." *Facilities Design and Management* 4, no. 5 (June): 76–79.

Designers' Journal (UK). 1985: "Reuters." 11 September, 38–39.

DeWald, Karen. 1987. "Looking into Fire Research." *ASID Report* 12, no. 4:8–10.

DiLaura, D. L., and R. G. Mistrick. 1985. ''Direct vs. Indirect Lighting in the Electronic Office.'' *Corporate Design and Realty* 4, no. 1: 138–40.

Drucker, Peter. 1985. ''Playing in the Information-Based Orchestra.'' *The Wall Street Journal,* 4 June, 22.

——. 1989. ''Information and the Future of the City.'' *The Wall Street Journal,* 4 April, 24.

Dubbs, Dana. 1989. ''Venting Health Complaints.'' *Contract,* March, 126–27.

Duffy, Francis, 1981a. ''Changing Offices.'' *The Architects' Journal* (UK) 174:5.

——. 1981b. ''Nine to Five.'' *The Architects' Journal* (UK) 174:495.

——. 1982. ''The Architect and Information Technology.'' *The Architects' Journal* (UK) 175:13

——. 1983. *The ORBIT Study: Information Technology and Office Design,* Maryanne Chandor, ed. London: DEGW and Eosys.

——. 1988a. ''The European Challenge.'' *The Architects' Journal* (UK), 17 August, 30–42.

——. 1988b. ''Hertzberger on the Slow Track.'' *The Architects' Journal* (UK), 13 January, 36–41.

——. 1987. ''Change Is Importunate.'' *The Architects' Journal* (UK), 19 and 26 August, 34–37.

Duffy, Francis, Colin Cave, and John Worthington. 1976. *Planning Office Space.* London: Architectural Press.

Duffy, Francis, and Roger Pye. 1979. ''Offices, the Future Landscape: Paper Factory or Room with a View.'' *The Architects' Journal* (UK) 170:669–75.

Duffy, Frank, and Paul Stansall. 1985. ''Growing Concerns.'' *Designers' Journal* (UK), October, 56–65.

Duke, Paul Jr. 1985. ''NASA Roots Out Earthly Cure for Polluted Air in Space Stations.'' *The Wall Street Journal,* 28 August, 23.

Dukes, Bernard. 1987. ''Cabling Trends.'' *Facilities* (UK), July, 8–9.

——. 1988. ''Is Your Floor Box Really Necessary?'' *Facilities* (UK), May, 18–19.

Dumesnil, Carla D. 1987. ''Office Case Study: Social Behavior in Relation to the Design of the Environment.'' *The Journal of Architectural and Planning Research* 4, no. 1:7–13.

Dykeman, John. 1988. ''Optical Disk a Technology on the Move.'' *Modern Office Technology,* June, 82–88.

Eakin, David B. 1989. ''The General Services Administration's Advanced-Technology Buildings Program: A Statement of Direction, Building Features and Applications.'' In Goumain, Pierre, ed., *High-Technology Workplaces.* London, New York, Toronto, Melbourne, Agincourt: Van Nostrand Reinhold.

Eley, Peter, and John Worthington. 1984. *Industrial Rehabilitation: The Use of Redundant Buildings for Small Enterprises.* London: The Architectural Press.

Ellis, Peter. 1984. ''Keyboard-Induced Injuries.'' *Facilities* (UK) 2, no. 12:2.

——. 1986a. ''Functional, Aesthetic and Symbolic Aspects of Lighting.'' In Jean D. Wineman, ed., *Behavioral Issues in Office Design,* 225–49. New York: Van Nostrand Reinhold.

——. 1986b. ''International Association of Applied Psychology Congress.'' Report, *Facilities* (UK), October, 2.

Ellis, Peter, and Francis Duffy. 1982. ''Building for Better Labour Relations.'' *Management Today* (UK), July.

Engel, Peter. 1987. ''Lighting Controls Shine from Reduced Energy Costs.'' *Facilities Design and Management,* June, 76–78.

Engelken, Larry J. 1984. ''CAD Applications for the HVAC Engineer.'' *Heating/Piping/Air Conditioning,* July, 59–62, 82.

Eosys. 1988. ''Cabling Guide.'' *The Architects' Journal* (UK), 8 June, 59–67; 15 June, 59–63; 22 June, 51–57; 29 June, 65–71; 6 July, 51–55.

Evans, Barrie. 1984. ''Building with Information Technology 5: Offices.'' *The Architects' Journal* (UK) 180, no. 29:61–66.

Facilities (UK). 1988. ''Choosing Office Furniture.'' March, 8.

Facilities Design and Management. 1987. ''Videoconferencing Demands: A Holistic Approach.'' July/August, 50–57.

——. 1990a. ''Big Blue Unveils Low-Key, Low Radiation Computer Monitors.'' March, 20.

——. 1990b. ''Standard Assures Indoor Air Quality.'' February, 14.
——. 1990c. ''VDT Rules: New York vs. New Jersey.'' January, 7.
Falluchi, Anne. 1982. ''There's Too Much at Stake to Ignore Tomorrow's Office.'' *Facilities Design and Management,* June, 39.
FCW/Contract. 1986. ''Partitions on Top of Carpet.'' February, A7.
Federal Design Matters. 1977. ''Army Word Processing Center.'' 4.
Fernberg, Patricia M. 1988. ''Ergonomic Seating: Finding the Chair That Fits Your Needs.'' *Modern Office Technology,* June, 50–54.
Fine, Brenda. 1988. ''Flying High . . . Tech: Passenger-Friendly Cabins.'' *Frequent Flyer,* September, 54–60.
Finlay, Douglas, 1987a. ''Global Integration the Seamless Way.'' *Administrative Management,* May, 18–23.
——. 1987b. ''Powered Systems Furnishings Ease Cabling Woes.'' *Administrative Management,* July, 40–44.
Francis, J., and D. L. Dressel. 1990. ''Workspace Influence on Worker Performance and Satisfaction: An Experimental Field Study.'' In Steven L. Sauter, Marvin J. Dainoff, and Michael J. Smith, eds., *Promoting Health and Productivity in the Computerized Office: Models of Successful Ergonomic Interventions.''* London and Philadelphia: Taylor & Francis. In press.
Freidin, H. Richard. 1982. ''Lighting: Specifying the Benefits.'' *The Construction Specifier,* March, 62–71.
Frequent Flyer. 1982. ''OAG Pocket Flight Guide'' Part 2. September, 14.
Freund, Eric C. 1987. ''Pursuing the Future to Preserve the Past.'' *The Construction Specifier,* July, 35–37.
Gerola, Humberto, and Ralph E. Gomery. 1984. ''Computers in Science and Technology: Early Indications.'' *Science* 225, no. 4657:11–18.
Gibson, Frank E. 1984. ''Selecting Access Flooring for Offices.'' *The Construction Specifier,* August, 38–41.
Ginzberg, Eli, and the Editorial Advisory Board. 1984. ''The Office Work Force of the 1990's.'' *Corporate Design,* July/August, 149–54.
Glickman, Michael. 1984. ''File Copy.'' *Designers' Journal* (UK), 98–100.
Goldstein, David B. 1984. ''Optimal Lighting Strategies: Designing to Prevent Wasted Light.'' *The Construction Specifier,* October, 38–45.
Goodrich, Ronald. 1986. ''The Perceived Office: The Office Environment as Experienced by Its Users.'' In Jean D. Wineman, ed. *Behavioral Issues in Office Design,* 190–33. New York: Van Nostrand Reinhold.
Gordon, Douglas E. 1987. ''Lighting Requirements for VDT's.'' *Architecture,* June, 106–8.
——. 1988. ''Professional Seminars Address Emerging Technologies.'' *Architecture,* 27, 30.
Gottschalk, Earl C., Jr. 1987. ''Tax Changes for Historic Preservation Lead Syndicators to Seek Smaller Investors.'' *The Wall Street Journal,* 2 March, 25.
Grandjean, E. 1980. *Fitting the Task to the Man,* 3d ed. London and Philadelphia: Taylor & Francis.
Grandjean, Etienne. 1985. ''Design of VDT Workstations.'' In G. Salvendy, ed., *Handbook on Human Factors/Ergonomics.* Santa Monica: Human Factors Society.
——. 1986. *Ergonomics in Computerized Offices.* London, New York, Philadelphia: Taylor & Francis.
Grandjean, Etienne, ed. 1984. *Ergonomics and Health in Modern Offices.* London and Philadelphia: Taylor & Francis.
Grandjean, E., W. Hunting, M. Piderman. 1983. ''A Field Study of Preferred Settings of an Adjustable VDT Workstation and Their Effects on Body Postures and Subjective Feelings.'' *Human Factors Journal* 25, no. 2:161–75.
Grandjean, E., K. Nishiyama, W. Hunting, and M. Piderman. 1982. ''A Laboratory Study on Preferred and Imposed Settings of a VDT Workstation.'' *Behaviour and Information Technology* 1, (UK) no. 3:289–304.
Grandjean, E., and E. Vigliani. 1980. *Ergonomic Aspects of Visual Display Terminals.* London and Philadelphia: Taylor & Francis.
Greenberg, Adam. 1988. ''Laptops Boost PC's Standing in Home Office.'' *hfd,* 25 July, 98.

Guenther, Robert. 1987. "Historic Rehabilitations Drop Despite Continued Tax Credit." *The Wall Street Journal,* 3 June, 33.

Gutman, Liz. 1988. "Fibre Optics in Communications Systems." *Facilities* (UK), February, 4–5.

Gupta, Amar. 1982. "An Overview of Contemporary Office Automation Technology." *Behaviour & Information Technology* (UK) 1, no. 3:217–36.

Haavind, Robert C. 1982. "Breaking Down Corporate Empires." *High Technology* 1, no. 1:30.

Hall, Edward T. 1970. Preface in Leon A. Pastalan and Daniel H. Carson, eds., *Spatial Behavior of Older People.* Ann Arbor: Institute of Gerontology, University of Michigan—Wayne State University.

Hall, Stephen S. 1983. "Biochips." *United,* December, 89–95.

Harack, Tom. 1987. "Illuminating Drawbacks of Lighting Trends." *Corporate Design and Realty,* January/February, 38–39.

Harbinger, Sims, William, and Becker, Franklin. 1985. *ORBIT 2.* London: DEGW.

Harris, George T. 1977. "Psychology of the New York Work Space." *New York* 10, no. 44 (31 October): 51–54.

Harrison, Andrew. 1988. "Practical Wiring Issues—Towards the Fourth Building Utility." *Facilities* (UK) 6, no. 10 (October): 6–7.

Harrison, John, and Anthony Pickering. 1987. "Sick Building Syndrome." *The Architects' Journal* (UK) 10 June, 59–60.

Hawkins, Phoebe, with Charlotte Low. 1986. "Going to Work by Staying at Home." *Insight,* 21 July, 44–45.

Heaton, Nigel. 1986. "Voice Recognition." *The Ergonomist* (UK), December, 1.

Hedberg, Augustin. 1989. "Plugging in the Home Office of Tomorrow." *New York Times Magazine,* 15 October, 60, 61.

Hedge, Alan. 1984. "Ill Health among Office Workers: An Examination of the Relationship between Office Design and Employee Well-Being." In E. Grandjean, ed., *Ergonomics and Health in Modern Offices,* 46–51. London and Philadelphia: Taylor & Francis.

——. 1987. "Office Health Hazards: An Annotated Bibliography." *Ergonomics* (UK), May, 733–72.

——. 1990. "Sick Building Syndrome Correlates with Complex Array of Factors." *IFMA Journal,* January/February, 52–58.

Hedge, Alan, Elia M. Sterling, and Theodore D. Sterling. 1986. "Evaluating Office Environments: The Case for a Macroergonomic Approach." In O. Brown, Jr. and Hal W. Hendrick, eds. *Human Factors in Organizational Design and Management,* vol. 2, 419–24. Amsterdam, New York, Oxford, Tokyo: North Holland, Elsevier.

Heerwagen, Judith H. 1987. "Windowscapes: The Psychology of a View." *The Construction Specifier,* August, 31–32.

Hembree, Diana. 1990. "Warning: Computing Can Be Hazardous to Your Health." *MacWorld,* January, 150, 154–57.

hfd, 1988a. "Link Survey: 2 Million Americans Began Working at Home in Last 12 Months." 4 July, 95.

——. 1988b. "Sears to Install Satellite Network for Conferencing." 11 April, 18.

——. 1988c. "Tandy CD Shocks Industry—Giants React to Inexpensive Record/Erase Device." 2 May, 145.

Hirsch, Richard H. 1984. "VDTs and the Human Factors Community: Tipping the Iceberg." *Human Factors Society Bulletin* 27, no. 6:1–3.

Hirtle, Parker. 1987. "Acoustics Baffle Even the Experts." *Corporate Design & Realty,* January/February, 50–52.

Hughes, David. 1990. "NASA Will Fly Computer Processor, Erasable Optical Disk on Space Shuttle." *Aviation Week and Space Technology,* 15 January, 47.

Human Factors Society. 1988. *American National Standard for Human Factors Engineering of Visual Display Terminal Workstations.*

Hunting, W., T. Laubli, and E. Grandjean. 1981. "Postural and Visual Loads at VDT Workplaces. I. Constrained Postures." *Ergonomics* (UK) 24, no. 12:917–32.

IFMA News. 1989. "Adjustable Furniture Required by Law." February, 4.

——. 1990. "New York Judge Overturns VDT Law." February, 7.

Inaba, Minoru. 1988. "Japan's 2nd Wave Videophones Due in U.S." *hfd* 2 May, 156.

Kaplan, Audrey G. 1985. "FUNDI Field Trial." DOC/OCS. Ottawa: Public Works Canada.

——. 1990. "Building Diagnosis Improves Overall Effectiveness of Facility." *IFMA Journal,* January/February, 42–49.

Kerr, Richard A. 1987. "Compact Discs Shrinking Data Storage Costs." *Science,* 7 August, 604.

Kimsey, Steven P., with Perry Jarrell, and Andrew Beldecos. 1988. "Comparative Analysis of Alternative Energy Efficient Lighting Systems." *Architecture,* June, 114–17.

Kirkpatrick, David. 1988. "How Safe Are Video Terminals?" *Fortune,* 29 August, 66–71.

Kleeman, Walter B, Jr. 1982. "Air Traffic Controllers' Chairs Evaluated for the Federal Aviation Administration." *Human Factors Society Bulletin* 25, no. 12 (December): 5–7.

——. 1982b. "The Future of the Office." *Environment and Behavior* 14, no. 5 (September): 593–610.

——. 1983. *The Challenge of Interior Design.* New York, Cincinnati, Toronto, London, Melbourne: Van Nostrand Reinhold.

——. 1986. "The Office of the Future." In Jean D. Wineman, ed., *Behavioral Issues in Office Design.* New York, Cincinnati, Toronto, London, Melbourne: Van Nostrand Reinhold.

——. 1988. "The Politics of Office Design." *Environment and Behavior* 20, no. 5 (September): 537–49.

——. 1989. "Gas Cylinder Dangers." *Human Factors Society Bulletin* 32, no. 2 (February): 8–9.

Kleeman, Walter B., Jr., and Thomas Prunier. 1982. "Evaluation of Chairs Used by Air Traffic Controllers of the U.S. Federal Aviation Administration—Implications for Design." In Ronald Easterby, K. H. E. Kroemer, and Don B. Chaffin, eds., *Anthropometry and Biomechanics: Theory and Application,* 235–39. NATO Series III: Human Factors. Proceedings of a NATO Symposium, 7–11 July, 1980. New York and London: Plenum Press.

Knobel, Lance. 1983. "Clearing the Cable Confusion." *Designers' Journal* (UK), November, 66–74.

Kodak. 1988. "The new vision of Kodak." Ad in *Fortune,* 6 June, 17.

Kroemer, K. H. E., H. J. Kroemer, and K. E. Kroemer-Elbert. 1986. *Engineering Physiology: Physiologic Bases of Human Factors/ Ergonomics,* A, 32. Amsterdam, Oxford, New York, Tokyo: Elsevier.

Kroemer, K. H. Eberhard, and Joan C. Robinette. 1968. *Ergonomics in the Design of Office Furniture: A Review of the European Literature.* Report no. AMRL-TR-68-80. Wright-Patterson Air Force Base: Aerospace Medical Research Laboratories.

Kron, Penny. 1986. "Security and Fire Protection." *Buildings Design Journal,* April, 16, 17, 24.

Krotz, Joanna L. 1990. "The Ultimate Office on Wheels." *Money,* March, 100–108.

Krouse, John K. 1983. "Selecting a Graphics-Input Device for CAD/CAM." *Machine Design,* October, 74–80.

Labranca, Tommaso. 1988. "The Sick Building Syndrome." *Habitat Ufficio* (Italy) 31 (April): 1330–35.

Lanctot, Roger C. 1988. "Link's Miller Gets a Handle on Home Office." *hfd,* May 2, 159.

Laubli, T., W. Hunting, and E. Grandjean. 1981. "Postural and Visual Loads at VDT Workplaces. II. Lighting Conditions and Visual Impairments." *Ergonomics* (UK) 24, no. 12:933–44.

Lob, M., M. Guillemin, P. Madelaine, and M.-A. Boillat. 1980. "Collective Dermatitis in a Modern Office." In E. Grandjean, ed., *Ergonomics and Health in Modern Offices,* 52–58. London and Philadelphia: Taylor & Francis.

Lord, David. 1988. "Simulation of Lighting Designs." *Architecture,* June, 106–8.

Lublin, Joann S. 1982. "Labor Letter." *The Wall Street Journal,* 16 February, 1.

Lueder, R. 1986. "Seat Height Revisited." *Human Factors Society Bulletin* 29, no. 11:4–5.

Lueder, Rani, ed. 1986. *The Ergonomics Payoff: Designing the Automated Office.* New York: Van Nostrand Reinhold.

Lueder, Rani Karen. 1983. ''Seat Comfort: A Review of the Construct in the Office Environment.'' *Human Factors* 25, no. 6:701-12.

Magliano, John V. 1985. ''Can Access Flooring Unsnarl the Wiring Jungle?'' *Corporate Design and Realty* 4, no. 5 (June): 96-99.

Maguire, Mary. 1989. ''Reproducing Documents: A Choice of Duplicators.'' *The Office,* November, 58.

Makower, Joel. 1981. *Office Hazards: How Your Job Can Make You Sick.* Washington, D.C.: Tilden Press.

Marberry, Sara O. 1987. ''Companies Spend Big Bucks on R&D.'' *Contract,* January, 190-193.

Marshall, Robert. 1970. ''Carpet as an Acoustical Material.'' *Canadian Interiors,* 7, no. 1:36-39.

Martin, Roger. 1981. Speech given at ''New Directions and Issues for Interior Design Practice and Education in the 80's,'' symposium at the University of Cincinnati.

Mauro, Charles. 1981. ''Human Factors Study Crucial for Future Office.'' *Industrial Design* 28, no. 2:29.

McCandless, David. 1987. ''Church Acoustics.'' *The Construction Specifier,* March, 54-62.

McFarlane, Robert E. 1987. ''PBX.'' *Interior Design,* 304-5.

McGregor, Douglas. 1960. *The Human Side of Enterprise.* New York: McGraw-Hill.

McKeon, Nancy. 1981. ''Wired for the Future.'' *New York,* 14, 34, 50.

McMillan, Lorel. 1985a. ''Carpet Tiles Are a Natural for Access Floors and Flat Wire.'' *Facilities Design and Management* 4, no. 4:102-5.

——. 1985b. ''High-Density Mobile Files Move—and Store—Mountains.'' *Facilities Design and Management* 4, no. 9:108-13.

——. 1986. ''ACT Puts Fabric Codes to the Test.'' *Facilities Design and Management,* September, 67-69.

——. 1987. ''Control Is the Key to Power-Full Flooring.'' *Facilities Design and Management,* April, 68-70.

Meade, Martin. 1984. ''Banque populaire.'' *The Architects' Journal* (UK), 28, no. 180:40-51.

Mechanical Engineering. 1983. ''Developing a Desktop Computer-Based Three-Dimensional Modeling System.'' November, 50-61.

Miller, John, and Jeff Charles. 1988. ''Risk and Remedies 2—Noise: The remedies.'' *The Architects' Journal* (UK), 10 February, 55-63.

Miller, Michael W. 1986. ''In this Futuristic Office, Intimacy Exists between Workers Separated by 500 Miles.'' *The Wall Street Journal,* 27 June, 31.

Miller, Win, and Thomas W. Suther, III. 1983. ''Display Station Anthropometrics: Preferred Height and Angle Settings of CRT and Keyboard.'' *Human Factors* 25, no. 4. 401-8.

Modern Office Technology. 1984. ''To Get Ahead, Get a Headset, Research Suggests.'' November, 36.

——. 1988a. ''Faster Fax, Coast to Coast.'' March, 24.

——. 1988b. ''Fiber Optic Cables: Do's and Don'ts.'' September, 38.

——. ''Portable 2400 bps Modem Debuts.'' August, 22.

Morris, Betsy. 1983. ''Hotels Start Luring Video Conferences.'' *The Wall Street Journal,* 25 February, 25.

Mullin, Stephen. 1976. ''Some Notes on an Activity.'' In Francis Duffy, Colin Cave, and John Worthington, eds., *Planning Office Space.* London: The Architectural Press.

Nachemson, A., and G. Elfstrom. 1970. ''Intravital Pressure Measurements in Lumbar Discs.'' *Scandinavian Journal of Rehabilitation,* Med. Suppl. 1.

National Aeronautics and Space Administration. 1971. *Architecture and Environment.* Habitatility Data Handbook, vol. 2, MSC-03909. Houston: Habitability Technology Section, Spacecraft Design Division, Manned Spacecraft Center.

National Lighting Bureau. 1988. *Office Lighting and Productivity.* Washington, D.C.

National Office Products Association in association with the University of Michigan. 1983. *The Future of the Office Furniture Industry.* Alexandria, Va.: National Office Products Association.

National Research Council. 1983. *Video Displays: Work and Vision.* Washington, D.C.: National Academy Press.

Neiss, Doug. 1988. Workbench Symposium Examines Needs of the Home-Based Worker.'' *hfd,* 25 July, 79.

Nemecek, J. and E. Grandjean. 1973. ''Results of an Ergonomic investigation of large-space offices.'' *Human Factors* 15:111–24.

The New York Times. 1987. Business Section, February 8.

Nightingale, Donald V. 1981. ''Work, Formal Participation and Employee Outcomes.'' *Sociology of Work and Occupations* 8, no. 3:277–91.

Nordwall, Bruce D. 1990. ''Aerospace Companies Capitalize on Benefits of Videoconferencing.'' *Aviation Week and Space Technology,* 1 January, 53, 55, 56.

Numark, David. 1987. ''Choosing Carpet.'' *Professional Office Design,* May/June, 57–58.

NYNEX Supplement to *The Wall Street Journal.* 1988. ''Where Business Is Headed: Top Executives Speak Out.'' 11 March.

OAG Pocket Flight Guide. 1982. Part 2: September, 14.

The Office. 1990. ''Rewritable Technology: Where Does It Fit?'' April, 77.

Office Administration and Automation. 1985. ''Verbatim Displays Erasable Optical Disk.'' 46; no. 9 (September): 17.

Ong, C. N. 1984. ''VDT Work Place Design and Physical Fatigue: A Case Study in Singapore.'' In E. Grandjean, ed., *Ergonomics and Health in Modern Offices,* 484–94. London and Philadelphia: Taylor & Francis.

——. 1985. Personal communication.

Ontario Hydro, Health and Safety Division, Safety Services Department. 1985. *Hazard Assessment of Video Display Units Final Report,* vols. 1 and 2. December. Toronto.

Ostberg, O., B. Warell, and L. Nordell. 1984. ''ComforTable® A Generic Desk for the Automated Office.'' In E. Grandjean, guest ed., *Behaviour and Information Technology* (UK) 3, no. 4:411–16.

Ott, James. 1985. ''Videoconference Use Expands to Meet Rising Business Needs.'' *Aviation Week and Space Technology* 123, no. 3: 157–64.

Ottaiano, Ralph A. 1987. ''Wiring for Flexibility: Access Flooring.'' *Corporate Design and Realty,* March, 44–46.

Owens-Corning Fiberglas Corporation. 1983. ''Noise Control Design Guide.'' Toledo.

——. 1984. ''Noise Control Manual.'' Toledo.

Parkinson, Kenneth. 1984. ''Buildings with Information Technology 1: Specifying Data Cabling.'' *The Architects' Journal* 24 (UK), no. 179: 71–79.

Paznik, M. Jill. 1986. ''Optical Character Readers and Image Scanners Can Reduce Workload.'' *Administrative Management,* July, 23–28.

Person, Sarah. 1988. ''Leasing Alternatives with Panache.'' *Professional Office Design,* July/August, 57–58.

Pesmen, Curtis. 1982. ''The Missing Link.'' *Frequent Flyer,* August, 47.

Pettus, Theodore. 1982. ''Home Is Where the Office Is.'' *New York,* 15, 15, 33.

Pianzola, Luisa. 1988. ''SAM: The Modular Office.'' *Habitat Ufficio* (Italy) no. 34 (October): 120–23.

Picasso, Gere, AT&T Communications. 1985. Personal communication.

Pile, John. 1977. ''The Open Office: Does It Work?'' *Progressive Architecture,* June, 66–81.

Pineault, R., and D. Berthelette. 1984. ''Health Hazards of VDTs.'' In E. Grandjean, ed., *Ergonomics and Health in Modern Offices,* 146–51. London and Philadelphia: Taylor & Francis.

PPG Industries Feneshield Fabrics. 1976. Pittsburgh: PPG Industries.

Radl, G. W. 1980. ''Experimental Investigations for Optimal Presentation-Mode and Colours of Symbols on the CRT-Screen.'' In E. Grandjean, and E. Vigliani, eds., *Ergonomic Aspects of Visual Display Terminals,* 127–35. London and Philadelphia: Taylor & Francis.

Ramazzini's Corner. 1989. ''Sick Building Syndrome.'' *At the Centre* (Canada) 12, no. 1 (June): 20.

Rand, George. 1985. ''Examining 'Sick' Buildings.'' *Architecture* 74, no. 1:80–83.

——. 1986. ''Whatever Happened to the Office of the Future?'' *Architecture* 75, no. 12:106–8.

——. 1988. "Indoor Pollution Isn't Going Away." *Architecture,* June, 99–102.

——. 1989. "Indoor Pollution: The Issue Continues to Build." *Architecture* 78, no. 3 (March): 117–20.

Randall, F. E., Albert Damon, Robert S. Benton, and Donald I. Patt. 1946. "Human Body Size in Military Aircraft and Personal Equipment." Army Air Forces Technical report no. 5501. Wright-Patterson Air Force Base, OH Air Materiel Command.

Reid, Chris. 1988. "Architectural Light 3: Lighting Offices." *The Architects' Journal* (UK), 13 April, 55–59.

Reis, Robert S. 1987. Personal communication.

Richardson, Walt R. 1986. "Sorting Out VAV 'Variables'." *Corporate Design and Realty,* 70–71.

Romei, Lura K. 1989. "Redefining the Office, Finnish Style." *Modern Office Technology,* April, 84, 86.

Rothchild, Edward S. 1984. "Optical Memories Eye Computer Markets." *High Technology,* February, 26–31.

Rothfeder, Jeffrey, 1982. "Computerized Community Being Built." *The New York Times* (New Jersey ed.), 8 August, 1 ff.

Rubin, Arthur. 1983. *The Automated Office—An Environment for Productive Work, or an Information Factory?: A Report on the State-of-the-Art.* National Technical Information Service report no. NBSIR 83-2784-1. Sponsored by Public Buildings Service, General Services Administration, Washington, D.C.

——. 1984. *Interim Design Guidelines for Automated Offices.* National Technical Information Service report no. NBSIR 84-2908. Sponsored by Public Buildings Service, General Services Administration, Washington, D.C.

——. 1986. *Revised Interim Guidelines for Automated Offices.* National Technical Information Service report no. NBSIR 86-3430. Sponsored by the General Services Administration, Washington, D.C.

Ruff, Carl. 1985. "Merck Case History." *Architecture* 74, no. 11:S5.

Sauer, David M. 1986. "Changing Roles." *Commercial Renovation,* February, 6.

Sauter, S. L., and R. Arndt. 1984. "Ergonomics in the Automated Office: Gaps in Knowledge and Practice." In G. Salvendy, ed., *Human-Computer Interaction,* 411–14. Amsterdam: Elsevier.

Sauter, Steven L., Marvin J. Dainoff, and Michael J. Smith, eds. 1990. *Promoting Health and Productivity in the Computerized Office: Models of Successful Ergonomic Interventions.* London: Taylor & Francis. In press.

Saxon, Richard. 1984. "Raising the Floor." *Designers' Journal,* September, 82–89.

Scalet, Elizabeth A. 1987. *VDT Health and Safety Issues and Solutions.* T. F. M. Stewart, cons. ed. Kate McGee, res. assoc. Lawrence, K., and London: Ergosyst Associates.

Schiller, Gail, et al. 1988. *Thermal Environments and Comfort in Office Buildings.* Berkeley: Center for Environmental Design Research, University of California.

Schlender, Brenton R. 1987. "Tandon to Unveil Hard-Disk Drives That Are Portable." *The Wall Street Journal,* 18 March, 9.

Schnipper, Scott. 1984. "Flat Cable's Next Generation Arrives." *Facilities Design and Management* 3, no. 9:106–9.

Sebastian, Pamela. 1988. "Nynex Unit Freezes Long Island Hiring, Plans to Close Office." *The Wall Street Journal,* 6 July, 29.

Shaffer, Richard A. 1982. "Satellite Transmission of Data May Take Off." *The Wall Street Journal,* 2 July, 27.

Showker, Kay. 1985. "An Office Away from the Office." *OAG Frequent Flyer,* February, 76–80.

Simmons-Forbes, M. 1986. "World Bank: New Workplace Standards." *Facilities* (UK) 4, no. 11:15.

——. 1987. Personal communication.

Skerritt, John. 1982. "Banking: Containing the Costs." *The Architects' Journal* (UK) 174, no. 34:42.

Smith, Desmond. 1981. "Info City." *New York* 14, no. 6:24–29.

——. 1982. "The City's Coming White-Collar Crisis." *New York* 15, no. 38:32.

Smith, E. D., 1989. "Burning Issues: State Toxicity Codes and Product Liability." *Contract,* November, 32.

Smith, G. Wentworth. 1987. ''Double Glue Carpet Foils Ugly-Out.'' *Facilities Design and Management,* February, 66–67.

——. ''Carpet 'Wear' Is Performance—But How Is Performance Defined?'' *Facilities Design and Management,* June, 29 and 34.

Smith, Wendy. 1988. ''Bucking the Systems?'' *Interior Design* (UK), July/August, 38–42.

Springer, T. J. 1982. *Visual Display Terminal Workstations: A Comparable Evaluation of Alternatives.* Bloomington, Ill.: State Farm Mutual Automobile Insurance Company.

——. 1986. *Improving Productivity in the Workplace: Reports from the Field.* St. Charles, Ill. Springer Associates.

Spinrad, R. J. 1982. ''Office Automation.'' *Science* 215, no. 4534:812.

Steelcase Inc. 1978. *Do They Work?* The Steelcase National Study of Office Environments: no. 1. Conducted by Louis Harris & Associates, Inc. Grand Rapids, Mich.: Steelcase Inc.

——. 1980. *Comfort and Productivity in the Office of the 80's.* The Steelcase National Study of Office Environments, no. 2. Conducted by Louis Harris & Associates. Grand Rapids, Mich.: Steelcase Inc.

——. 1983a. *Case Studies in Office Productivity.* Written by the American Productivity Center, Houston, Tex. Grand Rapids, Mich.: Steelcase Inc.

——. 1983b. *White Collar Productivity: The National Challenge.* Written by the American Productivity Center, Houston, Tex. Grand Rapids, Mich.: Steelcase Inc.

——. 1986. *Wiring and Cabling.* Grand Rapids, Mich.: Steelcase Inc.

——. 1987. *The Office Environment Index: 1987 Full Report.* Conducted by Louis Harris and Associates. Grand Rapids, Mich.: Steelcase Inc.

——. 1988. *The 1988 Office Environment Index.* Conducted by Louis Harris and Associates. Grand Rapids, Mich.: Steelcase Inc.

——. 1989. *The 1989 Office Environment Index.* Conducted by Louis Harris and Associates. Grand Rapids, Mich.: Steelcase Inc.

Steele, Fritz. 1986. ''The Dynamics of Power and Influence in Workplace Design and Management.'' In Jean D. Wineman, ed., *Behavioral Issues in Office Design,* 43–63. New York: Van Nostrand Reinhold.

Sterling, E. M., E. D. McIntyre, and T. D. Sterling. 1984. ''The Effects of Sealed Buildings on the Ambient Environment of Office Workers.'' In E. Grandjean, ed., *Ergonomics and Health in Modern Offices,* 70–76. London and Philadelphia: Taylor & Francis.

Stewart, T. F. M. 1980. ''Practical Experiences in Solving VDU Ergonomics Problems.'' In E. Grandjean, and E. Vigliani, eds., *Ergonomic Aspects of Visual Display Terminals,* 233–40. London and Philadelphia: Taylor & Francis.

Stewart, Tom. 1988. ''Ergonomics Training at Marks & Spencer.'' *Facilities (UK),* August, 8–9.

Stone, Philip J., and Robert Luchetti. 1985. ''Your Office is Where You Are.'' *Harvard Business Review,* March-April, 102–17.

Streeter, John. 1986. ''Security: All Under Control.'' *Designers Journal* (UK), 87–89.

Strehlo, Kevin. 1983. ''Power at Your Fingertips.'' *Personal Computing,* November, 37–42.

Stuckle, Don. TRW. 1985. Personal communication.

Sullivan, C. 1990. ''Employee Comfort, Satisfaction and Productivity: Recent Efforts at Aetna.'' In Steven L. Sauter, Marvin J. Dainoff, and Michael J. Smith, eds., *Promoting Health and Productivity in the Computerized Office: Models of Successful Ergonomic Interventions.* London: Taylor & Francis. In press.

Sutherland, Duncan B., Jr. 1990. ''The Office Is Dead. . . . Long Live The Office!'' *Facility Management Journal,* March/April, 40–42.

Taafe, Theodore. 1988. ''Riding the Waves.'' *Frequent Flyer,* April, 44–46.

Tandy Corporation. 1988. ''The First Record and Erase CD-Compatible Optical Disc.'' Ad in *The Wall Street Journal,* 22 April, 16.

Tannenbaum, Jeffrey A. 1981. ''Quality Circles Spread to Banks and Other Service Concerns.'' *The Wall Street Journal,* 3 February, 1.

Tate, Robert G., Jr. 1984. *Company Wide Quality Control Questions and Answers.* Red Bluff, Calif.: Quality Circle Institute.

Thomas, Marita. 1987. ''Sounding Off on Acoustics for Facilities.'' *Facilities Design and Management,* May, 82–85.

——. 1989. "Can Plants Purify Indoor Air? Yes, Says NASA." *Facilities Design and Management,* September, 56–59.

Tobin, John H. 1988. *Monday Morning Message.* August 15.

Todd, Colin, and David Tong. 1986. "New Generation Fire Systems." *Facilities* (UK), June, 9–12.

Toffler, Alvin. 1981. *The Third Wave.* New York: Bantam Books.

Tong, David, and Peter Ellis. 1986. "Activity Analysis: A Case Study of a New Trend in Office Planning." In Jean Wineman, Richard Barnes, and Craig Zimring, eds., *The Costs of Not Knowing . . . ,* 187–92. Proceedings of the 17th Annual Conference of the Environmental Design Assn.

Trickett, Terry. 1989. "Office Design towards the 1990's." *The Architects' Journal* 189, no. 14 (5 April): 69–74.

Trost, Cathy. 1986. "Study on VDT Use During Pregnancy Seen Lessening Concern of Health Risks." *The Wall Street Journal,* 30 September, 5.

Truppin, Andrea. 1989. "Office for the Third Millenium." *Interiors,* November, cover story.

Turiel, I., et al. 1982. "The Effects of Reduced Ventilation on Indoor Quality in an Office Building." *Atmospheric Environment* 17:51–64.

Turnbull, David. 1989. "Corridors of Power." *The Architects' Journal* (UK) 189, no. 13 (29 March): 46–53.

Ulrich, Roger S. 1984. "View through a Window May Influence Recovery from Surgery." *Science* 224, no. 4647:420–21.

Vanier, Lena. 1990. "Flat Wire Thrives as a Satellite Hook-Up." *Facilities Design and Management,* January, 54–56.

Vicker, Ray. 1981. "Computer Terminals Allow More People to Work at Home Instead of Commuting." *The Wall Street Journal,* 4 August, 46.

Vonier, Thomas. 1987. "PA Technics Skin Deep." *Progressive Architecture,* June, 99–103.

Waldman, Peter. 1988. "Reusable Optical Disks Expand Data Storage." *The Wall Street Journal,* 1 April, 13.

The Wall Street Journal. 1981a. "Developers Offer That Something Extra." 16 September, 25.

——. 1981b. "The Latest in Seminars: A TV Hookup." 15 October, 31.

——. 1981c. "Touche Ross Adds Apples." 4 November, 5.

——. 1982. "Business Conferences Via Global Television to Begin in December." 31 March, 14.

——. 1985a. "Device Controls a Computer with a Shake of the Head." 9 July, 38.

——. 1985b. "Study Targets VDT Effect on Pregnant Employees." 7 June, 10.

——. 1985c. "Technology in the Workplace: A Special Report." 16 September, 1C-92C.

——. 1985d. "Wang Message Service Takes Car-Phone Calls." 28 August, 4.

——. 1988a. "Apple Introduces Scanner, Beefs Up Macintosh Line." 11 August, 2.

——. 1988b. "Computer Maker Introduces Optical Disk-Storage System." 6 April, 2.

——. 1988c. "FAX Machines Sales Zoom as Prices Drop and Distribution Improves." 10 March, 1.

——. 1990. "The World's First Desktop Office Is Here." Ad for Canon's Navigator. 26 March, C26.

Warren, Peter. 1987. "Risks and Remedies: Indoor Air Quality—2: The Remedies." *The Architects' Journal* (UK), June, 57–59.

Watanabe, Hiroshi. 1985. "Hong Kong Steel-Corseted Bank Tower Gives the City a Needed Landmark." *Architecture* 74, no. 9:74–77.

Waters, Brian. 1985. "The Hong Kong Bank HQ." *Facilities* (UK) 3, no. 9 (September): 12–15.

Webb Associates, ed. 1978. *Anthropometric Source Book,* vols. 1, 2, and 3. NASA Reference Publication no. 1024. Washington, D.C.: NASA Scientific and Technical Office.

Weddle, David. 1990. "Aren't You Going to Work?" *California,* May, 65–71, 148–150.

Weinberg, Sanford B. 1983. "Conquering Computer Fear." *Impact OA,* May, 4 and 5.

Welsch, Manfred. 1988. Personal communication.
Wiggins, Phillip H. 1987. "Market Place, A Busy Sector: Office Supplies." *The New York Times*, 11 August, 32.
Williams, Bernard. 1986. "Premises Audit: Security." *Facilities* (UK), June, 4–8.
Wilson, Forrest. 1987. "The State of the Art of Technological Space." *Architecture*, March, 74–77.
——. 1989. "Meeting the Seemingly Insatiable Demands for Power in Buildings." *Architecture* 78, no. 4 (April): 101–3.
Wilson, Sheena. 1987a. "The Office Environment Survey." *Facilities* (UK), June, 12–13.
——. 1987b. "Sick Buildings." *The Architects' Journal* (UK), May, 22–23.
Wilson, Sheena, with Ziona Strelitz, and Jennifer O'Neill. 1986. *Premises of Excellence: How Successful Companies Manage Their Offices*. London: Building Use Studies, Ltd.
Wise, Barbara K., and James A. Wise. 1989. "Task Analysis in Workstation Design." June. The Center for Integrated Facilities Research, Grand Valley, MI.
Wise, James. 1984. "How to Make Teleconferencing Work." *Office Ergonomics Review* (Toronto) 1, no. 1, 1, 28.
Wise, A. James, and Barbara K. Wise, eds. 1984. *The Human Factors of Underground Environments*. Written by the Autumn Architecture Research Group. Seattle: Wise Associates.
Wolverton, B. C. 1988. "Harnessing Nature to Clean Polluted Water and Air." National Space Technology Laboratories, National Aeronautics and Space Administration. April, MS 39529.
Wortz, E. C., and Nowlis, D. P. 1975. "The Design of Habitable Environments." *Man-Environment Systems* 5, no. 5:280–88.
Yamaguchi, Y. and Ishinada, Y., "Sitting Posture: an electromyographic study on healthy and notalgic people." (1972): *J. Jap. Orthop. Assn.* 46, 51–56.
Zagami, Robert. 1987. "State-of-the-Art Report on Micrographics and Optical Disks." *Administrative Management*, April, 24–29.

Addresses

Here are addresses you might have trouble finding for some of the publications cited above:

The Architectural Press Ltd, 9 Queen Anne's Gate, London SW1H 9BY, England, UK, publishers of *The Architects' Journal* and *Designers' Journal* as well some books cited

The Business and Institutional Furniture Manufacturers Association, 2335 Burton S. E., Grand Rapids, MI 49506

The Bureau of National Affairs, Inc., RSPD, 1231 25th St., N. W., Washington, D.C. 20037

College of Real Estate Management, Publications, Whiteknights, Reading, Berkshire RG6 2AW, England, UK, publishers of the CALUS report

Cross Information Company, Canyon Center, 939 Pearl St., Boulder, CO 80302, publishers of *Intelligent Buildings/Information Systems—IBIS*

DEGW, Porters North, 8 Crinan Street, London N1 9SQ, England, UK, publishers of *Facilities* and the ORBIT reports

Quality Circle Institute, 1425 Vista Way, Airport Industrial Park, P.O. Box Q, Red Bluff, CA 96080-1335

Taylor & Francis Ltd, 4 John St., London WC1N 2 ET, England, UK; or Taylor & Francis, Inc., 242 Cherry St., Philadelphia, PA 19106-1906, publishers of several books cited, as well the journals *Ergonomics* and *Behaviour and Information Technology*

Wise Associates, P.O. Box 1759, Richland, WA 99352, publishers of *The Human Factors of Underground Work Environments* and *Task Analysis in Workstation Design*

Suggested Reading

Bettendorf, Robert F. 1990. ''Good Ergonomics Can Mean Good Economics.'' *The Office,* June, 111, no. 6:32, 37.

Burns, Robert J. 1990. ''Organization Invests in Nationwide Video Teleconferencing System.'' *Facility Management Journal,* May-June, 64–73.

Dubin, Fred S. 1990. ''Intelligent Buildings: HVAC, Lighting, and Other Design Trends.'' *The Construction Specifier,* February, 43, no. 2:50–57.

Freiman, Ziva. 1990. ''Essay: The Office of the Present.'' *Progressive Architecture,* September, LXXI, no. 9:137–38.

hfd. 1990. ''Home Office Ranks Up 23 Percent, Survey Finds.'' 20 August, 77, 93.

Linn, Charles. 1990. ''Workers in Cornell Study Favor Indirect Lighting in VDT Offices.'' *Facilities Design & Management,* July, 9, no. 7:27.

——. 1990. ''Shedding New Light on the Computerized Office.'' *Facilities Design & Management,* July, 9, no. 7:42–45.

Loftness, Vivian, Volker Hartkopf and Peter A. D. Mill, 1990. ''The Intelligent Office.'' *Progressive Architecture,* September, LXXI, no. 9:47–52.

Morell, Jonathan A., and David Sutherland. 1990. ''Managerial Employment and Information Technology—An Exploration of Organizational Dynamics.'' *Office Systems Research Journal,* Spring, 8, no. 2:15–25.

Nelson, D. L., and M. G. Kletke. 1990. ''Impact of IT at the Individual Level.'' *Behaviour & Information Technology* (UK), July-August, 9, no. 4:257–271.

Rubin, Arthur. 1990. *Post Occupancy Evaluation of Federal Buildings—The Portland Federal Building and Others.* Gaithersburg, MD: National Institute of Standards and Technology, U. S. Department of Commerce NISTIR 4307, April.

——. 1990. *High Technology Office Evaluation Survey—A Pilot Study.* Gaithersburg, MD: National Institute of Standards and Technology, U. S. Department of Commerce NISTIR 4354, June.

Rubin, Arthur, and Gary Gillette. 1989. *Guideline for Work Station Design.* Gaithersburg, MD: National Institute of Standards and Technology, U.S. Department of Commerce NISTIR 89-4163, September.

Veilleux, C. Thomas. 1989. ''Home Office Sales Continue to Grow.'' *hfd,* 18 December, 143–144.

Index